Minority Nationalist Parties and European Integration

This book examines the attitudes of minority nationalist parties towards European integration from the 1970s until the present day. The findings of the study challenge the notion prevalent in the scholarly literature that minority nationalist parties are increasingly pro-European.

Taking into account recent developments in European integration, and improved state channels for minority nationalist parties to achieve their policy goals, the author contends that the European dimension has become de-emphasised in nationalist politics. A theoretical framework is proposed in the book that distinguishes between different dimensions of party attitudes towards Europe, and identifies different factors that may shape party positions towards Europe.

The volume provides:

- a systematic analysis of the ways in which minority nationalist party attitudes towards European integration have evolved from 1979 to 2007
- original empirical data on hitherto under-researched minority nationalist parties in Wales, Galicia and Corsica
- major new insights into the European attitudes of minority nationalist parties.

It will be of strong interest to students and scholars interested in minority nationalism, the Europeanisation of political parties, comparative research on regional politics and in contemporary debates about nationalism.

Anwen Elias is Lecturer in European Politics at the Department of International Politics, Aberystwyth University, UK.

Routledge/UACES Contemporary European Studies

Edited by Tanja Börzel, *Free University of Berlin*, Michelle Cini, *University of Bristol*, Roger Scully, *University of Wales, Aberystwyth* on behalf of the University Association for Contemporary European Studies.

Editorial Board:
Grainne De Búrca, *European University Institute and Columbia University*
Andreas Føllesdal, *Norwegian Centre for Human Rights, University of Oslo*
Peter Holmes, *University of Sussex*
Liesbet Hooghe, *University of North Carolina at Chapel Hill, and Vrije Universiteit Amsterdam*
David Phinnemore, *Queen's University Belfast*
Mark Pollack, *Temple University*
Ben Rosamond, *University of Warwick*
Vivien Ann Schmidt, *University of Boston*
Jo Shaw, *University of Edinburgh*
Mike Smith, *University of Loughborough*
Loukas Tsoukalis, *ELIAMEP, University of Athens and European University Institute*

The primary objective of the new Contemporary European Studies series is to provide a research outlet for scholars of European Studies from all disciplines. The series publishes important scholarly works and aims to forge for itself an international reputation.

1 **The EU and Conflict Resolution**
   Promoting peace in the backyard
   Nathalie Tocci

2 **Central Banking Governance in the European Union**
   A comparative analysis
   Lucia Quaglia

3 **New Security Issues in Northern Europe**
   The Nordic and Baltic states and the ESDP
   Edited by Clive Archer

4 **The European Union and International Development**
   The politics of foreign aid
   Maurizio Carbone

5 **The End of European Integration**
   Anti-Europeanism examined
   Paul Taylor

6 **The European Union and the Asia-Pacific**
   Media, public and elite perceptions of the EU
   Edited by Natalia Chaban and Martin Holland

7 **The History of the European Union**
   Origins of a trans- and supranational polity 1950–72
   Edited by Wolfram Kaiser, Brigitte Leucht and Morten Rasmussen

8 **International Actors, Democratization and the Rule of Law**
   Anchoring democracy?
   Edited by Amichai Magen and Leonardo Morlino

9 **Minority Nationalist Parties and European Integration**
   A comparative study
   Anwen Elias

Minority Nationalist Parties and European Integration
A comparative study

Anwen Elias

LONDON AND NEW YORK

First published 2009
by Routledge
2 Park Square, Milton Park, Abingdon, Oxon OX14 4RN

Simultaneously published in the USA and Canada
by Routledge
711 Third Ave, New York NY 10017

Routledge is an imprint of the Taylor & Francis Group, an Informa business

First issued in paperback 2013

© 2009 Anwen Elias

Typeset in Times New Roman by
Exeter Premedia Services Private Ltd.

All rights reserved. No part of this book may be reprinted or reproduced or utilised in any form or by any electronic, mechanical, or other means, now known or hereafter invented, including photocopying and recording, or in any information storage or retrieval system, without permission in writing from the publishers.

British Library Cataloguing in Publication Data
A catalogue record for this book is available from the British Library

Library of Congress Cataloging-in-Publication Data
Elias, Anwen.
  Minority nationalist parties and European integration: a comparative study/Anwen Elias.
    p. cm.
  Includes bibliographical references and index.
1. Minorities – Europe – Political activity. 2. Minorities – Europe – Case studies. 3. Nationalism – Europe. I. Title.
JN94.A38M52 2008
324.2'183094 – dc22
2008019118

ISBN 978-0-415-46803-9 (hbk)
ISBN 978-0-415-86072-7 (pbk)
ISBN 978-0-203-88864-3 (ebk)

Contents

	List of illustrations	vi
	Acknowledgements	vii
	List of acronyms	ix
1	Introduction: minority nationalist parties and European integration	1
2	Theorising the European attitudes of minority nationalist parties	16
3	Wales: Plaid Cymru	43
4	Galicia: The Bloque Nacionalista Galego	76
5	Corsica: a comparison of moderate and radical Corsican nationalist parties	110
6	Conclusions: a comparative analysis of minority nationalist party attitudes towards European integration	140
	Appendix	168
	Notes	170
	Bibliography	178
	Index	193

Illustrations

Figures

2.1	Typology of minority nationalist party attitudes towards European integration	26
6.1	Typology of minority nationalist party attitudes towards European integration	141
6.2	The European attitudes of minority nationalist parties: (a) 1975 and (b) 2007	143

Tables

3.1	European Parliament election results for Wales, 1979–2004	46
3.2	General election results in Wales, 1979–2005	46
3.3	National Assembly for Wales election results, 1999–2007	47
3.4	Constitutional preferences in Wales, 1997–2003 (%)	71
3.5	Constitutional preferences for Wales in the UK and Europe, 1999–2003 (%)	72
4.1	Composition of the BNG	78
4.2	Election results for the Congress of Deputies in Galicia, 1977–2004	81
4.3	Results of autonomous elections in Galicia, 1981–2005	91
4.4	European Parliament election results for Galicia, 1987–2004 (%)	98
4.5	Do you consider European integration to be beneficial or prejudicial for your autonomous community (Galicia)? (%)	105
4.6	How do you evaluate Spain's membership of the EU?	106
5.1	Results of Corsican regional elections, 1982–2004 (%)	120
5.2	European Parliament election results for Corsica, 1984–2004 (%)	124

Acknowledgements

There were plenty of times when it felt like this book would never be completed. That it finally has been is due in no small part to the on-going support and encouragement of several people. Two individuals in particular have been a constant source of advice and inspiration. During four years at the European University Institute (EUI) in Florence, Michael Keating helped me develop vague ideas about regionalism in Europe into a coherent PhD on minority nationalist parties and European integration. In Aberystwyth, Roger Scully read several drafts of the revised book manuscript, and I am deeply indebted to him for being so thorough and incisive in his comments.

I am also grateful to numerous other colleagues for sharing their thoughts on different aspects of the book. Donatella della Porta, Lieven De Winter and Ramón Maíz all read an earlier version of this study, whilst Richard Wyn Jones, Filippo Tronconi and Marga Gómez-Reino were kind enough to offer suggestions on the rewriting and reorganisation of different chapters. The research on which the book is based has also been presented in various workshops and conferences in Santiago de Compostela, Florence, Edinburgh, Siena and Montreal. These were invaluable occasions for exchanging and refining ideas and arguments, as well as for making new contacts and several good friends.

Conducting empirical research for this study allowed me to spend time in some truly wonderful places, and to get to know many inspirational figures who continue to fight for their nation's right to self-determination. In Paris, Ajaccio, Bastia, Santiago de Compostela, Aberystwyth and Cardiff, party representatives and other individuals went out of their way to facilitate access to primary sources, and willingly gave up their time to talk about the challenges of nation building within Europe. This book could not have been written without their insights.

The final draft of the book was completed whilst I was an ESRC postdoctoral fellow at the Department of International Politics, Aberystwyth University. I am grateful to the department for allowing me to organise my teaching commitments in such a way as to have time to dedicate to rewriting and updating my PhD research. My thanks also to my colleagues, who could always be persuaded to join me for coffee or a few pints when my enthusiasm for research was waning. The postdoctoral fellowship also enabled me to spend several months in Lugo (Galicia), where most of the final draft of the book was written. I am indebted to Jose for allowing me to turn his spare room into an office.

I would like to thank the team at Routledge for their assistance with getting the manuscript ready for publication. Permission was also given by Routledge to reproduce the chapter on Plaid Cymru, a previous draft of which was published in M. Keating and J. McGarry (2006) *European Integration and the Nationalities Question*.

During the final stages of completing the book, Scott was a much needed reminder that there are more important things in life than minority nationalist parties. My biggest debt of gratitude, however, goes to my parents, Eurig and Llinos, for their unwavering support. They have never tried to dissuade me from pursuing any of the projects that I've undertaken in my academic or personal life, however ill advised or poorly thought out they have been. And for that, I will always be deeply grateful. Diolch.

Acronyms

aCN	A Cuncolta Naziunalista
ANC	Accolta Naziunale Corsa
AN-PG	Asamblea Nacional-Popular Galega
AP	Alianza Popular
APC	Associu di u Patriotti Corsi
ARC	Action Régionaliste Corse
BNG	Bloque Nacionalista Galego
BN-PG	Bloque Nacional-Popular Galego
CAP	Common Agricultural Policy
CCN	Cuncolta di i Cumitati Naziunalisti
CDC	Convergència Democràtica de Catalunya
CG	Coalición Galega
CiU	Convergència i Unió
CONSEO	Conference of Nations without a State in Western Europe
EA	Eusko Alkartasuna
EEC	European Economic Community
EFA	European Free Alliance
EG	Esquerda Galega
ELDR	European Liberal-Democrat Reform Party
EMU	European and Monetary Union
EN	Esquerda Nacionalista
EPP-ED	European People's Party and European Democrats
ERC	Esquerra Republicana de Catalunya
ETA	Euskadi 'Ta Askatasuna
EU	European Union
FLNC	Front de Libération Nationale de la Corse
FRC	Fronte Régionaliste Corse
GUE	European United Left/Nordic Green Left
HB	Herri Batasuna
ID	Independence/Democracy Group
IMEDOC	Îles de la Méditerranée Occidentale
ITS	Identity, Tradition and Sovereignty group
MCA	Muvimentu Corsu per l'Autodeterminazione

MEP	Member of the European Parliament
MPA	Movimentu pà l'Autodeterminazione
MRG	Mouvement des Radicaux de Gauche
NATO	North Atlantic Treaty Organisation
NAW	National Assembly for Wales
Nós-UP	Nós-Unidade Popular
PCE	Partido Comunista de España
PES	Party of European Socialists
PG	Partido Galegista
PGP	Partido Galego do Proletariado
PNV	Partido Nacionalista Vasco
PNC	Parti National de la Corse
PNG-PG	Partido Nacionalista Galego-Partido Galeguista
POG	Partido Obrero Galego
PP	Partido Popular
PPdeG	Partido Popular de Galicia
PSdeG-PSOE	Partido Socialista de Galicia
PSG	Partido Socialista Galego
PSG-EG	Partido Socialista Galego-Esquerda Galega
PSI	Partitu Sucialistu per l'Indipendenza
PSOE	Partido Socialista Obrero Español
RN	Rinnovu Naziunale
RPR	Rassemblement pour la République
SEA	Single European Act
SF	Sinn Fein
SNP	Scottish National Party
TEU	Treaty on European Union
UCD	Unión de Centro Democrático
UDC	Unió Democràtica de Catalunya
UDF	Unione pour la Démocratie Française
UEN	Union for Europe of the Nations
UG	Unidade Galega
UMP	Union pour un Mouvement Populaire
UPC	Unione di u Populu Corsu
UPG	Unión do Povo Galego

1 Introduction
Minority nationalist parties and European integration

In different parts of Europe, minority nationalist parties have been rewriting centuries of history in an attempt to legitimise demands for a right to national self-determination. In recent years, these parties have claimed to have found a new ally in the quest for territorial autonomy: the European Union (EU). If this nationalist rhetoric is to be believed, then European integration has created new opportunities for the reassertion of collective identities below the state.

Claims that European integration provides new solutions to the 'nationalities question' (Keating, 2004) have come to prominence as minority nationalist parties themselves have acquired unprecedented political and electoral salience. Minority nationalist contestation has long existed in the territorial peripheries of many states in western Europe (Rokkan and Urwin, 1983). During the latter half of the twentieth century, however, minority nationalist parties have become major political players in different regional and statewide political arenas. Many old minority nationalist parties have experienced a revival in their electoral fortunes. In other places, new minority nationalist parties have been created to defend the cultural, linguistic and political rights of historic nations situated within the borders of larger sovereign states (De Winter *et al.*, 2006b: 7–8).

The rise of minority nationalist parties has had a major impact on the territorial organisation of sovereign states in western Europe. The main goal of these parties is to reconfigure the distribution of political authority between the centre and the periphery in favour of the latter. As minority nationalist parties have become more electorally and politically successful, state authorities have been forced to respond by decentralising or devolving new policy-making responsibilities to the sub-state level. Minority nationalist parties in Belgium were key actors in the transformation of the country from a unitary to a strongly federal state (Beulens and Van Dyck, 1998: 65; De Winter, 2006: 31–32). In Spain, the creation of a 'state of autonomies' at the end of the 1970s, which granted substantial policy responsibilities to autonomous communities below the state, was a concession to the demands of Catalan and Basque nationalists. In subsequent years, the Catalan Convergència i Unió (CiU) and the Basque Partido Nacionalista Vasco (PNV) were able to extract further policy concessions for their respective minority nations in return for parliamentary support for minority Spanish governments (Calvet Crespo, 2003; Guerrero Salom, 2003). In the UK, the electoral growth of Scottish nationalism during the 1980s was one factor that led the British Labour Party to adopt a commitment to devolve power to the UK's component nations (Mitchell, 1998). Since the establishment of the Scottish Parliament and the National Assembly for Wales (NAW) in 1999, the Scottish National Party (SNP) and Plaid Cymru have used their positions as main parties of opposition, and then as parties of regional government since 2007, to push for a further redistribution of power away from Westminster. The Lega Nord's electoral breakthrough in the 1990s enabled the party to negotiate new institutional reforms to strengthen regional government in Italy (Ruzza, 2006: 243–44). Even in France, a state with a tradition of strong ideological antipathy to recognising the existence of cultural and linguistic diversity within its borders, a limited degree of administrative devolution has been granted to Corsica to assuage the political demands of the island's minority nationalist movement (Olivesi, 1998).

Minority nationalist parties have often legitimated their demands for greater autonomy within the state by referring to a more far-reaching transformation of the territorial organisation of political authority in western Europe. It has often been claimed by these actors that the challenge they pose to the state's authority from below is closely linked to a similar pressure emanating from above the state, as a result of European integration. The rise of minority nationalism on the one hand, and progress in European integration on the other, are presented as twin processes that are challenging the existing state order in western Europe in fundamental ways. The linkage between these two dynamics has been expressed by many minority nationalist parties in terms of the potential to create a new political order based on an alternative territorial configuration of political authority. The notion of a 'Europe of the Regions', or some version thereof, has been employed by these parties to articulate a vision of a future European polity where nationalist demands for greater political autonomy would be achieved within a supranational legal and institutional framework. Several scholars have argued that the potential of European integration to resolve key nationalist demands in the long term has led minority nationalist parties to become ardent supporters of Europe (Keating, 2001a, c, 2004; Hix and Lord, 1997). Indeed, and as noted above, one of the most striking features of the electoral growth of minority nationalist parties in recent decades was the overwhelming pro-Europeanness of these parties. Much of the political appeal of these parties seemed to derive from their ability to link core nationalist demands with progressive ideas about the transformative potential of European integration.

This book examines how minority nationalist parties have sought to use the emerging European order to repackage and reassert their nationalist demands for self-determination. Its aim is to evaluate the degree to which European integration has facilitated the reassertion of collective identities below the state. The main argument to be developed throughout the subsequent chapters can be summarised as follows. Whilst European integration has encouraged minority nationalist parties to imagine alternative solutions to their territorial demands, in other respects there have been major constraints on the ability of these actors to realise their long-term constitutional goals within the EU. The findings of this study challenge the frequent portrayal of minority nationalist parties as Europeanists *par excellence* in two ways: (i) by highlighting the different (and not always positive) ways in which European integration impacts upon the political programmes of these actors; and (ii) by identifying different factors that facilitate, but also constrain, the ability of minority nationalist parties to resolve dilemmas arising from the centre–periphery cleavage in the European context.

The remainder of this chapter introduces the main issues with which this study is concerned. The next section begins by reviewing the existing academic literature on minority nationalist party attitudes towards European integration. Accounts of the pro-Europeanism of minority nationalist parties have multiplied in recent years. The basic tenets of minority nationalist party positions on the European question, and the explanations that have been provided for such attitudes, are summarised. Existing accounts of minority nationalist party attitudes towards European integration, however, are problematic in several respects; the limitations of this scholarly literature are identified. This leads on to a statement of the main objectives of this study, and how they will be met in the analytical and empirical chapters that follow. The research design adopted by the study is then specified, before the chapter concludes with an overview of the remainder of the book.

Minority nationalist parties: Europeanists *par excellence*?

A survey of academic accounts of minority nationalist party attitudes towards European integration reveals a party family that is overwhelming supportive of Europe. Even though many minority nationalist parties were initially critical of the European Economic Community (EEC) (Hermant, 1992; Lynch, 1996; Nagel, 2004: 61), since the 1980s opposition to European integration has been replaced by growing levels of support for this process. The degree to which minority nationalist parties have converged around a strongly pro-European position is remarkable when one considers that in many other respects – ideology, long-term constitutional goals, organisational profile and socio-economic appeal – minority nationalist parties are extremely heterogeneous (De Winter, 1998; Ugarte and Gómez-Reino, 2003; Newman, 1994; Keating, 2001a; De Winter and Gómez-Reino, 2002). Ray's (1999) comparative statistical analysis of the European attitudes of different party families reveals the minority nationalist party family to be among the most pro-European of all party families in western Europe. Hix and Lord (1997: 27) go even further to suggest that minority nationalist parties[1] are *the* most pro-European parties.

The vast majority of minority nationalist parties have acknowledged the potential of European integration to empower minority nations to take control over their own destinies. Some, like the CiU in Catalonia, have always espoused the idea of national self-determination in a European context. For CiU, Catalan autonomy can be achieved only within a pluri-national Spanish state in a regionalised Europe, where sovereignty is shared and divided across different territorial levels (Keating, 2001c: 72–73). Other minority nationalist parties have redefined long-term constitutional goals that were once formulated with the state as their exclusive frame of reference, to demand greater national autonomy within a European framework.

The SNP and Plaid Cymru in Wales were emphatically opposed to economic integration within the framework of the EEC in the 1970s. By the mid-1980s, both parties had developed a more sympathetic position towards European integration. Both now demand 'independence in Europe' for their respective minority nations (Hepburn, 2006; Elias, 2006). A similar 'Europeanisation' of party goals (Lynch, 1996: 198) has been identified in the cases of the Basque PNV (Keating, 2000), the Belgian Volksunie (Lynch, 1996) and others.[2] This pro-Europeanist consensus among minority nationalist parties even constituted the basis for the creation of a new European party family from scratch, namely the European Free Alliance (EFA) (De Winter and Gómez-Reino, 2002).

Scholars have offered three main explanations for minority nationalist party support for European integration. They all identify different ways in which European integration is challenging the historical centre–periphery cleavage around which these parties mobilised. Firstly, minority nationalist parties have been favourable towards European integration because it has undermined the functional purpose of the nation-state. The internationalisation of economic and political relationships, and the emergence of new dimensions to traditional policy issues that the state is ill-equipped to deal with in isolation, have forced the reallocation of decision-making capacities upwards to supranational bodies, and downwards through decentralisation and devolution (Marks and Hooghe, 2000). As a result, the sovereign state has been emptied of much of its substantive content, and can no longer lay exclusive claim to the exercise of legitimate political authority within a territorially bounded political system. European integration has thus challenged the centre–periphery cleavage that pitted the centralising state against countervailing political, economic and cultural forces within the state's territorial peripheries (Rokkan and Urwin, 1983). If historically minority nationalist parties emerged in response to, and in confrontation with, the state, European integration has transformed this 'apposition and opposition' between the two (Keating, 2004: 367). Changes in the territorial organisation of political decision making have prompted minority nationalist parties to explore new connections between function, representation and institutions (Keating, 2001b, d). Very different models of functional organisation have been proposed which reject the assumption that sovereignty is a prerequisite for the exercise of legitimate political authority. The notion of a Europe of the Regions has frequently been employed by minority nationalist parties to invoke such a future European polity where sovereign states have withered away. Instead, political power and authority would be exercised jointly by regional and supranational actors (Nagel, 2004: 59). From a minority nationalist perspective, this is clearly an attractive prospect since minority nations would enjoy a degree of decision-making responsibility unimaginable within the framework of the sovereign state.

Secondly, European integration has fuelled new theoretical and philosophical debates about the nature of sovereignty and statehood. Some scholars have challenged the idea that state sovereignty has defined the international political system since the seventeenth century (Krasner, 1999, 2001; Keating, 2001b, d). It is claimed that the intellectual preponderance of the statist discourse has overlooked the existence of alternative ways of organising political authority that do not necessarily entail statehood at all. Others have argued that within the specific context of European integration, where states have willingly transferred sovereignty over certain policy domains to non-state organs, the notion of 'indivisible sovereignty' as a zero-sum commodity has become increasingly untenable. Alternative conceptualisations such as 'divided sovereignty' (MacCormick, 1999) and 'constitutional pluralism' (Walker, 2001) have been proposed as more innovative ways of conceptualising the sources of legitimate authority. These debates are appealing to minority nationalist parties because 'if we recognize that neither nationalism nor sovereignty are absolutes and that both can change and evolve over time, and that the nation-state as it had existed since the nineteenth century is merely one way of doing this, then we open up a large array of possibilities for managing nationality issues' (Keating, 2001d: 42). Many minority nationalist parties have adopted 'post-sovereigntist' conceptualisations of the nation's place within the new European order. Such arguments have been based on the assumption that traditional understandings of sovereignty are no longer appropriate in contemporary society (Keating, 2001c). In Spain, for example, the 'Plan Ibarretxe' was formulated by the Basque PNV in 2004 as a third way between classic statehood and devolution (Keating and Bray, 2006). The proposed reform of the Basque Country's constitutional status envisaged a Basque nation 'freely associated' with the Spanish nation within a Europe of the Regions.

Thirdly, the European arena has provided minority nationalist parties with new opportunity structures for pursuing national self-determination (Keating and McGarry, 2001: 4; Lynch, 1996). The EU constitutes an external support structure that makes arguments about the feasibility and sustainability of self-determination much easier. As such, the EU enables minority nationalist parties to overcome key obstacles to self-determination that could not easily be resolved otherwise (Keating and McGarry, 2001: 7). Attempts by the EU to develop a transnational security and defence regime, for example, may reduce some of the risks and costs associated with seceding from a sovereign state. Similarly, arguments relating to the economic viability of self-determination are easier to make in the context of an integrated European economic space. Minority nations can seek competitive advantage within a European common market rather than depend on state contributions. European regional policies may also be available to tackle economic underdevelopment and encourage diversification and innovation as the basis of a new social prosperity (Keating, 1998; Gren, 1999). Within a system of economic and monetary union, minority nations would also no longer be required to develop their own 'national' monetary policies. In principle, therefore, economic integration at the European level offers favourable conditions for minority nations to promote economic competitiveness whilst safeguarding territorial autonomy.

European integration has also offered minority nationalist parties several opportunities to represent nationalist interests directly at the supranational level. The introduction of direct elections to the European Parliament in 1979 provided minority nationalist parties with direct access to the supranational level for the first time. The Maastricht Treaty on European Union (TEU) created a Committee of the Regions to represent sub-state interests, introduced a right for representatives from sub-state governments to be included in member-state delegations to the Council of Ministers, and contained a commitment to the principle of subsidiarity (Hooghe, 1995; Hooghe and Marks, 1996; Keating and Hooghe, 2001). The latter in particular was interpreted by many minority nationalist parties and other sub-state actors as the basis for the future reallocation of decision-making authority to sub-state levels of government.

Finally, the fact that steps were taken on the supranational level to promote and protect minority rights resonated with key minority nationalist concerns to do with safeguarding cultural and linguistic traditions. The European Parliament, in particular, pushed the agenda of minority languages and cultural diversity by commissioning reports and passing resolutions on these issues, and was instrumental in the creation of the European Bureau for Lesser-Used Languages in 1982 (Ó Riagáin, 2001). Article 128 of the Maastricht Treaty underlined the importance of the diversity of European cultures. The EU also made the fair treatment of minorities a condition of accession for candidate countries wishing to accede to the European club (Sasse, 2005). Even though these initiatives in cultural matters have been highly controversial and less far-reaching than European co-operation in other policy areas (O'Reilly, 2001), for minority nationalist parties they demonstrated a fundamental commitment by the EU to defend the right of cultural and linguistic groups.

To summarise, it has often been argued in the scholarly literature that the growing support of minority nationalist parties for Europe in recent decades reflects a fundamental conviction on the part of these actors that European integration has created new opportunities for meeting core nationalist demands. European integration has undermined hitherto closed state systems of political, institutional, functional and cultural relationships. At the same time, minority nationalist parties have been motivated to propose new territorial solutions for reconciling national loyalties with a more legitimate and democratic political and institutional framework. European integration thus promised to rectify the incongruence between the political and the national that had consigned Europe's historic nationalities to the peripheries of sovereign states for far too long. For these reasons, it has been argued, minority nationalist parties have redefined their nation-building projects in such a way that the achievement of national self-determination has become inextricably linked to the future development of the European polity.

Reassessing minority nationalist party attitudes towards Europe

The evidence cited thus far suggests that European integration has provided a powerful impetus for minority nationalist parties to reframe their territorial demands in European terms. There are several reasons, however, why the frequent portrayal of minority nationalist parties as pro-Europeanists *par excellence*, and the explanations for this pro-Europeanism, are unsatisfactory.

A first problem relates to the empirical accuracy of existing accounts of minority nationalist party attitudes towards Europe: minority nationalist party support for European is not as uniform as is usually asserted in the scholarly literature. Taking a closer look at what exactly minority nationalist parties want from Europe reveals a range of party attitudes that are much more complex than simple unqualified support for European integration. For one thing, individual minority nationalist parties have proposed very different conceptualisations of the minority nation's place within a future regional Europe. In his survey of the constitutional aims of different minority nationalist parties, Keating (2001c: 56–57) distinguishes three broad categories of minority nationalist position vis-à-vis Europe: those who see transnational regimes as facilitating independence at a lower cost than in the past; those who are less overtly separatist and support a continuing link with the state as necessary for managing interdependence; and those that adopt a more radical 'post-sovereigntist' stance which embraces globalisation and transnational integration to the point of believing that sovereignty in the classic sense has little meaning anymore. The SNP falls into the first category. The party adopted the slogan 'independence in Europe' in 1988, based on the notion of an intergovernmental European polity where Scotland would take up its place alongside other European member states, and would participle fully and equally within the EU (Lynch, 1996). Less radical than the SNP, the CiU in Catalonia falls into Keating's second category. The party has rejected full sovereignty within the EU as a long-term goal for Catalonia. Instead, a transformation of Spain into a plurinational confederation is proposed, within a broader European framework that recognises the rights of regions and historic nations (Keating, 2000; Barberà and Barrio, 2006). Until 2003 (when the party adopted 'independence in Europe' as its long-term goal), Plaid Cymru fitted clearly into Keating's third category, as a party that has a long tradition of rejecting sovereign statehood as irrelevant for the modern world.[3] Throughout the 1980s and 1990s, the party campaigned for 'full national status' for Wales within a Europe of the Regions. This long-term goal envisaged a future European polity where state sovereignty had withered away, and where political authority would be exercised jointly by European institutions and Europe's historic nationalities and regions (Elias, 2006). These examples demonstrate some of the different forms that minority nationalist party support for European integration can assume. However, the existing academic literature is silent on why this variation in minority nationalist party support exists; there have been no serious attempts to examine the factors that give rise to such diverse conceptualisations of the minority nation's place within Europe.

The frequent portrayal of minority nationalist parties as ardent supporters of European integration also overlooks the fact that some minority nationalist parties, despite adopting formal positions in support of Europe, have been hostile towards significant aspects of European integration. In Galicia, the Bloque Nacionalista Galego (BNG) has formally supported the ideal of a Europe of the Peoples since the mid-1990s. At the same time, however, the party has always been highly critical of the economic, political and institutional realities of the EU. The BNG has even been categorised as a Euro-sceptic party by some authors

(Gómez-Reino, Llamazares and Ramiro, 2008; Gómez-Reino, 2006). A similar dissonance between principled support for European integration and critique of the concrete structures and policies of the EU has been identified in the case of the Lega Nord in northern Italy. Diamanti (1993) has argued that the Lega Nord always placed the north of Italy firmly into a European context, and showed a general, mostly symbolic, support for Europe. Nevertheless, the party always considered the 'real Europe' to be too big, too bureaucratic, too centralist, and too tightly integrated. The Lega Nord's Euro-scepticism has become increasingly evident since the end of the 1990s (Chari et al., 2004; Giordano, 2004).

This tendency towards Euro-scepticism among minority nationalist parties is not limited to these two cases. In recent years, an increasing number of minority nationalist parties – including the most ardent supporters of the EU – have demonstrated a growing unease with the trajectory of European integration, whilst at the same time remaining committed to the European project in principle. Recent debates on the proposed European Constitution revealed a growing pessimism among many minority nationalist parties with regard to the benefits of European integration for their respective minority nations. In the referendum on the European Constitution in Spain, held on 20 February 2005, minority nationalist parties disagreed on the implications of the proposed constitutional document for their respective territories. Campaigning for a 'yes' vote, the CiU (albeit internally divided) and the PNV interpreted the proposed constitution as a step forward in the recognition of the historical, cultural and political rights of Europe's historic nations. Other parties, including Esquerra Republicana de Catalunya (ERC), Eusko Alkartasuna (EA) in the Basque Country and the BNG campaigned to reject a constitution that was deemed to protect state interests at the expense of the political, cultural and linguistic rights of national communities below the state. Elsewhere in western Europe, other minority nationalist parties came to similarly divergent conclusions about the virtues of the European Constitution. These debates revealed a party family divided over, rather than wholeheartedly supportive of, European integration. These observations do not fit easily with the categorisation of minority nationalist parties as 'uniformly pro-European' (Hix and Lord, 1997: 27). However, to date there have been very few attempts at explaining the basis of minority nationalist party Euro-scepticism.[4] It remains unclear how, if at all, such a policy position can be reconciled with the formal support of minority nationalist parties for a regional Europe.

A second problem with the existing academic literature relates to explanations of the basis of minority nationalist party support for European integration. As outlined above, such explanations have rested on the general assumption that minority nationalist parties have more to gain than to lose from European integration. And yet there is considerable evidence that, in practice, the process of European integration has fallen far short of providing a definitive solution for the territorial grievances of minority nationalist parties. The ways in which European integration's offer to minority nationalist parties has been 'flawed' (Nagel, 2004: 59) are well documented in the academic literature, and are summarised in the following paragraphs. These are limitations that have often constrained the mobilisation of sub-state actors in general, rather than just minority nationalist parties. However, whereas scholars have documented the ways in which other sub-state actors have adapted their political discourses and territorial strategies to the concrete realities of European policy making (for example, Macneill *et al.*, 2007; Moore, 2007), no comparable effort has been made with regard to minority nationalist parties. If minority nationalist parties were initially favourable towards European integration because of the potential of this process to satisfy nationalist demands for self-determination, it is reasonable to expect that the persistent failure to meet these expectations may well compromise this support. As yet, however, this hypothesis has not been investigated systematically. We still know very little about how minority nationalist parties have responded to developments in European integration that have not necessarily been advantageous to their nation-building projects.

The shortcomings of European integration are evident in the limited degree to which the sovereign state has been transformed, the continued salience of state actors in the process of European integration, and the mixed bag of opportunities that are available to minority nationalist parties within the EU. Theoretical and philosophical arguments about the transformative capacity of European integration, for example, belie a reality where sovereign states remain in control of key policy areas and continue to play a privileged role in defining the scope and speed of European integration. Even though European integration has assumed many of the functional responsibilities of sovereign states in western Europe, there is little evidence that minority nations, or sub-state actors more generally, have benefited from this redistribution of policy responsibilities. A new model of 'multilevel governance' within the EU, much touted during the 1990s (Marks, 1993; Hooghe, 1996), has not materialised. Sovereign states have proved remarkably resilient in the face of pressure to reallocate political authority upwards to the supranational level, and downwards to the sub-state level. Instead, state actors continue to control access to the supranational level for sub-state actors, and only the most entrepreneurial and well resourced of regional authorities and governments have succeeded in mobilising directly on the supranational level (Hooghe, 1995; Jeffery, 2000; Bache, 1998; Bache and Jones, 2000; Nagel, 2004). A Europe with some regions, rather than a Europe of the Regions, offers a more accurate picture of the supranational status quo. Faced with such a European reality, demands by minority nationalist parties for some kind of specialist status appear increasingly fanciful and irrelevant.

Similarly, whilst the supranational arena has provided some new resources and opportunities for minority nationalist parties in their pursuit of self-determination, in other ways European integration has given rise to a set of conditions that undermine, rather than promote, this nationalist agenda. The EU may well make arguments in favour of independence more attractive for some minority nationalist parties. However, Keating (2001e: 32) notes that 'transition costs may be high, transaction costs of various sorts may be raised by independence, and institutions may have to be reinvented'. Arguments in favour of independence in Europe also ignore the political difficulties of achieving such a goal. The prospects of a minority nation seceding from a state's territory, and becoming a full member of the EU in its own right, would undoubtedly lead other member states to oppose the move, not least because of fears that this could encourage similar demands from nationalist groups within their own territories.

Being part of a European economic space may also not be as beneficial as some scholars and many minority nationalist parties have suggested. Integrating into the European economy might be an attractive option for richer minority nations who can expect to compete favourably under such conditions. Economically underdeveloped minority nations, however, are likely to be further disadvantaged. Market pressures may come to bear unfavourably on protected and heavily subsidised regional industries that cannot compete favourably with more competitive regions, and the occurrence of asymmetrical shocks can no longer be countered by state intervention policies. And whilst many poorer minority nations have undoubtedly benefited from receipt of European regional funds, enlargement to central and eastern Europe has meant many are now ineligible for these European monies. Attempts to sustain economic development may be endangered as a result.

With regard to opportunities for representing minority nationalist party interests directly at the supranational level, it is often the case that these opportunities are either not available to minority nationalist parties (because access is exclusively for parties in regional government), or that the scope of influence that can be exercised is highly constrained. The participation of regional representatives in member-state delegations to the Council of Ministers remains at the behest of the state authorities. To date, only regional representatives from Germany, Belgium, the UK and Spain have participated in Council of Ministers meetings (Hooghe and Marks, 2001: 83; Bulmer et al., 2002; Elias, 2005). As far as the European Parliament is concerned, many minority nationalist parties have faced huge difficulties in passing the threshold of representation in order to get a member of the European Parliament (MEP) elected. In countries such as Spain and (until 1999) France, for example, minority nationalist parties with territorially concentrated support have been disadvantaged by having to compete within a single statewide constituency (Nagel, 2004: 60). As a result, the number of minority nationalist MEPs has always been relatively small. Many are members of the EFA, but this group has never managed to constitute its own party group within the European Parliament.[5] The Committee of the Regions has proved to be a weak and ineffectual body, due to its lack of formal authority, internal divisions and its excessive bureaucratisation (Christiansen, 1996; Jeffery, 2000; Hooghe and Marks, 2001: 81–82). The fact that the criteria for selecting representatives for the Committee of the Regions is usually defined by state authorities also means that minority nationalist parties have no guaranteed presence within this institution. Furthermore, the principle of subsidiarity has predominantly been applied in a very narrow way to decide the legal basis of competence between member states and the European institutions, rather than as a mechanism for empowering the sub-state level (Peterson, 1994; Van Hecke, 2003). This state-centric bias is deeply ingrained in European law, where the transfer of power is conceptualised as being exclusively between the member states and European institutions (Evans, 2002).

Finally, despite initial moves to protect minority rights as set out above, the EU's member states have resisted demands to recognise the cultural and linguistic specificities of minority nations. In particular, member states with minority nations with strong language-based identities within their territories – the UK, France and Spain – have jealously guarded their rights to deal with their minorities in their own way. As a result, initiatives such as the Charter on Regional or Minority Languages have had little concrete impact on the status of minority languages within the EU.[6] The official languages of the EU remain those of the member states, regardless of the number of speakers; with some minority nations boasting languages with more speakers than some state languages, the EU's failure to extend the same official recognition to minority languages is a particular difficulty for many minority nationalists. Attempts to develop a system of minority rights at the supranational level has proved similarly disappointing for minority nationalist parties, not least because these have been defined as basic rights pertaining to individuals, rather than ethnic or cultural groups. A regime to protect the latter is highly unlikely to develop within the EU since 'defining a national minority or ethnic group is scientifically impossible, politically fraught, and ethnically dubious, since it reifies the group and prevents evolution and change' (Keating, 2001c: 147).

The ways in which European integration has been claimed to boost the prospect of territorial re-organisation thus seem to have been grossly overestimated by minority nationalist parties and (some) academic observers (Nagel, 2004: 74). The ways in which minority nationalist parties have sought to make sense of the harsher realities of European integration remain little understood. Explanations of these actors' pro-Europeanism due to the transformative potential of the process of European integration continue to predominate in the academic literature.

The limitations already identified above in existing accounts of minority nationalist party attitudes towards European integration can be attributed to a third problem, namely the paucity of scholarly work on this dimension of minority nationalist party politics. Even though European integration has clearly impacted in significant ways on minority nationalist parties, there have been surprisingly few attempts to study the linkage between these two phenomena systematically. Observations of the ways in which minority nationalist parties have perceived and responded to Europe have, on the whole, been descriptive and offered on a case-by-case basis.[7] Some cross-national studies of party family attitudes towards European integration have included the minority nationalist party family. However, the data gathered and analysed for the purpose of mapping attitudinal trends across a large number of political party families – either drawing on general evaluations of party positions provided by expert judgements (Ray, 1999; Marks, Wilson and Ray, 2002; Hooghe, Marks and Wilson, 2002), on content analyses of party programmes (for example, Gabel and Hix, 2004), or on mass public opinion surveys (Hix and Lord, 1997) – do not allow the researcher to probe beyond formal statements of party positions on Europe (Mair, 2006). Very few studies have offered in-depth systematic empirical analyses that aim to get to grips with the complex ways in which minority nationalist parties have interpreted and responded to European integration.[8] The factors influencing the formation of party attitudes, and the pressures that may lead minority nationalist parties to change or modify their position on Europe, have been insufficiently theorised and poorly hypothesised. As a result, many questions about how and why minority nationalist parties have attempted to make sense of Europe have either been answered unsatisfactorily, or not at all.

Aims of the book

In response to the limitations of existing academic accounts of minority nationalist party attitudes towards European integration, this book aims to answer two key questions. Firstly, how have minority nationalist parties perceived and responded to European integration? Secondly, what factors have shaped the European attitudes adopted by these actors? In answering these questions, the book has three major aims.

Firstly, the book aims to address the theoretical and analytical deficiencies of previous work. The study of minority nationalist party attitudes towards European integration lags considerably behind the study of the European attitudes of other party families. As part of a growing scholarly interest in the 'Europeanisation' of political parties in recent years, an important literature has examined the positions adopted by different political parties on Europe, and the factors that shape these attitudes. This literature is discussed in detail in Chapter 2. Along with more general theories of party and party-system change, it provides a starting point for formulating theoretically and empirically informed hypotheses about how minority nationalist parties are expected to respond to European integration. This approach brings much-needed analytical rigour to the examination of minority nationalist party attitudes towards European integration.

The second aim of the study is to make a major empirical advance on existing accounts of minority nationalist party attitudes towards European integration. As noted above, the vast majority of scholars have based their judgements on the European attitudes of these parties on an evaluation of formal party positions on Europe. Such analyses do not tell us anything about how Europe actually plays in parties' political discourses, and the ways in which Europe is conceived by these actors (Mair, 2006: 163). The goal of this study, in contrast, is to generate systematic in-depth empirical data with a view to providing comparative evidence of how and why minority nationalist parties adapt their programmes to Europe. The research design adopted to this end is summarised in the next section.

Thirdly, the study will consider what an examination of minority nationalist party attitudes towards Europe can tell us more generally about the nature of politics in Wales, Galicia and Corsica, and the ways in which minority nationalist parties can be understood and studied. These questions are addressed in Chapter 6. The implications of the findings of this study for research on the EU are also considered, and a case is made for bringing nationalism back into the study of European politics.

Research design

The research design employed to investigate how and why minority nationalist parties have responded to European integration is predicated upon qualitative case studies of a limited number of minority nationalist parties. Given the paucity of systematic comparative research in this area, this design was chosen in order to generate rich in-depth data on the processes through which minority nationalist parties interpret and respond to Europe, and to trace the impact of different variables on this attitude-formation process. The three cases were chosen according to the logic of a 'most different systems' design (Prezeworski and Teune, 1970). Chapter 2 identifies three broad sets of factors that are expected to shape minority nationalist party attitudes towards European integration, these being intra-party factors, factors within the domestic political context and factors relating to the supranational level. Case studies were thus sought that would allow maximum variation along three dimensions: (i) the origins, evolution and organisation of the minority nationalist movement; (ii) the institutional and political structure of the state context within which minority nationalist parties have mobilised; and (iii) the length of membership of the EU. With these considerations in mind, the following territories were chosen: Wales, Galicia and Corsica. This choice has the added virtue of generating original empirical data on cases that have hitherto received relatively little scholarly attention. Most research has focused on minority nationalist politics in places such as Scotland, Catalonia, the Basque Country and Flanders, where the electoral and political impact of minority nationalist parties has been most pronounced; this has been at the expense of other cases where minority nationalist parties have made significant breakthroughs since the 1990s. This choice of case studies thus serves the broader purpose of expanding on extant knowledge of members of the minority nationalist party family.

Within these three territories, the study focuses on the most important minority nationalist parties in terms of the role played within the nationalist movement over a sustained period of time. In Wales, this means focusing on Plaid Cymru, the main mouthpiece of Welsh nationalist for over eighty years. In Galicia, the main focus is on the BNG, although consideration is also given to the most important nationalist parties that preceded the BNG's creation in 1982, and those that were its main competitors until their integration into the BNG during the early 1990s. The choice of parties was most problematic in the Corsican case, given the highly fragmented and unstable nature of the Corsican nationalist movement. This study has chosen to focus on the dominant parties within the moderate and radical tendencies that have long characterised the nationalist movement. Empirical data is thus mainly provided on the Unione di u Populu Corsu (UPC) (and its predecessors and successors) as the most important moderate nationalist party; and the Front de Libération Nationale de la Corse (FLNC) and its main legal public front since the early 1990s, Corsica Nazione, as the most important parties within the radical nationalist movement. However, other smaller parties within the nationalist movement are referred to when they have

14 *Introduction*

had a significant impact upon the European attitudes of their more dominant nationalist competitors.

The empirical data on party attitudes towards Europe was gathered from two main sources. Firstly, party documents were analysed. Formal party positions on Europe were garnered from a qualitative analysis of election manifestos, as documents that constitute the only medium-term plans for the whole of society regularly produced by a political party (Klingemann, Hofferbert and Budge, 1994). A range of other party documents where the party's position on Europe was discussed were also analysed in order to map the process of attitude formation prior to the adoption of a formal party position. These included party newspapers, internal briefing papers and minutes of meetings where Europe was discussed. There was inevitable variation in terms of the availability of this documentation, although all three case studies draw on a sufficiently broad variety of sources to be able to map general patterns of attitude change towards Europe over time. Secondly, semi-structured interviews were conducted with key individuals within each minority nationalist party. These individuals were identified as being: parties' current or recent leaders; their general secretaries; party representatives on the regional and/or state level; past and present MEPs (if applicable); and any party staff with responsibilities for EU-related affairs. It was not always possible to interview the identified individual, although in most cases either the formal holder of the relevant office or the office holder's key assistant was interviewed instead. A list of the interviews conducted is provided in the Appendix. Twenty-eight interviews were conducted in total. The semi-structured interviews were particularly important in establishing the impact of different variables on party attitudes, given that such causal inferences were not always apparent from party documents. Explicit questioning about *why* parties adopted the attitudes they did vis-à-vis Europe contributed to the validity of the findings with regard to this aspect of the study. Finally, quantitative data in the form of public opinion data is employed in each case study to evaluate public attitudes towards Europe, in order to evaluate the coincidence of minority nationalist party and popular attitudes on this issue dimension.

The time period covered by the study spans just over thirty years, from the mid-1970s until the fiftieth anniversary of the Treaty of Rome in May 2007. However, the case studies also provide a longer historical overview of minority nationalist party attitudes to earlier stages in European integration when this is considered essential for understanding party positions from the mid-1970s onwards.

Plan of the book

The remainder of the book is organised as follows. Chapter 2 outlines the framework of analysis that is employed to examine minority nationalist party attitudes towards Europe. The chapter begins by situating this study in the broader Europeanisation literature. The chapter then draws on recent scholarly work on the Europeanisation of political parties, and on political parties and party systems more generally, to formulate several hypotheses about how and why minority nationalist parties adopt the attitudes that they do towards European integration. This framework is then used to structure an analysis of minority nationalist party attitudes towards European integration in three different territories: Wales, Galicia and Corsica. These case studies are presented in Chapters 3, 4 and 5. The chapters adopt a similar structure so as to facilitate comparative analysis. They thus begin by providing a brief overview of the origins and evolution of the minority nationalist party or movement. This provides the necessary background before proceeding to analyse party attitudes towards European integration, and the different factors that have shaped the nature of, and changes in, these positions.

Chapter 6 concludes by summarising the main findings with regard to how minority nationalist parties have perceived and responded to European integration, and the factors that have shaped these attitudes. Different ways of categorising and mapping attitudinal trends are proposed and evaluated, and the relative importance of different variables in shaping party positions on Europe is assessed. The chapter concludes by examining the broader implications of these findings for the three minority nations that have featured in the book, for future research on minority nationalist parties, and for the way in which the EU is studied.

2 Theorising the European attitudes of minority nationalist parties

European integration has opened up a new array of opportunities for minority nationalist parties to pursue their nation-building projects, even if, as argued in Chapter 1, it is not necessarily the case that minority nations will emerge as clear winners from the integration process. But minority nationalist parties are certainly not the only ones to have mobilised in response to advances in European integration. Developments on the supranational level are no longer something that any political party can, or is advised to, ignore. If the early years of European integration were characterised by a 'permissive consensus' on the part of most domestic political actors, as the scope of European integration has extended to new – often politically sensitive – areas of co-operation, the EU has become an increasingly contested issue that has divided political actors of all colours across western Europe (Van der Eijk and Franklin, 2004). European integration is no longer the preserve of national governing elites and civil servants in Brussels. Rather, it is often a matter of contentious public debate as different actors seek to advance their own understanding of the virtues and/or ills of the European project, and compete to shape the future trajectory of European integration.

For analysts of EU politics, understanding the ways in which different actors perceive and respond to European integration has become an increasingly salient concern. In recent years, significant new research has been conducted into the way European attitudes are constructed, and the factors that come to bear on these processes of opinion formation. In particular, a growing literature on the Europeanisation of political parties offers important analytical and empirical insights into how and why political parties adopt the positions that they do on the issue of European integration. This research, along with a broader theoretical and empirical literature on political parties and party systems, constitutes the basis of this chapter. It provides a starting point for developing a framework of analysis for mapping the evolving European attitudes of minority nationalist parties, and the factors that shape these views of European integration. The chapter begins by summarising the main challenges posed by European integration to political parties in the domestic sphere. Advances in the study of the Europeanisation of political parties are then considered, and the understanding of Europeanisation adopted by this study is specified. The chapter then turns to the elaboration of a framework of analysis that will enable a systematic study of the two themes of central concern to this study: the nature of minority nationalist party attitudes towards European integration, and the factors that influence these European attitudes.

How do political parties adapt to Europe?

As European integration increasingly impinges upon the political processes of its member states, political parties within these state contexts are compelled to discuss and take up positions on a range of EU issues. Political parties may also be under pressure to reconfigure their internal structures and strategic behaviour to take this new supranational arena into account (Ladrech, 2002; Poguntke et al., 2003). Failing to adapt to Europe may risk a party's survival as a political organisation (Panebianco, 1988).

However, if adapting to European integration is an imperative for political parties, it is not always clear how this should be done. The difficulties of doing so is attested by the fact that the European issue has frequently divided otherwise coherent political parties in several western European party systems (Taggart, 1998; Sitter, 2002; Hix and Lord, 1997). Until very recently, however, researchers of European politics and party politics alike paid very little attention to what national political parties had to win or lose from Europe. There is certainly a substantial literature that has documented the emergence of a 'European' party system and the formation of so-called Europarties within and around the European Parliament.[1] However, even though the EU is defined and run by party politicians, very few studies attempted to think of the role of national party politics in the process of European integration, in the sense that the political party in the state context is taken as the unit of analysis rather than being assumed to be a participant in more general processes of European institution building and policy making (Hix and Lord, 1997: 7; Carter et al., 2007: 1–2).

More recent attempts at evaluating the impact of European integration on political parties have demonstrated that the way in which European integration impacts upon political parties is far from clear-cut. On the one hand, European integration has thus far had a limited direct effect on both national party systems (Mair, 2000; 2006)[2] and individual political parties operating within these systems. There is no European legislation that directly impacts upon the freedom of manoeuvrability of political parties in their respective national contexts, and their activities and financing are not subject to regulation by EU legislative or judicial decisions (Poguntke et al., 2003: 2–3). On the other hand, the indirect effects of European integration on national political parties are potentially more far-reaching. For political parties in national government, the growing policy competencies of the EU reduce the options available for domestic policy making. Europe may also exert an indirect influence on the way in which parties compete with one another, and may encourage alternative forms of non-partisan interest representation (Mair, 2006: 157). The fact that European integration has also become a highly politicised issue in the domestic public sphere of the EU's member states makes public opinion on the EU a further potential constraint on the abilities of governing parties to negotiate in intergovernmental decision making. The 'no' votes in the referendums on the European Constitution held in France (29 May 2005) and the Netherlands (1 June 2005) illustrated that party politicians who are out of tune with public sentiment on such questions run the risk of damaging their political credibility and electoral appeal.[3]

However, if these indirect impacts upon national party politics cannot be avoided, developing a strategy for participating in European decision making is not straightforward. It may be in the strategic interests of political parties to mobilise on the European level in so far as new options are created in the pursuit of domestic policy goals. This is particularly the case as the globalisation and internationalisation of economic and political affairs has made it increasingly difficult for political parties in government to 'deliver the goods' to their welfare-consuming publics (Gaffney, 1996; Hix and Lord, 1997; Goetz and Hix, 2001: 12–14). However, the opportunities for political parties to mobilise on the European level are not evenly distributed. Access to the Council of Ministers is exclusively the prerogative of political parties holding government office. A directly elected European Parliament, and the incremental increase in its legislative powers with successive treaty revisions, have certainly enabled a larger array of political parties to ensure a presence on the supranational level. However, the parliament's role continues to be inferior to that of the Council of Ministers (Hix and Lord, 1997: 2). Moreover, it is still difficult for many political parties to cross the threshold of representation for the European parliamentary arena, and thus they remain excluded from this supranational institutional sphere. In short, the opportunities for political parties to participate in European decision-making depends on a variety of structural, legal, institutional and organisational variables at different political levels.

The Europeanisation of political parties

In order to better understand the relationship between political parties and European integration, scholars have increasingly focused on how political parties have adapted to European integration, and how political parties have become Europeanised. First attempts at studying the adaptation of political parties to Europe were primarily descriptive. The concern was more with documenting the general rhetoric and evolution of these parties' European policies than probing the underlying factors that could explain these positions. The term 'Europeanisation' was invoked loosely to simply mean 'becoming favourable towards the EU' (Gaffney, 1996; Daniels, 1998; Moxon-Browne, 1999).

In contrast, more recent work has sought to unpack and specify the relationship between Europeanisation and domestic political parties and party systems. For example, Ladrech (2002) proposes a framework for exploring changes in political parties resulting from the impact of the EU. By identifying different dimensions of such an adaptation, 'one ought to be able systematically to compare party responses across political systems, bearing in mind of course that each political system represents a bundle of national-specific factors that condition party responses' (ibid.: 401). Ladrech identifies five such dimensions along which a process of Europeanisation may take place. These are: (i) modifications in party programmes, with increasing references to the EU; (ii) organisational change, either to co-ordinate and control new European functions/representatives or actors outside the national territory; (iii) changing patterns of party competition in the domestic political arena as the EU becomes politicised; (iv) changes in the nature of the party–government relationship over time;[4] and (v) a change in the nature of relations beyond the party system, via transnational co-operation with other actors. Other scholars have made important contributions towards improving theoretical and empirical understandings of these different aspects of Europeanisation. There is a growing literature on the European attitudes of different political parties, and especially the phenomenon of Euro-scepticism (for example, Johansson and Raunio, 2001; Aylott, 2002; Sherrington, 2006; Kopecký and Mudde, 2002; Szczerbiak and Taggart, 2003; Harmsen and Siering, 2004; Taggart and Szczerbiak, 2008; Neumayer, 2008). Poguntke *et al.* (2007) provide a comprehensive analysis of the impact of European integration on the internal organisational dynamics of national political parties. An important literature has also examined the emergence and consolidation of a European party system (Bardi, 2002; Hix, 2002; Gabel and Hix, 2002; Marks and Steenbergen, 2004; McElroy and Benoit, 2007), although research on the third and fourth aspects of Europeanisation identified by Ladrech remains underdeveloped (Mair, 2006: 161).

Whilst this growing literature has been inspired by a general interest in Europeanisation, however, the concept itself has tended to be understood in two different ways (Mair, 2006: 155–56). Some scholars have understood Europeanisation in the sense of European integration as an external factor that impacts upon national political systems; evidence of Europeanisation is thus usually sought with respect to the programmes, organisation or strategies of political parties within the domestic arena. Others have used Europeanisation to refer to the emergence and development of a distinct political system at the European level; research on transnational political parties and the European party system adopts such a definition of Europeanisation.

Differing conceptualisations of Europeanisation are certainly not exclusive to the party politics literature. The term has been used in a number of ways to describe such a variety of phenomena and processes of change in different contexts and disciplines, that its continued usefulness as a meaningful concept for political analysis has been questioned by some scholars (Radaelli, 2000; Kassim, 2000: 238).[5] For the purposes of this study, the definition of Europeanisation adopted draws on the first one noted above: Europeanisation is a process by which political parties (in this case minority nationalist parties) adapt their political programmes in response to developments in European integration. The nature of the adaptive pressure arising from European integration, and how minority nationalist parties are likely to respond to this external factor, can be further specified as follows.

Firstly, even though few authors have explicitly examined the European attitudes of minority nationalist parties through the conceptual lenses of Europeanisation,[6] in work that has evaluated the positions that these actors have adopted on Europe, an implicit 'top-down' conceptualisation of Europeanisation predominates. In other words, minority nationalist party attitudes towards Europe are conventionally understood as a function of changes at the supranational level. These changes do not necessarily create a *pressure* for adaptation, such as is generated when there is a 'misfit' or 'mismatch' between European and domestic policies, processes and institutions (Börzel and Risse, 2000: 5; Risse *et al.*, 2001). Nevertheless, the direction of influence clearly runs in a downward direction, with developments in European integration stimulating a response on the part of minority nationalist parties. Thus the growing support among minority nationalist parties for Europe during the 1980s and 1990s has usually been explained as a response to developments in European integration during these decades which promised to create a new European order within which the territorial goals of these actors would be much easier to achieve. These developments are summarised in Chapter 1, and are linked to the redistribution of functional responsibilities across different territorial levels, the challenges to established normative conceptualisations of legitimate power and authority, and the new supranational opportunity structures generated, all as a consequence of European integration. Such a top-down understanding of Europeanisation is not exclusive to research on minority nationalist parties. Many authors have explicitly adopted such an analytical definition of Europeanisation, even though it is usually acknowledged that in practice Europeanisation is a much more complex process whereby actors seek to shape European integration as well as being affected by it (cf. Risse *et al.*, 2001; Bomberg, 2002; Börzel, 2002; Poguntke *et al.*, 2007).

Such a top-down conceptualisation of the relationship between minority nationalist parties and European integration, however, is of limited use in explaining the range of positions that minority nationalist parties have adopted on Europe (summarised in Chapter 1). There is simply too much variance in what minority nationalist parties have had to say about Europe that cannot be explained as an outcome of the top-down effects of developments in European integration alone. Firstly, it is worth recalling that whilst the vast majority of minority nationalist parties have established a linkage between their long-term territorial demands and the process of European integration, this linkage has been defined in a myriad of ways. The fact that there is no single shared understanding of what the nation's role should be within a future regional Europe strongly suggests that other factors have also shaped party responses to developments in European integration, thus giving rise to contrasting versions of the 'Europe of the Regions' narrative. Secondly, Chapter 1 also noted that whilst some minority nationalist parties reacted positively to specific policy and institutional developments at the supranational level, others adopted highly sceptical positions vis-à-vis these same developments. That minority nationalist parties have adopted such divergent stances with regard to the practical realities of European politics is a further reason to assume that there are other factors that shape party attitudes towards Europe, apart from changes in European integration itself.

For these reasons, this study adopts a 'bottom-up' conceptualisation of Europeanisation. Such an approach 'starts and finishes at the level of domestic actors' (Radaelli and Pasquier, 2006: 41). In other words, the goal is to begin with an analysis of the domestic context prior to the impact derived from European integration, and then to evaluate if, when and how European integration leads to a change in the domestic political system. This approach explicitly recognises that advances in European integration will not be perceived in the same way by all political actors. The west European political order is composed of political units with long and varied political histories, where processes of state and nation building have taken very different trajectories, and where political authorities lay claim to a diversity of resources and capabilities. As a result, 'European signals are interpreted and modified through domestic traditions, institutions, identities and resources in ways that limit the degree of convergence and homogenization' (Olsen, 2002: 936). Developments on the supranational level are perceived and interpreted by contextually embedded actors who filter their external environment through a specific set of interpretative lenses constituted by ideology, experience and objectives (Díez Medrano, 2003). Responses to European integration are thus highly differentiated, since they are both actor and context specific. European integration is therefore treated as one independent variable that can modify domestic political systems and behaviour, but there are also other historical, political, institutional and cultural variables that may explain these changes (Goetz, 2000: 225). A bottom-up approach enables this study to examine alternative explanations of minority nationalist party attitudes towards Europe, and to elucidate the causal mechanisms through which European integration actually matters for minority nationalist parties. These alternative explanations are hypothesised on the basis of more general theories of party programmatic change. The potential impact of European integration can thus be assessed against other factors that are also known to impact upon the programmes of political parties (Mair, 2006: 162).

In addition to specifying the source of adaptive pressure on minority nationalist party attitudes towards European integration, it is necessary to specify how Europe matters to minority nationalist parties, and the different ways in which these actors are likely to respond to developments in European integration. Most scholars who have examined the changing attitudes of minority nationalist parties towards Europe have assumed that Europe is important to these actors because of the new opportunities that are created to resolve their territorial demands (see Chapter 1). Evidence of attitudinal adaptation in response to European integration has thus mostly been sought through an analysis of the constitutional goals espoused by these parties; it is on this basis that arguments about the growing pro-Europeanism of these parties have been made.

However, whilst minority nationalist parties may be defined first and foremost by their relationship to the centre–periphery cleavage (De Winter, 1998: 204–8), this does not exhaust the ideological profile of the vast majority of these actors. The 'core business' of minority nationalist parties is usually complemented by other, more traditional ideological values (Freeden, 1998). This is not surprising, given that these actors are also concerned with questions about how to organise the national territory as a viable socio-economic unit whilst at the same time maintaining its cultural (and often linguistic) distinctiveness. European integration may thus matter to minority nationalist parties in the way that it impacts upon these other policy goals that are additional to the primary goal of securing territorial autonomy. The impact of European integration on this dimension of minority nationalist party programmes is as yet very poorly understood. For this reason, this study aims to examine how minority nationalist parties perceive and respond to developments in European integration that not only have implications for their long-term constitutional goals, but also other socio-economic, political and cultural goals that make up these parties' political programmes.

To summarise, therefore, this study departs from the following two assumptions. Firstly, minority nationalist party attitudes towards Europe will be shaped by a range of actor-specific and context-specific factors; these will inform the ways in which minority nationalist parties perceive and respond to developments in European integration. Secondly, European integration will impact on a whole range of short and medium-term policy goals espoused by minority nationalist parties, in addition to the longer-term constitutional goals that constitute the *raison d'être* of these parties. Evidence of programmatic change must therefore be sought along these different policy dimensions if the full significance of Europe for these actors is to be understood.

The rest of this chapter is devoted to elaborating a framework of analysis for exploring minority nationalist party attitudes towards Europe in greater detail. The framework draws on the specific literature concerned with the Europeanisation of party programmes, as well as a broader literature on political parties and party systems, to formulate specific hypotheses about how and why minority nationalist parties adapt their programmes with regard to Europe.

At the same time, however, the framework of analysis is sensitive to the ways in which minority nationalist parties differ from the major traditional party families on which much of this literature is based. The specificities of the minority nationalist party family may mediate the ways in which these parties perceive and evaluate European integration. To begin with, minority nationalist parties are historically rooted in the centre–periphery cleavage, as opposed to the left–right cleavage that shaped the mobilisation of many traditional party families. Minority nationalist parties thus have a different ranking of priorities compared to other major political parties. Moreover, while some minority nationalist parties have a long history (such as the Basque PNV and Plaid Cymru) others have been established much more recently, and may therefore be at earlier stages of their lifespan (Pedersen, 1982) compared to the long-established major political parties in western Europe. Finally, minority nationalist parties are non-statewide parties, in the sense that they limit their expansion to a well-defined area of the state's territory and do not intend to go beyond it, since it corresponds to the view the party has of the nation (Seiler, 1995:15).[7] At the same time, however, minority nationalist parties often compete at several different territorial levels: local, regional, state and European (Elias and Tronconi, 2006: 3–4). The multilevel nature of party competition may also come to bear on party attitudes towards European integration. The ways in which these distinctive features of the minority nationalist party family may shape party attitudes towards Europe are considered throughout the remaining sections of this chapter.

Mapping the changing European attitudes of minority nationalist parties

A party's programme is defined as a party's stance on a variety of policy issues, including European affairs. Several studies have sought to map the European attitudes of political parties. The majority have done so by categorising parties according to whether they are anti- or pro-European (for example, Hix and Lord, 1997; Ray, 1999). The categorisation of political parties along such a unidimensional scale is justified when the number of political parties and party families being studied is very large, or when the nature of the available data restricts the analysis to a pro or anti classification.

The drawback of this approach, however, is that it fails to capture the complexity of party attitudes towards European integration. European integration is not a single and straightforward process that has a uniform effect on all spheres within its scope, but a highly complex and multidimensional one that defies simple definition and analytical specification. It is a process that has proceeded unevenly over time, as well as across institutional spheres and policy areas. The adaptive pressure exerted by European integration on different political actors and institutions also varies considerably. Given the multifaceted nature of European integration, it is reasonable to expect that political parties will also perceive their interests to be affected by different aspects of integration in different ways (Marks and Wilson, 2000: 436). Reducing party attitudes towards European integration to an assessment of whether they are more or less favourable to European integration thus fails to reflect the complexity of party evaluations of what exactly Europe has to offer.

In order to understand the different aspects of European integration that political parties take into account when deciding upon a position on Europe, therefore, it is necessary to begin by unpacking the nature of European integration. The possible impact of European integration upon minority nationalist parties was considered in Chapter 1, and the opportunities and challenges for this party family within the EU were set out. It was argued that European integration has important implications for minority nationalist parties in two distinct ways. Firstly, in the longer term, European integration holds the potential for resolving the fundamental territorial dilemma that constitutes the *raison d'être* of these parties. As argued in Chapter 1, this potential derives from the role of European integration in undermining the functional and the normative hegemony of the sovereign state within which minority nationalist parties have mobilised. Secondly, and in the shorter term, the European arena offers minority nationalist parties new opportunity structures for achieving concrete domestic policy goals and developing alternative strategies in pursuit of their territorial demands.

Based on this distinction between the long-term aspirations of minority nationalist parties within Europe, and the short-term opportunity structures created as a result of European integration, it is proposed that minority nationalist parties will evaluate the impact of European integration for the minority nation along two dimensions: the general idea of Europe, and the EU as a concrete political, institutional and policy-making reality. The distinction draws on that proposed by

Kopecký and Mudde (2002) between diffuse support for European integration, characterised by support for the general ideas of integration that underlie the EU, and specific support for the EU; that is, for the general practices of the EU as it is and as it is developing.[8]

The first dimension – the basic idea of Europe – refers to the attitude of minority nationalist parties towards the basic values that inform the process of European integration. The priority for any minority nationalist party is to resolve the tension arising from the centre–periphery cleavage. Minority nationalist party support for the principle of European integration, therefore, is likely to depend on the degree to which European integration is perceived to hold the potential for redistributing political authority in a more equitable way across different territorial levels. Minority nationalist parties who perceive European integration to offer the possibility of resolving their key territorial demands and securing the reorganisation of political authority in such a way that better accommodates the interests of the minority nation, will support further European integration as a matter of principle. They believe in such ideas regardless of how the EU is defined and realised in practice, and independently of the specific rewards which are obtained from belonging to the system (Kopecký and Mudde, 2002: 301; Easton, 1965: 125). Where such a linkage between the fundamental aims of minority nationalism and European integration is made, then minority nationalist parties are likely to reformulate their long-term constitutional goals to take this European dimension into account. The rhetoric of a 'Europe of the Regions' may be adopted as an expression of the transformative capacity of European integration, in contrast to the constraining nature of the existing centre–periphery relationship. The opposite scenario is that a party does not see in European integration any potential whatsoever to secure national self-determination. Such parties will be unsympathetic to the general idea of European integration, and will formulate their long-term goals for the minority nation in altogether different legal and political terms which are deemed to be more compatible with minority nationalist aspirations. No principled linkage will be made between the long-term goals of the minority nationalist party and European integration.

The second dimension – Europe as a concrete reality – reflects the legal, political, institutional and policy realities of the EU. It seeks to capture the attitudes of minority nationalist parties towards the EU beyond the idea of European integration as a general process, and refers to the specific benefits that these actors derive from being part of the EU. For most party families, this would mean taking stock of developments in economic and political integration (Marks and Wilson, 2000). In addition to economic and political integration, however, minority nationalist parties will also be concerned with supranational initiatives that relate to cultural and linguistic matters, since these may have direct implications for the identity-based concerns that are a core feature of these parties' agendas. Thus the concrete European reality taken into account by minority nationalist parties will encapsulate developments in economic, political and cultural integration, since these are the aspects that will have the greatest impact upon the territorial project that minority nationalist parties claim to represent (Rokkan and Urwin, 1983;

Sitter, 2002). Minority nationalist parties who are satisfied with the way the European polity is working and perceive a range of economic, political and cultural benefits to be available which serve their nationalist agendas well, will strongly support the European polity in its actual form. They will favour further integration in so far as it continues along these lines. Other minority nationalist parties may be highly dissatisfied with the shape of the European polity since the economic, political and cultural benefits for the minority nation are perceived to be minimal. They may also be pessimistic about the way Europe will develop in the future. These parties will propose radical changes to the kind of Europe being built, and will support further European integration only in so far as it is seen to put these changes into place.

These two dimensions give rise to a fourfold categorisation of the types of attitude minority nationalist parties may adopt towards Europe, illustrated in Figure 2.1.

(i) Minority nationalist parties who are *Euro-enthusiasts* will combine support in principle for Europe as a framework for national self-determination, with a positive evaluation of the EEC/EU in its current form, since the minority nation is seen to benefit from a range of economic, political and cultural opportunities on the supranational level. A party's long-term aims for the minority nation will be altered to take the European dimension into account, and achieving self-determination will be linked intrinsically to the future evolution of a regional Europe. This normative vision will be complemented by a deeply rooted commitment to Europe as a concrete reality. The European polity will be integrated thoroughly into party thinking, becoming the starting point for policy making previously defined in domestic terms.

(ii) In contrast, parties can be categorised as *Euro-rejects* when they reject the notion that European integration can resolve the centre–periphery conflict in the long term, and they are opposed to the way in which Europe is developing in practice. A party's long-term constitutional goals will not be adapted to take the European context into account, while the economic, political and cultural benefits of European integration for the minority nation will be perceived to be minimal. In other words, minority nationalist parties who belong to this category will reject European integration in all its forms. This rejection may take the form of unqualified and clearly articulated opposition to the European project, although it may also be the case that European integration is simply ignored in favour of alternative long- and short-term strategies for achieving minority nationalist aims.

The remaining two scenarios reflect the possibility that parties may not necessarily evaluate the two dimensions of European integration in the same way. The analytical distinction between 'European integration in principle' and 'Europe as concrete reality' creates the possibility of a divergence between attitudes towards the general idea of European integration and the specific nature of the European polity as it has thus far developed. In such cases, a minority nationalist party may

26 *Theorising party attitudes towards Europe*

		Support for the idea of Europe	
		Strong	Weak
Support for Europe as a concrete reality	Strong	Euro-enthusiasts	Euro-pragmatists
	Weak	Euro-sceptics	Euro-rejects

Figure 2.1 Typology of minority nationalist party attitudes towards European integration.

conclude that not all the different elements of European integration – either the basic idea of European integration or Europe as a concrete reality – are equally beneficial for the minority nation.

(iii) *Euro-sceptics* will recognise the potential of Europe integration to resolve the centre–periphery cleavage, but will perceive the European polity in its current form as being far from putting this normative ideal into practice. Symbolic rhetoric outlining a vision for a future regional Europe may be a salient feature of these parties' European discourses, but the EEC/EU's concrete institutional set-up and policy scope will be considered to be highly unsatisfactory. Further European integration will be supported only if these deficiencies are redressed, and steps are taken towards creating a European polity that is closer to the party's idea of what Europe should look like. Principled support for European integration is thus qualified by specific criticism of developments in areas of economic, political and cultural integration.

(iv) Parties that are *Euro-pragmatists* will support the EEC/EU on the basis of pragmatic, often utilitarian, considerations since doing so is profitable in some way for their own national constituencies. European integration may also help achieve prior domestic policy goals, goals which would otherwise not have been met. However, these parties will reject the basic principles underlying the integration process and do not recognise the long-term potential of European integration for facilitating national self-determination. Further European integration will be supported only in so far as it continues to serve their immediate policy interests, but the symbolic rhetoric of a regionalised or federal Europe will not be a feature of the party's European discourse. The linkage between the future direction of European integration and the resolution of the centre–periphery cleavage will not be made.

This fourfold typology constitutes a first attempt at conceptualising minority nationalist party attitudes towards Europe. These four categories are conceived as ideal types that can help us begin to understand different minority nationalist perceptions of European integration. Within each category, there is scope for variation in the precise form of a party's position on Europe. Neither is it assumed that the categorisation of parties will be stable and enduring. Rather, by evaluating the attitudes of minority nationalist parties at different points in time, this typology enables the variation in the European positions of minority nationalist parties to be mapped, thus providing a dynamic account of minority nationalist party attitudes towards Europe. Moreover, by unpacking the notion of European integration, the typology proposed above can provide a more sophisticated account of minority nationalist party positions on the issue of Europe than has hitherto been attempted in the academic literature. Other scholars have argued that the diversity of party positions on Europe requires a larger number of categories if the whole range of party attitudes on Europe is to be captured. Flood (2002) proposes a six-fold categorisation, while Conti (2003) opts for five. However, 'the more complex and fine grain the typology, the more difficult it is to operationalise and categorise parties' (Szczerbiak and Taggart, 2003: 10). The fact that this study considers only a small number of minority nationalist parties is a further justification for not disaggregating these four categories further. As stated above, the usefulness of this schematic representation is as a heuristic device to assist the preliminary analysis of the European attitudes of minority nationalist parties. Chapter 6 will return to a critical evaluation of the usefulness of this typology in light of its application in the empirical analyses that follow in Chapters 3, 4 and 5.

Thus far, this chapter has identified the different dimensions of minority nationalist party attitudes towards Europe. The remainder of the chapter considers the different factors that may impact upon the way in which minority nationalist parties perceive and evaluate developments in European integration.

Identifying the factors that shape the European attitudes of minority nationalist parties

A bottom-up approach to studying the European attitudes of political actors aims to understand the complex interaction between different supranational, domestic and intra-party dynamics that may shape positions taken up by these actors. This, in turn, requires entering into the context of each object of study in order to understand what informs perceptions and evaluations of the process of European integration and how the EU impacts upon predefined political projects. For this study, this means understanding minority nationalist perceptions of Europe as seen from their specific historical, ideological, political and institutional viewpoint. Such an approach is not without its problems. As Olsen (2002) points out, doing so risks the intervention of an increasing number of variables whose influence may be difficult to isolate analytically, rendering causal explications significantly more difficult and complex.

In order to avoid this pitfall, this study draws on the work of scholars who have examined different factors that influence political party attitudes towards Europe. Featherstone (1988) analysed twelve social democratic parties from the 1950s until the mid-1980s, and proposed three broad types of factor that influence the way parties position themselves on the European issue: (i) internal influences within the party (ideology, the role of internal elites, public opinion and whether the party is in government or opposition); (ii) influences from the wider political context (the impact of other political parties, perceptions of economic interest, and historical context); and (iii) the external dimension (external events and influences, and co-operation between political parties). He concluded that 'it has been the influence of individual national circumstances which has most noticeably shaped the parties' policies towards European integration ... The extent to which there have been influences independent of a particular national situation is very limited' (1988: 303, 333). Arguing the need for further investigation of the influence of cross-national variables in particular, Johansson and Raunio (2001) proposed disaggregating Featherstone's trifold categorisation further, and provided a list of seven factors which account for party positions on European integration: basic ideology, public opinion, factionalism, leadership influence, party competition, transnational links, and the development of integration. In their comparison of the responses of Swedish and Finnish political parties to European integration, it was found that party competition and leadership influence were the strongest factors in the Finnish case, while public opinion and factionalism were the strongest factors in Sweden.

The work of these authors, in combination with the theoretical and empirical insights of a broader literature on political parties and party systems, provides the basis for identifying different sets of factors that are likely to shape the attitudes of minority nationalist parties towards Europe. Accordingly, the way in which minority nationalist parties have respond to European integration is expected to be shaped by a combination of three broad types of factor: factors internal to the party, factors arising from the domestic political context and factors emanating from the supranational level. The nature, strength and timing of these influences may vary not only from case to case, but also over time. A party's ideology is expected to be an enduring and stable influence on its broad orientation towards European integration. In contrast, patterns of party competition, public opinion, and the nature and trajectory of European integration are likely to be more fluid, and may thus exert an influence on party attitudes towards European integration that is more punctual and short term. These different sets of factors, and their potential impact on minority nationalist party attitudes towards Europe, are considered in more detail in the remainder of this chapter.

Factors from within the party

The influence of basic ideology

A party's basic ideology can be understood as the core set of beliefs that constitute a party's identity and which allows it to distinguish itself from other political parties. Contrary to Downs's contention that politicians construct ideology opportunistically as a weapon in the struggle for office (Downs, 1957: 96–101), party identity is an enduring feature that reflects a party's historical origins and experiences. Party identity, in turn, is rooted in one of several social cleavages which define the main axes of political competition in modern political systems (Lipset and Rokkan, 1967). Although political competition in contemporary party systems is no longer 'frozen' along the cleavages identified by Lipset and Rokkan, these cleavages still play a powerful role in determining the ideological preferences of political parties and the way in which political parties respond to new issues (Bartolini and Mair, 1990; Crewe and Denver, 1985; Franklin, Mackie and Valen, 1992). In other words, political parties are 'organisations with historically rooted orientations that guide their response to new issues' (Marks and Wilson, 2000: 434). Thus, while party ideology is not immutable, it nevertheless serves as an enduring touchstone of identification for party elites, members and voters, as well as the basis upon which a more pragmatic policy package is developed (Freeden, 1998; Volkens and Klingemann, 2002).

How does a party's identity influence the position it takes on European integration? A growing body of empirical research suggests that, rather than constituting a new cleavage that cuts across existing social cleavages, European integration is assimilated into pre-existing ideological predilections that reflect the long-standing political orientations of political party families (Bartolini 2000; Marks et al., 2002; Marks and Wilson, 2000; Hooghe et al., 2002; Hix, 1999; Hix and Lord, 1997; Gabel and Hix, 2002; Ladrech, 2000). A party's identity – as defined by its ideology and political values – constitutes a prism through which European issues are filtered. Since the majority of west European party families are categorised according to their position along the left–right cleavage, the response of such parties is to squeeze European issues into the left–right axis of conflict. Thus the kinds of attitude major party families adopt towards the EU are dictated, first and foremost, by their left–right positioning within the domestic arena of party competition (Hooghe et al., 2002; Marks and Wilson, 2000; Hix and Lord, 1997).[9] Left-wing parties have generally become more pro-European over time, as the EU has increasingly been perceived to offer opportunities for achieving social democratic goals such as greater equality, increased welfare spending and market regulation. In contrast, right-wing parties have historically demonstrated higher levels of support for European integration based on advancements in market liberalisation. This support has declined more recently as the EU has endeavoured to regulate market capitalism, with these parties opposed to the development of policies such as employment and cohesion policies.

In contrast, minority nationalist parties mobilised historically around the centre–periphery cleavage, in protest at the exclusion of the periphery from the process of state building (Rokkan and Urwin, 1983). What defines this party family is the shared advocacy of a reform of the territorial structure of the state in which they operate, although the precise nature and degree of such reform varies from party to party (De Winter, 1998: 204–8, 241; Hix and Lord, 1997: 44). One would expect, therefore, minority nationalist parties to interpret developments in European integration through the lenses of the centre–periphery cleavage. In other words, the way in which minority nationalist parties respond to European integration will be determined by their understanding of the centre–periphery cleavage, their relationship with the central state, and their proposals for modifying this constitutional set-up (Giordano and Roller, 2002: 99). To the extent that European integration is perceived to undermine the sovereign state – the organisation in opposition to which minority nationalist parties have mobilised – minority nationalist parties will support European integration (Hix and Lord, 1997: 44). This support is likely to be expressed as support for European integration in principle given that European integration offers the prospects of satisfying the core territorial demands that constitute the *raison d'être* of these parties.

The historical rootedness of minority nationalist parties in the centre–periphery cleavage, therefore, will constitute the primary determinant of minority nationalist party attitudes towards the general idea of Europe. However, as noted above, other ideological values may come to bear on the positions taken up on the concrete economic, political and cultural developments associated with European integration. Minority nationalist parties have positioned themselves at different points along the traditional left–right ideological axis (Hix and Lord, 1997; Ugarte and Gómez-Reino, 2003). For example, whilst the BNG in Galicia has been categorised as a social democratic party, CiU in Catalonia has been described as socially conservative, with an ideological platform loosely based on liberal and Christian democratic ideas (Giordano and Roller, 2002; Keating, 2001a). These two examples by no means exhaust the range of left–right positions adopted by different minority nationalist parties. The implication is that, whilst a minority nationalist party's broad attitudinal orientation towards European integration may be defined by centre–periphery concerns, pragmatic evaluations of the impact of European integration on the minority nation are just as likely to reflect the minority nationalist party's left–right leanings. The way in which this left–right dimension is likely to impact on minority nationalist party attitudes towards European integration can be hypothesised on the basis of evidence from mainstream left- and right-wing parties (Ray, 1999; Marks and Wilson, 2000; Hooghe *et al.*, 2002; Gabel and Hix, 2002). Thus, on a range of socio-economic issues, it is expected that minority nationalist parties situated on the left of the political spectrum will become more supportive of European integration over time, as issues that resonate with this policy agenda are increasingly taken up on the supranational level. On the contrary, right-wing parties will be supportive of supranational attempts to liberalise European markets, but will be suspicious of any moves in the opposite direction, namely towards regulation and the development of policies that undermine the free-market ethos.

Finally, the left–right ideological dimension is not the only one that must be taken into account when mapping the spectrum of ideational influences on minority nationalist party attitudes towards European integration. Minority nationalist parties are frequently categorised together with 'green' parties and radical right-wing groups as examples of the 'new politics' wave of political mobilisation that has emerged in several advanced liberal democracies since the 1980s (for example, Newman, 1996). The new politics agenda originates from a shift in the value structures of voting publics away from the traditional socio-economic concerns that underlie the left–right ideological spectrum, to a concern with other social and quality of life issues. Inglehart (1977) referred to this shift as one from material values to post-material values. This transformation manifested itself not only in the emergence of green and ecological groups, but also radical right-wing groups that defend traditional ways of life and challenge the existing political and social order (Ignazi, 2005). There is some evidence that many minority nationalist parties have adopted new politics values into their political agendas. Parties like the BNG in Galicia and Plaid Cymru have incorporated green/libertarian issues into their political programmes, including ecological protection, sustainable development and anti-war stances (Lynch, 1995; Van Atta, 2003). In contrast, the Lega Nord in Italy and the Vlaams Blok/Vlaams Belang in Belgium combine the idiom of minority nationalism with themes associated with right-wing extremism, such as xenophobia and opposition to immigration (Ruzza, 2006; De Winter, Gómez-Reino Cachafeiro and Buelens, 2006). The impact of these ideological values on minority nationalist party attitudes towards Europe can be hypothesised on the basis of patterns observed with regard to other radical right and Green parties. Hooghe et al. (2002: 977–81) have argued that parties on the radical right tend to be by far the most Euro-sceptic of parties, their ideological opposition to European integration being grounded in their defence of national sovereignty and traditional values. In contrast, Green parties have generally become more pro-European over time, as the EU has taken up many key green issues, such as the development of environmental policy and strengthening democracy (Hooghe et al., 2002: 983–84; Bomberg, 2002; Rüdig, 1996). To the extent that minority nationalist parties have new politics propensities – towards the radical right or towards the ecological left – then these ideological values are expected to influence their European attitudes in similar ways.

To summarise, this section has argued that the ideological convictions that constrain minority nationalist party positioning in domestic political arenas will also constrain party positioning on the issue of European integration. In other words, 'European politics is domestic politics by other means' (Hooghe et al., 2002: 985). Given that party ideology and values are features of a party's identity that have evolved gradually over time, the influence of basic ideology is expected to be an enduring determinant of minority nationalist party attitudes towards European integration.

And yet, party ideology does not tell us all that we need to know about political party attitudes towards European integration. In his study of the European positions adopted by socialist parties in several different west European countries,

Featherstone (1988: 307–9) observed that the values broadly held in common by these members of the same party family prompted very different policy formulations vis-à-vis Europe, variation that cannot be explained by ideology alone. Taggart (1998: 378) makes a similar observation in his survey of party attitudes towards Europe, to the effect that 'even within ideological families there are differences'. While ideology may determine the long-term orientations of political party attitudes towards European integration, there are other shorter-term influences that may also exert an influence on how political parties perceive the EU. As suggested above, these include factors originating from the domestic political context as well as from the supranational level.

However, balancing long-term ideological commitments with the shorter-term considerations of party strategy within the domestic party competitive system, and developments and experiences on the supranational level, may lead to new tensions over a party's position on the European issue. These tensions may, in turn, undermine internal party cohesion on the issue of Europe. It is well documented that the issue of European integration has proved particularly divisive for many otherwise coherent political parties (Gaffney, 1996; Taggart, 1998). The presence of internal differentiation related to the EU may hamper the ability of a political party to articulate a coherent European policy. The ways in which this may happen are considered below, before the chapter turns to consider the short-term changes in the domestic and supranational arenas that may trigger such internal tensions.

Internal party cohesion on the issue of Europe

Factions are defined by Janda (1980: 118) as the degree of congruence in the attitudes and conduct of party members. Factions are a fact of life within most political parties (Sartori, 1976/2005; Janda, 1980), and minority nationalist parties seem particularly prone to such intra-party divisions (Newman, 1994: 46–53; De Winter, 1998: 222–35). Both Panebianco (1988) and Harmel et al. (1995) have linked programmatic change with changes in the power relations between different sub-party units that compose a party. The efficacy of factions depends on their degree of organisation, their resources and their durability. Their motivation may also be important; that is, whether they seek power within the organisation, contest different strategies, or represent different ideological currents competing for predominance. However, the difficulty of identifying different factions within the party, identifying their motivations and their degree of organisational solidity, makes studying the nature and impact of factions difficult and essentially impressionistic (Hine, 1982). Nevertheless, it is important to consider how the presence of intra-party dissent might impact upon a minority nationalist party's attitude towards European integration.

Both Taggart (1998) and Sitter (2002) have argued that factions within established political parties specifically on the issue of European integration tend to be confined to those parties that are central to the political system; for example, the major political parties that are either in government, or the main opposition parties. While in some cases, such as within the British Conservative Party, these factions are motivated by an ideological position which is contrary to that of the party leadership, in other cases, factions may emerge as a result of changes in the nature of party competition. Thus, for example, electoral defeat may lead to the emergence of factions, as different groups take the opportunity to challenge the leadership's European policy or strategy, and replace it with an alternative European policy or strategy. The degree to which these factions will succeed in changing a party's position on Europe depends on how organised they are, how much support they command within the party, and how much resources they have to support their mobilisation. Johansson and Raunio (2001: 228) have suggested that, in some cases, it might be better to speak of different issue groups instead of factions, which seek to 'influence the way in which power is exercised (by others) on given questions' to do with the EU rather than constitute 'solidly organized, disciplined, self-aware groups, enjoying a relatively stable and cohesive personnel over time' (Hine, 1982: 38–39). The deeper these internal divisions go, the more constrained the party will be in the articulation of its European discourse.

Intra-party divisions are very rarely seen as advantageous. On the contrary, 'being seen as divided undermines the degree of certainty that electors have about parties' trajectories' (Taggart, 1998: 373) and is, therefore, something that political parties will try to avoid at all costs. In cases where such divisions on the issue of Europe do exist, parties may develop different strategies for coping with this internal incoherence. Ignoring such divisions, attempting to suppress dissent on Europe, or expelling activists with views that do not echo those of the party leadership are risky strategies, since they may rob the leadership of legitimacy and may lead to the formation of new challenger parties competing directly on the European issue. Rather, Aylott's (2002) research on the internal divisions on Europe within Scandinavian political parties has led him to argue that political parties will instead seek to manage internal division carefully. In particular, the leadership of a political party will seek to compartmentalise the European issue; that is, to confine divisions on Europe to specific arenas within the party in order to 'isolate the potentially damaging effects that divisive European questions have' on party unity and, therefore, vote maximisation (ibid.: 454). Thus, for example, a political party might decide to hold an internal referendum to finally decide its position on Europe, in order to remove the European issue from the political agenda. A party might also make positive moves to acknowledge, tolerate or even co-opt activists with divergent views on Europe, since doing so takes the 'sting' out of internal dissent and does not allow factionalism to escalate into a serious threat to party unity. Political parties may, therefore, attempt to direct debate on the European questions to specific political arenas, thus keeping the European issue out of other arenas where such divisions would be electorally damaging (for example, general elections). Parties that are not successful in managing internal divisions over Europe will risk a decline in their electoral performance, since divided parties are unattractive to voters (ibid.: 442). In the worst-case scenario, internal dissidents may leave the political party to create their own distinct group to compete on the European issue.

Factors from the domestic political context

Within the broad parameters set by a party's identity and ideology, shorter-term changes in party strategy and tactics within the context of the domestic party system can also affect a party's position on European integration. Party strategy and tactics will be shaped, in turn, by the structure of the domestic political system, and the opportunities available to political actors to articulate their interests within this arena. Several authors have explored these effects. The status of the party within the party system, whether a party aspires to hold public office or not, the degree of competition between different parties on the issue of Europe, and public attitudes towards European issues have all been identified as being important in shaping political party attitudes towards Europe (Featherstone, 1988; Johansson and Raunio, 2001; Sitter, 2002; Batory and Sitter, 2004). However, influences emanating from the domestic context may push and pull parties in a different direction over Europe, and may not necessarily sit easily with the basic ideological preferences of the party. Policy changes for shorter-term electoral gains may well enter into conflict with a party's fundamental ideological principles. Conflicting views within parties on the issue of Europe may also lead to the emergence of factions divided over how best to approach the issue of European integration, as discussed above. In such a situation, the dilemma facing any political party is whether there is any space to adapt the details of party policy on Europe in response to short-term contextual political changes, whilst remaining faithful to basic party values. Taking a closer look at the different aspects of the domestic political context will help to grasp the nature of this dilemma.

The dynamics of party competition

The changing dynamics of party competition within the domestic political arena, and the strategic and tactical decisions taken by political parties as they pursue their goals of influencing policy, maximising votes and achieving public office, will impact upon party positions on European integration (Sitter, 2002). In the first place, the position of the party within the political system is important. A party adopting an anti-system strategy (Seiler, 1982) will position itself at the fringes of the political system and, since it declares itself in clear opposition to that system, will refuse to participate in electoral competition or aim to participate within its governing institutions.[10] Taggart (1998: 372) notes that peripherality in the party system often leads to Euro-scepticism, as opposition to European integration is adopted as 'an ideological appendage to a more general system critique'. In other words, opposition to European integration is justified on the grounds that the EU is merely an extension and amplification of the failures of the domestic political system (Sitter, 2002). Such ideologically motivated anti-Europeanism can be found in protest parties on both the left and the right wings of the political spectrum. Positioning within the party system, therefore, can be a more important determinant of party position on European integration than ideology alone (Taggart, 1998: 383). Opposition to Europe becomes 'a secondary issue which can relatively costlessly be appropriated to strengthen [the party's] claims to be an alternative to the political centre' (ibid.: 384). Minority nationalist parties who adopt such an anti-system strategy are expected to be similarly opposed to European integration, regardless of where they are situated on the left–right ideological spectrum.

However, if a party takes the decision to compete in elections and aims for representation in public office on the regional or state level, the direction of party competition changes from the centrifugal dynamic maintained by anti-system parties at the fringes of the political system, to a centripetal one in which parties move towards the centre ground. The general experiences of other small or new parties upon entering the competitive party arena suggests that going down the avenue of electoral competition will generate a pressure on parties to adapt their political message in two ways: to broaden its content and moderate its tone (Pedersen, 1982; Harmel, 1985; Müller-Rommel and Pridham, 1991; Poguntke, 2001; Müller-Rommel, 2002). Not only must parties rise to the challenge of competing with other parties on a range of socio-economic issues that may go beyond their 'core business', but they must also broaden their appeal beyond their traditional support base if they are to achieve the coveted goal of public office. The closer a party comes to participation in government, the greater the pressure to adapt its political message in these ways becomes. Such a pattern of programmatic broadening and moderation is more likely in a multiparty system where coalition government is the norm, rather than in a two-party system where it is much more difficult for small parties such as minority nationalist parties to gain access to governing arenas.

If these dynamics are applied to minority nationalist parties and the issue of Europe, then one can expect that the closer a minority nationalist party comes to achieving public office – whether on the state or regional level – the more likely it is that the party will moderate the general tone of its European discourse and thrash out the details of its position on specific EU policies. In the event that a minority nationalist party began this transition towards the centre ground from the periphery of the political system, then the party's position on European integration may undergo a complete revision, from opposition to support for Europe. This expectation is based, in part, on Sitter's (2002: 16) observation that 'catch-all' political parties competing for the centre ground have very little incentive to be anything but pro-European. Firstly, these parties' quest for executive office makes it difficult to oppose a European project that they either have in the past been, or might be in the future, deeply involved in as a party of national government. Secondly, the need for catch-all parties to appeal to a broad coalition of social and political interests means it is 'easier to build a cross-class alliance in favour of integration than against it' (ibid.: 22). In the event that a party crosses the threshold of government, these pressures for moderating and specifying the party's position on Europe will be exacerbated. In coalition government, political parties have to negotiate and compromise on policy goals, and will have to prioritise their agendas and focus on those ideas that can be realistically achieved (Heinisch, 2003: 101–2). For minority nationalist parties, this may lead to a playing down of the symbolic rhetoric of a Europe of the Regions, in favour of concentrating on the details of how European policy making impacts upon the minority nation in question. However, adaptation to these new roles and requirements will not be without its problems. A moderate catch-all European discourse may alienate the party's core voters. The constraints on party action in government office may also force a minority nationalist party to act in a way that goes against the party's fundamental ideological principles. At best, a failure to resolve these internal tensions may risk the party's political and electoral credibility (see the discussion on factionalism above). At worst, the party's survival as a political organisation may be at risk.

Political space on the issue of Europe

The degree of political space a party has within a political system will determine the scope it has to exploit the European dimension. This refers not only to the number of parties competing against each other, but also to the degree to which other parties have colonised the European issue. A party that is alone in promoting a European dimension may have a considerably freer hand to explore different formulations than when there is electoral competition from other parties playing the European card. In the latter case, parties may come under pressure to make themselves more distinctive vis-à-vis their partisan opponents, which may lead to a change or radicalisation in the party's position on the EU. Again, however, too much change or excessive radicalism runs the same risk of violating the party's basic ideological principles or alienating its core support base. On the contrary, no changes at all would make it difficult for voters to distinguish between the party's European credentials and that of other political parties, thus reducing the party's capacity to exploit the European dimensions for political gain in the competition against other political parties.

The structure of the domestic political system

Thus far, these propositions about the impact of party competitive dynamics on the European attitudes of minority nationalist parties have assumed that such competition occurs within a single territorial arena, usually that of the state. For the majority of political party families, this arena of competition is indeed the most important one. For minority nationalist parties, however, it is the regional level that constitutes what Deschouwer (2003: 216) calls the 'core level'. This is because the ultimate goal of minority nationalist parties is to reorganise political authority within the state in such a way that greater autonomy is granted to the minority nation. Moreover, minority nationalist parties have no organisation at a higher territorial level, and seek to mobilise electoral support only within the minority nation they claim to represent. The regional level is thus intrinsically the most important level for the minority nationalist political project.

This does not mean that minority nationalist parties confine party behaviour to the regional level. On the contrary, minority nationalist parties frequently seek representation at several different territorial levels: local, regional, state and European. The state level, for example, will always be an important focus for minority nationalist political activity, since the reorganisation of the state power structure in order to increase the degree of regional self-government can be approved only by legislative bodies at the state level (De Winter, 1998: 211–12). Achieving policy influence at the state level is thus crucial in order to secure further rights for the minority nation. Minority nationalist parties may also place importance on competing at the European and local levels, although the way in which these levels matter may differ from regional and state levels. Thus, for example, European elections may be less important in the sense that the European Parliament does not have a direct impact on the territorial redistribution of political authority within any member state. However, representation within the European Parliament may be symbolically important, since it enables minority nationalist parties to claim that they can bypass the state and represent their nation's interests directly on the supranational level. Having an MEP may be particularly important if the party is excluded from institutional arenas on the regional and state levels. Similarly, securing a presence within local institutions may also be a priority if other levels of representation are closed off.

For minority nationalist parties, therefore, the reality of party competition is very often that of acting at multiple political levels simultaneously. This may generate complex tensions between party behaviour at different political levels, which in turn may constitute different and competing pressures on what a minority nationalist party can say about Europe. It is expected that the level of party competition which exerts the strongest influence on a party's attitude towards Europe will be the one where the party is most 'relevant' in its impact on the political system, whether this be due to the degree of political representation or its pivotal position vis-à-vis other parties (Sartori, 1976/2005). Changes in the relative importance of these different spheres of competition may lead to corresponding changes in the nature and degree of influence exerted on the European attitudes of a minority nationalist party.

Public attitudes towards European integration

Even if a party has clear political space on the European issue vis-à-vis its partisan competitors, it would make little sense to pursue such a policy if it had little appeal to the electorate that the party is targeting. Empirical studies have shown that when one party has a clear-cut advantage on an issue with regard to popular appeal, it regularly emphasises that issue, while another party which does not have such an advantage will prefer to focus on another policy issue where it does have a clear advantage (Riker, 1993). The nature of public opinion on European integration may, therefore, bolster or hinder the translation of a party's attitude towards Europe into concrete political and/or electoral appeal. A Euro-sceptic public, for example, will have little time for a zealously pro-European party, and vice versa. A party that is out of tune with public opinion is likely to de-emphasise the European issue and focus on another issue that is more likely to translate into electoral gain. On the contrary, a party in tune with public opinion will make a great deal more of this issue, since doing so may yield significant electoral gains.

The role of European Parliament elections

General party dynamics played out at state and sub-state levels are expected to exert the greatest influence on minority nationalist party attitudes towards European integration. However, there is good cause to pay specific attention to the role that European Parliament elections may play in the formulation of minority nationalist party attitudes towards European integration. Securing representation within the European Parliament will be important for minority nationalist parties for several reasons. Firstly, Raunio (2003), drawing on the work of Reif and Schmitt (1980), argues that the second-order nature of European elections means that small parties such as minority nationalist parties often do better in European elections than in other statewide or regional elections. Electoral success in European elections can be useful in order to boost the image of a minority nationalist party as being 'electable'. Secondly, for minority nationalist parties who are supportive of further European integration as a way of securing greater national self-determination, achieving representation within the European Parliament can serve to establish a direct connection between the territorial agenda of the party and the EU as a potential arena for resolving key party concerns in this respect. In particular, having an MEP may be symbolically important if the party is excluded from statewide and regional institutional arenas, and may bolster claims that the minority nationalist party can bypass the state and go straight to Europe.

However, if gaining representation within the European Parliament may be strategically important for minority nationalist parties, crossing this threshold of representation is neither automatic nor guaranteed, since a party must meet the entry conditions for the European parliamentary sphere. The specification of these conditions will vary, and their definition may be out of the hands of nationalist parties themselves since the rules are usually defined by state authorities. Where the threshold of representation is low, and where a party gets better than average results in European Parliament elections, minority nationalist parties will perceive European elections to be a positive opportunity for advancing its nation-building project. On the contrary, in cases where the threshold of representation is very high and the supranational political arena is closed off for these parties, competing in European elections will not be a strategic priority since the political gains are negligible. Moreover, it is possible that these disadvantageous conditions will be taken as proof of the limited value of the supranational polity for the minority nation, and will contribute to a more sceptical evaluation of the concrete benefits of European integration for the minority nation.

Factors at the supranational level

It is not only factors emanating from the domestic political context that will influence minority nationalist party attitudes towards European integration.

Developments in European integration, and specific experiences of co-operation with other actors directly on the supranational level, also constitute a further set of variables that may influence minority nationalist party attitudes towards European integration. It is to consider the impact of these factors emanating from the supranational level that this chapter now turns.

Developments in European integration

European integration is an incremental process that, in fifty years, has transformed the European polity, and will continue to do so in the future. Political actors contemplating the effects of integration are thus engaged in a dynamic and reflexive process, since European integration may affect their interests in different ways at different times. Political party positions towards Europe are therefore unlikely to be static, based on a one-off evaluation of what Europe has to offer. Just as European integration itself is a dynamic and ongoing process, so political parties will be constantly engaged with, and will reflect upon, these developments at the supranational level.

Evidence from research on other party families attests the degree to which party attitudes are indeed responsive to such changes. When European integration is seen to be developing in tune with a party's political priorities, support for the EU will be more forthcoming and easier to justify (Hooghe *et al.*, 2002). Thus social democratic parties that were opposed to the market-making dynamic of integration in the 1980s have, on the whole, become distinctly more pro-integration as regulated capitalism has increasingly come onto the European agenda, and have increasingly come to view European integration as a means for projecting social democratic goals onto a liberalising world economy (Hix and Lord, 1997; Ladrech, 2000; Hooghe *et al.*, 2002). Similarly, with regard to Green parties in different European states, Bomberg (2002: 34) notes that while 'the EU has always provided much grist for the Greens' mill ... recent EU policies have provided new (or newly revived) issues especially amenable to Green campaigns'.

Minority nationalist parties are also expected to assess the degree to which developments on the supranational level resonate with their own political agendas. As 'ethnic entrepreneurs' (Türsan, 1998: 6–7) involved in the ongoing construction of the nation as an imagined community of shared symbols and common identification, minority nationalist parties will be highly aware of developments in European integration that may impinge upon their political projects. As argued above, minority nationalist parties will evaluate European integration along two dimensions: the general potential of European integration to resolve the centre–periphery confrontation within which these parties are embroiled, and the more specific role that the EU can play in providing solutions for the socio-economic, political and cultural needs of the minority nation (the EU as a concrete reality). As noted in Chapter 1, given that many developments in European integration since the 1980s seemed to convince many minority nationalist parties that a very different kind of European polity was being created – a regional Europe with the potential for satisfying minority nationalist demands for greater autonomy – one would expect to see minority nationalist parties becoming more supportive of the general idea of Europe over time. In the event that European integration ceases to move in this general direction, then this diffuse support may be compromised, and the fundamental linkage between European integration and national self-determination may be questioned and ultimately abandoned. With regard to specific support for the EU in its concrete form, minority nationalist parties will assess the more immediate benefits for the nation of being a part of the supranational polity. If the EU consistently fails to meet the specific demands of minority nationalist parties, then support for the EU as a concrete reality is likely to decline.

Transnational links and co-operation on the supranational level

For many political parties, minority nationalist parties included, the European Parliament represents the only institutional arena within which direct representation on the supranational level can be achieved, provided the party succeeds in satisfying the criteria for passing this threshold of representation. Once such representation is achieved, there are clear incentives to join one of the party groups within the parliament, often referred to as 'Europarties'. These include financial benefits, the right to address the European Parliament and to take part in various deliberative processes, and the exchange of information and experiences. There are currently eight party groupings within the European Parliament.[11]

Participation in party groups within the European Parliament may exert an important influence on a political party's attitude towards Europe. Ladrech (2000) conceptualises this in terms of a process of socialisation, which in turn may serve as a top-down influence on the party at home. Drawing on evidence from his study of the Party of European Socialists (PES) within the European Parliament, Ladrech argues that the PES 'exists for its members, of its members, but also autonomous from its members' (ibid.: 14). This top-down influence is a consequence of interaction with like-minded people, resulting in a policy/programmatic diffusion through a mutual exchange of information and ideas, which may trickle down and be incorporated on the level of the individual party. It is not necessarily the case, however, that such a process of socialisation will make parties more pro-European, an effect often referred to in academic circles and journalistic spheres alike as 'going native'. Scully's (2005) authoritative study of MEPs within the European Parliament has shown that there is no evidence that MEPs become more pro-European once they are elected to, and spend several years in, the European Parliament. Rather, the effect of participation in Europarties is expected to be more of a reinforcing and deepening of existing attitudes towards European integration, or the incorporation of ideas and notions complimentary to those already espoused by the individual political party.

Such a top-down influence may equally be expected in the case of minority nationalist parties who succeed in gaining representation within the European Parliament. Most minority nationalist parties who have been represented in the European Parliament have sat with the Greens/EFA group (Hix and Lord, 1997: 46–47). The EFA was established in 1981, with six members. Since then, its membership has increased dramatically to include over twenty parties. The EFA defines itself as a genuine European political party, and is treated as such within the European Parliament. De Winter and Gómez-Reino (2002) have argued that the EFA constitutes a truly European party family built from scratch, which has succeeded in defining a common regionalist European agenda for minority nationalist parties that are otherwise ideologically highly diverse and weakly institutionalised. As an organisation, the EFA provides material and financial support for its members, and offers an institutional and strategic framework for articulating minority nationalist interests within the European Parliament. Minority nationalist parties who join the EFA will do so because they sign up to the regionalist vision of Europe offered by this organisation. Membership of the EFA is likely to further reinforce this Europeanist rhetoric, will encourage parties to develop such a discourse in more depth, and will allow parties to develop a more sophisticated European policy agenda in co-operation with other like-minded minority nationalist parties.

Of course, the EFA is not the only option for minority nationalist parties within the European Parliament. Preliminary research on the ideological nature of the different Europarties suggest that they can be differentiated in terms of their position on the traditional left–right axis, and on their degree of support for European integration (McElroy and Benoit, 2007). Minority nationalist parties, like other political parties, are most likely to sit with the Europarty that most resembles their own ideological orientations. Since minority nationalist parties differ widely in terms of their position on the left–right ideological spectrum, it is not surprising that many have chosen to be members of alternative groups within the European Parliament. Thus, for example, the Basque PNV sits with the European People's Party-European Democrats (EPP-ED), while the Italian Lega Nord currently sits with the Union for European Nations (UEN) group. Interestingly, the two parties that form the coalition party CiU in Catalonia sit in different groups in the European Parliament, with Unió Democrática de Catalunya (UDC) a member of the EPP-ED, while Convergéncia Democrática de Catalunya (CDC) sits with the European Liberal and Democrat Reform Party (ELDR). Whatever Europarty a minority nationalist party decides to join, a similar bolstering effect of its attitude towards European integration is to be expected. On the contrary, parties who are not able to cross the threshold of representation on the European level, or choose not to join one of the established Europarties, will not be subject to such a reinforcement effect.

Conclusion

This chapter has outlined a framework for analysing minority nationalist party attitudes towards European integration. By drawing on the theoretical and empirical insights of a growing scholarly interest in the Europeanisation of political parties, and a broader literature on political parties and party systems, several propositions have been formulated about how and why minority nationalist parties will change their attitudes towards Europe.

The proposed framework of analysis is composed of two dimensions, the first aimed at conceptualising and measuring the content of minority nationalist party attitudes towards Europe, and the second focusing on the identification of factors that may come to bear on the process by which parties arrive at a stance on Europe. With regard to the content of minority nationalist party attitudes towards Europe, it is proposed that a distinction must be made between diffuse support for the basic idea of Europe, and support for the concrete reality of European integration. While the former relates to the potential of Europe to resolve the centre–periphery confrontation, the latter refers to the impact in real terms that different European economic, political and cultural policies may have on the minority nation in question. Depending on how minority nationalist parties evaluate European integration along each of these dimensions, one of four possible types of attitude towards European integration will be adopted: Euro-enthusiast, Euro-reject, Euro-sceptic or Euro-pragmatist. As far as the factors shaping minority nationalist party attitudes towards Europe are concerned, three broad sets of factors have been identified that are expected to impact upon how minority nationalist parties make sense of European integration. These are: factors internal to the party itself, factors arising from the domestic political context and factors emanating from the supranational arena. In each case, the chapter has undertaken a detailed examination of what kind of influence each factor is expected to exert, and how its impact may alter in strength and significance over time.

In the next three chapters, this analytical framework is applied to the study of minority nationalist party attitudes towards Europe in Wales, Galicia and Corsica.

3 Wales
Plaid Cymru

This chapter examines the European attitudes of Plaid Cymru, the Welsh nationalist party established in 1924, and the main mouthpiece of minority nationalist demands in Wales ever since. During Plaid Cymru's lifetime, the party's attitude towards European integration has undergone several important transformations. The chapter identifies three stages in the evolution of Plaid Cymru's position on Europe. Firstly, during the mid-1970s, Plaid Cymru combined a strong ideological commitment to an international framework for Welsh self-determination with vitriolic opposition to the EEC as it was developing at the time, not least due to the negative implications of economic integration for the Welsh economy. By the mid-1980s, however, Plaid Cymru had abandoned its opposition to the EEC. In its place, the party adopted a passionately Europeanist discourse that called for 'full national status for Wales within Europe'. This European dimension provided the framework for rethinking how best to achieve other policy goals that had hitherto been conceptualised in exclusively domestic terms. This second stage of zealous Euro-enthusiasm was to characterise Plaid Cymru's attitude towards European integration until the late 1990s. More recently, however, developments in European integration, combined with the transformation of the Welsh political environment in the wake of devolution in 1999, have forced Plaid Cymru to reconsider its position on European integration once again. The failure of European integration to create a Europe of the Regions, and growing disillusionment with actually existing Europe, led Plaid Cymru to abandon its post-sovereigntist rhetoric in favour of a more conventional demand for 'independence for Wales in Europe'. At the same time, a growing Euro-scepticism among the Welsh electorate and new pressures on Plaid Cymru to transform itself into a credible political party of potential regional government, have led the party to de-emphasise a 'Wales in Europe' discourse that no longer serves as an attractive vote-winning agenda in post-devolution Wales. Instead, the party has sought other, more promising, ways of advancing its nationalist goals via domestic political channels. Plaid Cymru's entry into coalition government in May 2007 has opened up new opportunities for influencing European policy making and bolstering Welsh autonomy. With such opportunities not forthcoming at the European level, the party's commitment to 'independence in Europe' has been relegated to the domain of symbolic politics.

The chapter argues that these various attempts at making sense of European integration reflect an ongoing struggle within Plaid Cymru to reconcile a fundamental ideological commitment to Wales as a European nation with the ever-changing dynamics of Welsh, British and European politics. At times, the political context in these three political arenas has made it easy to translate this principled support for European co-operation into a concrete project that sets out the opportunities for the Welsh nation within the framework of the EEC and, after 1992, the EU. At other times, however, the dynamics of party competition at home and developments on the supranational level have made it very difficult for Plaid Cymru to defend a political project that posits a strengthening of Welsh self-government within a framework of European co-operation. The case of Plaid Cymru demonstrates clearly that, whilst basic party ideology dictates the broad parameters of minority nationalist party attitudes towards European integration, the substance of European policy is contingent on the shorter-term changes in domestic and European politics. The latter in particular has played a determining role in shaping Plaid Cymru's attitude towards European integration.

The origins and development of Plaid Cymru

Plaid Cymru was established as a result of the joining of forces of two smaller nationalist groups, the Welsh Nationalist Party and Mudiad Cymreig. Most commentators divide Plaid Cymru's subsequent evolution into three periods: from 1925 to 1939 under the leadership of Saunders Lewis; from 1945 to 1981 under the leadership of Gwynfor Evans; and from 1981 onwards with Dafydd Wigley and Dafydd Elis Thomas alternating as party presidents (Christiansen, 1998; McAllister, 2001; Gwilym, 2000; Wyn Jones, 2007).

In its earliest years, Plaid Cymru was first and foremost a pressure group for the protection and promotion of the Welsh language, its political agenda informed by the Catholic conservatism of the poet and prominent cultural figure, Saunders Lewis (Wyn Jones, 1999). However, for the first forty years of its existence, the party made very little impact upon the Welsh political scene, due to a combination of lack of members, lack of finance and lack of political motivation (Davies, 1983: 262). Gwynfor Evans's presidency from 1945 until 1981 was characterised by an attempt to bring Plaid Cymru out of the political and electoral wilderness. Party energies and resources were focused on fighting elections and contesting an incremental number of parliamentary constituencies. Plaid Cymru also abandoned the ideological purity of its forefathers and adopted a more detailed socio-economic programme inspired by the principles of 'community socialism'. As a result, 'Plaid Cymru's politics became more practical, more concrete, and more "normal"' (Wyn Jones, 1999: 189). By the end of the 1960s, this was a strategy that seemed finally to be paying off, bringing to an end the period of 'drift and fragmentation' (Butt Philip, 1975: 85) that had characterised Plaid Cymru's political fortunes in the post-war era. Plaid Cymru won its first Westminster parliamentary seat in the 1966 Carmarthen by-election. This was followed by further electoral successes in the late 1960s and 1970s in local and general elections (Butt Philip, 1975: 105–23; McAllister, 2001: 112–13).

A third stage in Plaid Cymru's evolution began with Dafydd Wigley's presidency in 1981. Wigley oversaw renewed attempts at broadening the party's electoral appeal beyond its geographical concentration in the Welsh-speaking heartlands of Wales. This strategy was continued under Dafydd Elis Thomas's leadership from 1984 to 1991. Thomas's aim was to create a dynamic, modern and inclusive party firmly anchored in the centre–left of Welsh politics (Lynch, 1995; Wyn Jones, 1996). The electoral dividends of this strategy coincided with Wigley's return to the presidency for a second time, in 1991. From 1991 until Wigley's resignation in 2000, Plaid Cymru experienced a period of electoral growth unprecedented in the party's history (McAllister, 2001: 83; see Tables 3.1, 3.2 and 3.3). The party's electoral performance peaked in 1999, in the first elections to the newly established National Assembly for Wales (NAW) (Table 3.3). It is arguable that the creation of this institution constituted a fourth stage in the party's development. After eight years of being the main party of opposition within this institution, Plaid Cymru entered into coalition government with the Labour Party in June 2007. Over a period of just over eighty years, therefore, Plaid Cymru has been transformed from being an educational and cultural movement in defence of the Welsh language on the margins of British politics, to a mainstream political party at the heart of Welsh politics.

During this lifetime, Plaid Cymru has shown varying degrees of interest in, and enthusiasm for, European affairs generally and, from the 1950s onwards, the specific project of European integration. The remainder of this chapter examines how a party that was, from its earliest years, ideologically committed to the idea of Wales as a nation with both a European past and a European destiny, sought to come to terms with concrete attempts at fostering European unity through co-operation in economic and, later, political affairs.

The ideological heritage: Wales as a European nation

Plaid Cymru has a long tradition of looking beyond its own borders in the articulation and legitimation of Welsh self-determination (Nairn, 1977: 198). It is an internationalism that was bequeathed to the party by one of its founding fathers, Saunders Lewis. For Lewis, Wales was a European nation by virtue of having shared in the European Christian heritage of the Middle Ages (Lewis, 1926: 2). Within a Europe united under the rule of the Vatican, Wales and other nations were 'free' to cultivate their cultural and linguistic diversity within the framework of Christian morality and values. This golden age had come to an end towards the close of the sixteenth century, with the rise of nationalism across Europe. The monarchical challenge to the power of the Roman Catholic Church, the threat of Protestantism, and the rise of centralised bureaucracies with their privileging of the material over the spiritual, brought an end to the political, cultural and social freedom enjoyed by Europe's small nations. For Lewis, the aim of Welsh nationalism should be to re-establish this respect for tradition within a continental community of shared morality, such as Wales enjoyed in the Middle Ages.

Table 3.1 European Parliament election results for Wales, 1979–2004

Party	1979 %	1979 Seats	1984 %	1984 Seats	1989 %	1989 Seats	1994 %	1994 Seats	1999 %	1999 Seats	2004 %	2004 Seats
Labour	41.5	3	44.5	3	48.9	4	55.9	4	31.9	2	32.5	2
Conservative	36.6	1	25.4	1	23.4	0	14.6	0	22.8	1	19.4	1
Liberal Democrat	9.6	0	17.4	0	3.6	0	8.7	0	8.2	0	10.5	0
Plaid Cymru	11.7	0	12.2	0	12.9	0	17.1	0	29.6	2	17.4	1
Others	0.6	0	0.6	0	11.2	0	3.7	0	7.5	0	20.2	0
Total	100	4	100	4	100	4	100	4	100	5	100	4

Source: Thrasher and Rallings (2007).

Table 3.2 General election results in Wales, 1979–2005

Party	1979 %	1979 Seats	1983 %	1983 Seats	1987 %	1987 Seats	1992 %	1992 Seats	1997 %	1997 Seats	2001 %	2001 Seats	2005 %	2005 Seats
Labour	47.0	22	37.5	20	45.1	24	49.5	27	54.7	34	48.6	34	42.7	29
Conservative	32.2	11	31.0	14	29.5	8	28.6	6	19.6	0	21.0	0	21.4	3
Liberal Democrat	10.6	1	23.2	2	17.9	3	17.9	1	12.4	2	13.8	2	18.4	4
Plaid Cymru	8.1	2	7.8	2	7.3	3	8.8	4	9.9	4	14.3	4	12.6	3
Others	2.2	0	0.4	0	0.2	0	0.7	0	3.4	0	2.3	0	4.9	0
Total	100	36	100	38	100	38	100	38	100	40	100	40	100	40

Source: Thrasher and Rallings (2007).

Table 3.3 National Assembly for Wales election results, 1999–2007

Party	1999			2003			2007		
	1st vote %	2nd vote %	Total seats	1st vote %	2nd vote %	Total seats	1st vote %	2nd vote %	Total seats
Labour	37.6	35.5	28	40.0	36.6	30	32.2	29.6	26
Conservative	15.8	16.5	9	19.9	19.2	11	22.4	21.5	12
Liberal Democrat	13.5	12.5	6	14.1	12.7	6	14.8	11.7	6
Plaid Cymru	28.4	30.6	17	21.2	19.7	12	22.4	21.0	15
Others	4.7	4.9	0	4.8	11.8	1	8.3	16.3	1
Total	100	100	60	100	100	60	100	100	60

Sources: Wyn Jones and Tristan (2000); Wyn Jones and Scully (2004a); Scully and Elias (2008).

'Freedom' was the terminology chosen by Lewis to denote this final aim of Welsh nationalist mobilisation, a status that was clearly distinguished from 'independence'. Lewis rejected the latter, which he equated to full sovereignty, on the grounds that it was contradictory to his Christian beliefs, as well as being undesirable.

> The principle of independence ... is anti-Christian and I cannot accept it in view of that ... Above all, let us not seek independence for Wales. Not because it isn't practical, but because it isn't worth having ... it is a materialist and evil thing, leading to violence and oppression.
>
> (Lewis, 1926: 4)

Instead, the nebulous notion of 'freedom' drew on a conceptualisation of authority characteristic of the Middle Ages where a shared Christian morality was wedded to national linguistic, cultural, legal and political diversity. Lewis paid little heed to the constitutional, institutional or political form that such freedom should assume. As long as Wales had the capacity to pursue its own interests, and to do so through the medium of Welsh, the concrete manifestation of this idea of freedom was of secondary importance (Wyn Jones, 1999: 176).

This distinction between 'freedom' and 'independence' was certainly more apparent than substantial. For one thing, Lewis's constitutional thinking idealised the degree of freedom enjoyed by Wales within the Roman Empire in the Middle Ages, despite evidence that Welsh culture and language had not in fact prospered to the same degree as asserted by Lewis. Lewis was also too dismissive of the rise of modern nationalism which premised the formulation of the principles of popular sovereignty and representative democracy (Wyn Jones, 1999: 178). It was also not the case that the rise of modern nationalism brought an end to all forms of supranational co-operation, as asserted by Lewis; on the contrary, such co-operation has continued to be a feature of the modern era. In short, 'from a historical perspective, the moral distinction made by Lewis between "freedom" and "independence" was a castle built on sand' (Wyn Jones, 1999: 177).

Nevertheless, Lewis's Europeanist ideas would shape Plaid Cymru's constitutional thinking for generations to come. An alternative agenda of co-operative small nation politics within a broader international context would become deeply ingrained in Plaid Cymru's political mindset, even if Lewis's particular Catholic anti-modernist interpretation of this Europeanist discourse was abandoned for being anachronistic and at odds with the radical nonconformist Protestantism and left-wing orientation of the majority of Plaid Cymru's membership (Wyn Jones, 1999). Firstly, Welsh nationality claims were not to be advocated in a vacuum, but as part of a European and world community (Davies, 1983: 81). Gwynfor Evans, Lewis's successor as Plaid Cymru president, argued several years later that 'Wales is a European nation, one that kept its uniqueness throughout the centuries and until the present day, despite having been terribly injured and divided given the lack of institutions to defend and nurture her' (Evans, 1966, quoted in Wyn Jones, 2007: 125). Secondly, the ultimate aim of Welsh self-government would always be understood as something falling short of full sovereign independence, although the precise form of such a status was left open for elaboration. In the 1930s, for example, Plaid Cymru was wedded to the idea of 'dominion status' within the British Commonwealth as its long-term ambition for the Welsh nation; whilst, by the 1950s, this had been replaced by a demand for greater autonomy for Wales within a Britannic confederation. In subsequent years, these two principles would provide the ideational parameters for defining Plaid Cymru's position on European integration.

'Europe YES, the EEC NO': divided over Europe

Given this long-standing Europeanist commitment, one would have expected Plaid Cymru to respond enthusiastically to the process of European integration embarked upon in the 1950s, as a project that would put into place the kind of overarching continental framework so central to the party's constitutional thinking (Davies, 1996). Such enthusiasm for European integration was not, however, forthcoming. Instead, Plaid Cymru was largely disinterested in European affairs until the 1970s. It would take the party until 1975 to formulate a European policy worthy of the name.

This is not to say that Plaid Cymru was completely unaware of the advances in European co-operation. During the 1960s, Gwynfor Evans frequently referred to the European Common Market as a model for a British common market of which Wales would be a member (Wyn Jones, 2007: 151). However, there is no evidence of either a significant engagement with, or enthusiasm for, European integration. Europe simply did not feature in Plaid Cymru's world view, which was defined instead through British Commonwealth, and later – with the dismantling of the British Empire – British frames of reference (Lynch, 1996: 58–59). Until well into the 1980s, for example, the party's constitutional policies aimed for a Welsh government within a British federation, complemented by an internal market for the British Isles, with authority for certain issues (defence and macroeconomic policy) residing with the British state. Rather, during these early years of European integration, Plaid Cymru's attention was firmly fixed on events much closer to home. In particular, the increasing militancy of the Welsh-language group Cymdeithas yr Iaith in the late 1960s and early 1970s, and the negative repercussions this had on Plaid Cymru's image as a serious and moderate political party, meant that Plaid Cymru's leadership had little time to discuss any other major policy issues, European integration included (Evans, 2005: 337).

The European issue was nevertheless forced onto Plaid Cymru's agenda as a result of two political developments. Firstly, in 1961 the UK government announced its intention to apply for membership of the EEC, even though it would take until 1973 for the application to be finally accepted. Secondly, Gwynfor Evans's election to Westminster in 1966 brought with it unprecedented political and media scrutiny of the party's political programme. Plaid Cymru was required to adopt a position on a number of issues which had hitherto not featured in the party's manifestos, among them the European question.

The first clues as to the nature of Plaid Cymru's attitudes towards the EEC were provided in May 1967 during a debate in the House of Commons on the EEC. Gwynfor Evans's intervention is worth quoting at length.

> I do not want to give the impression that I am against the Common Market as an idea. I am simply saying that, if we enter in the present conditions, the effect on Wales could be disastrous. I think the Common Market could be an effective device for protecting the existence and development of Europe's small countries, by ensuring their political freedom whilst also providing them with the advantages of large economic units. It offers the possibility that Europe's heritage will be much richer as a result of giving national communities the right conditions for developing their potential fully. This would be a Europe of Nations, and not a Europe of States. Wales, Scotland, Brittany and many other nations could benefit immensely from such a Europe, and they would have a major contribution to make.
>
> (Evans, 1967: 30)

This declaration revealed the basic parameters of Plaid Cymru's attitude towards Europe until the late 1970s: a commitment in principle to the idea of a Europe of small historic nations, but a rejection of the EEC as it had developed up to that point as being damaging for Welsh economic and political interests. This position was further elaborated upon in the campaign for the referendum to be held on 5 June 1975 on continued British membership of the EEC.

Plaid Cymru's slogan for the referendum campaign – 'Europe, YES; EEC, NO' – attempted (ultimately unsuccessfully) to reconcile two fundamentally opposed currents of thought within the party. On the one hand, there was a hankering for independent membership of the EEC for Wales if the conditions were right, as expressed by a reluctance to dismiss the European project outright and a commitment to a European alliance in principle. Plaid Cymru's preference was for some kind of Europe, although nothing more concrete was offered as an alternative beyond the frequent invocations of Lewis's romanticised Europeanism. On the other hand, British membership of the EEC raised a specific set of concerns about the potential impact of European integration on the Welsh nation. Plaid Cymru's campaign for a 'no' vote in the referendum was motivated by three main critiques of the developments in European integration up to that point.

Firstly, the lack of representation for Wales within the centralised and state-dominated European institutions was deemed incompatible with the stated aims of Welsh self-government. Membership of the EEC represented yet another layer of remote, bureaucratic and undemocratic government (Turner, 1998: 75). Informed by a similar line of reasoning, two years later Plaid Cymru would vote against the introduction of direct elections to the European Parliament as nothing more than a 'democratic charade' (Williams, 1979).

A second, more virulent, basis of opposition took issue with the economic principles underlying the EEC, and was to prove a more enduring tenet of Plaid Cymru's anti-integrationist rhetoric. Although the word 'socialism' would not formally be incorporated into the party's core aims until 1981, Plaid Cymru's economic policies had been inspired by broadly socialist principles since the 1930s.[1] A distinctly Welsh version of socialism at that, which rejected the centralisation of economic control in the hands of the state, in favour of a social model inspired by the twin themes of decentralisation and co-operation within a mixed modern economy (Davies, 1931/1958: 57–65; Wyn Jones, 2007: 136–46). The same basic ideas informed the rethinking of Plaid Cymru's economic policies by its newly constituted research group in the early 1970s (Wigley, 1992). The presence of committed left-wingers such as Dafydd Elis Thomas, Phil Williams and Gwyn Alf Williams in the higher echelons of Plaid Cymru by the mid-1970s led to a hardening of these socialist sympathies. Predictably, these left-wingers had very little sympathy for the liberal deregulatory policies being implemented as a part of European economic integration. For these 'anti-marketeers' (Wigley, 1992: 323), the EEC was a capitalist club whose common market would leave Wales economically isolated on the periphery of Europe. The Welsh economy, still largely dominated by heavy industries such as coal and steel, with a large agricultural sector, and plagued by high levels of unemployment (Morgan, 1998: 336) could never hope to compete successfully in such an unregulated economic arena (*Welsh Nation*, 1978; 1979). Wales would only enter the free market when it could negotiate its own terms of membership as a fully self-governing nation, at which point a renegotiation of the Treaty of Rome would be a priority (Mathews, 1971).

A third strand of opposition concluded that any kind of political co-operation meant that, in future, 'foreign policy and common defence policy would be predicated on nuclear weapons' (Williams, 1975). The militarisation of European co-operation would also threaten international peace and stability, a prospect at odds with the strong pacifist credentials which had become more prominent in Plaid Cymru's political rhetoric under Gwynfor Evans's presidency (Evans, 2005: 38–57).

It was not only on ideological grounds that Plaid Cymru opposed the UK's continued membership of the EEC. Its opposition was also driven by a tactical consideration: rejecting the EEC served the politically useful purpose of demarcating a clear nationalist political space vis-à-vis the Labour Party, Plaid Cymru's main political opponent in Wales and the party of government in Westminster at the time. Opposing Europe thus made sense in the context of the party competitive dynamics within Welsh and British politics at that moment. The fact that the EEC was presented by the Labour Party during the referendum campaign in narrowly domestic terms, 'as a means to prop up the old political order, itself threatened by economic decline, the loss of world power status and the breakdown of political consensus' (Keating and Jones, 1991: 314), meant opposition to the EEC from the Welsh periphery translated into a vote of no confidence in the state order itself. Plaid Cymru could also boast that only it had consistently argued against the EEC, in contrast to the chopping and changing of the Labour Party on the issue (Keating and Jones, 1991: 315).[2] The deep internal divisions within the latter on the issue of Europe were contrasted to the unity of Plaid Cymru in opposition to the EEC.

In fact, Plaid Cymru was less united in opposition to the EEC than it liked to claim, although internal dissent was confined to a very small group of activists who did not constitute a serious challenge to the party's formal campaigning position. Supporters of a 'yes' vote in the referendum included Plaid Cymru's first long-serving president, Saunders Lewis, and the future party president Dafydd Wigley. Lewis criticised Plaid Cymru for voting 'in favour of Westminster sovereignty and against Europe' (Saunders Lewis, quoted in Evans, 2005: 363), a move which he considered a betrayal of Plaid Cymru's core belief in the moral and political value of supranational co-operation (Evans, 2005: 363). Wigley, like Lewis, had also long recognised the importance of contextualising Welsh nation building in a broader European and international context (Wigley, 1992: 302–11). Wigley's pragmatic, as opposed to ideological, take on Europe was that not only was Plaid Cymru ignoring the long-term opportunities that co-operating with other European 'micro-nations' could bring for Wales, but Wales was also a long way from achieving the self-government that was touted by opponents to the EEC as a precondition of any possible Welsh membership of the EEC (Wigley, 1972). The EEC was something Plaid Cymru simply had to come to terms with. As such, reforming the European project along more accommodating and beneficial lines could be achieved only from within (Wigley, 1992: 308–12). During the referendum campaign, Wigley openly campaigned against his own party in favour of a 'yes' vote alongside Labour, Conservative and Liberal campaigners.

The eventual result of the referendum on the UK's membership of the EEC demonstrated that Lewis and Wigley were far more in tune with the British electorate than the majority of people within their own party. On a turnout of 64.5%, 67.2% of British voters favoured the UK's continued membership of the EEC. Within Wales, voting patterns left Plaid Cymru in no doubt as to the failure of its policy to appeal to Welsh voters, and especially its core support base in the Welsh-speaking heartlands of rural north and west Wales. The Welsh turnout was the highest in the UK (66.7%) and the proportion voting 'yes' to continued British membership of the EEC was almost as high as in England, and significantly greater than that in either Scotland or Northern Ireland (Jones, 1985: 61). The most intriguing result came in the north Wales county of Gwynedd, Plaid Cymru's electoral stronghold, where over 70% voted 'yes'. Elsewhere, rural Welsh-speaking constituencies also gave their enthusiastic support to the EEC, while industrial south Wales – not a strong Plaid Cymru support base – showed a more reluctant endorsement of British membership of the EEC. The overwhelming defeat of the 'no' campaign in the 1975 referendum would be the first of several events that would push Plaid Cymru to re-evaluate its position on Europe, and abandon its outright opposition to European integration over the next ten years.

Four years later, a referendum was held on devolution to Scotland and Wales.[3] The proposals put to the vote in Wales on 1 March 1979 were rejected by an overwhelming 79.74% of the Welsh electorate, on a turnout of 58.8%. It was the second disappointing referendum result for Plaid Cymru in four years. Not only did the result confound the impression that the party was fundamentally out of touch with Welsh public opinion. The campaign had also been very damaging for Plaid Cymru's political credibility, since the party had been forced to campaign for a programme of devolution that was opposed by a significant number of the Labour government's own MPs (Wigley, 1992: 319). By being too closely identified in the eyes of the electorate with devolution and the incumbent Labour administration, a vote for Plaid Cymru was also a vote of sanction for the deeply unpopular Wilson government.

The landslide win of Margaret Thatcher's Conservative Party in the general election a few months after the referendum sounded the death knell to any hopes that Plaid Cymru had of keeping the devolution issue on the British political agenda for years to come. In the words of Morgan (1998: 407), 'the 1979 general election seemed to mark the end of a distinct chapter in Welsh political history, with nationalism in full retreat'. Having lost referendums in 1975 and 1979, and with a Conservative government in Westminster that had little sympathy for the political demands of Welsh nationalists, Plaid Cymru was relegated to the margins of the British political system, a party devoid of political purpose and electoral appeal.[4]

Political crisis and the rediscovery of Europe

Wyn Jones (2007) argues that the result of the 1979 referendum was a catalyst for the most important re-evaluation of Plaid Cymru's ideology and political programme in its history. As a part of this process, a European dimension would be incorporated into Plaid Cymru's constitutional thinking that would lead to a fundamental redefinition of the party's long-term aspirations for Welsh self-government. Plaid Cymru's rediscovery of Europe throughout the 1980s began, therefore, with the profound self-examination prompted by the succession of electoral disasters suffered by the party at the end of the 1970s.

And yet, in the first few years after 1979, there seemed to be little change in the party's thinking on Europe. Plaid Cymru's European manifesto for the 1979 European Parliament elections was largely consistent with the tone and content of the party's rhetoric four years earlier (Plaid Cymru, 1979). The final report by a commission of inquiry, set up to consider the reasons for Plaid Cymru's spate of political failures, noted on the issue of European integration that 'it will be necessary to determine whether we should seek to amend and improve the structure and functioning of the EEC (as well as fighting for proper representation for Wales) or whether we should promote the collapse of the EEC' (Plaid Cymru, 1981: 9). It was the second of these two options that was favoured by the party in the early years of the 1980s, at least in its formal statements on Europe.

This continuity in Plaid Cymru's European policy can be attributed to the struggle for control of the party's ideological and strategic direction in the aftermath of 1979. As noted above, there had been a left-wing orientation to Plaid Cymru's policies throughout its existence, despite a resistance by party elites to formally position the party along the left–right ideological spectrum. The sympathy for a more overtly socialist agenda had been growing within Plaid Cymru throughout the 1970s. Several prominent individuals had began organising themselves into a clearly identifiable faction pushing for a more distinctly left-wing orientation in Plaid Cymru's policies. In the political, ideational and strategic wilderness that the party found itself in after 1979, the 'National Left', as they called themselves (Wyn Jones, 1996), proved itself to be the only group capable of stepping into the breach in an attempt to define a new course for Welsh nationalism. For this new generation of party activists, it was clear that the politics and strategies adopted by Plaid Cymru traditionalists in the past had failed completely to advance the goals of the Welsh nationalist movement. The only solution was to position the party unambiguously on the left of the political spectrum, and create a new left-nationalist synthesis that would see Plaid Cymru join in the struggle of the Welsh working class (Elis Thomas, 1979). Strategically, this meant working alongside other movements and organisations – trade unions, women's groups, the unemployed – to mobilise support for a Welsh 'decentralised socialist state' (Plaid Cymru, 1983: 3).

Given this shift in the internal balance of power within Plaid Cymru by the end of the 1970s, it is not surprising that opposition to the EEC continued to be the party's policy. The National Left articulated a political programme inspired by the principles of 'democratic socialism' that did not tire of pointing out the ills of European economic integration; these included the discriminatory effects of the Common Agricultural Policy (CAP), the undermining of the Welsh coal and steel industry, and the detrimental social effects of rising unemployment as a result of European free-market initiatives.[5] The neo-liberal and capitalist forces at work on the European continent were fundamentally irreconcilable with the radical socialist principles of this new generation of Plaid Cymru leaders. The fact that the issue of Europe was not discussed at all at the party's annual conferences in 1981 and 1982 suggested that it was a European policy that was not contested by Plaid Cymru members.

And yet, for all the anti-European rhetoric of the National Left, behind the scenes, changes were afoot that would gradually steer the party towards a more positive stance on the European issue. Evans (2005: 364) notes that the very first weekend after the failed referendum in 1975, a meeting of senior figures within Plaid Cymru decided that outright opposition to the EEC would have to be abandoned, so unpopular had such a position proved to be when put to the popular vote. Turner (1998: 109–10) also states that, by 1978, Gwynfor Evans was actively pushing for Plaid Cymru to make campaigning for better representation for Wales within the European institutions a priority. Moreover, the results of the 1979 European Parliament elections were crucial in persuading many party members of the opportunities that existed for Plaid Cymru on the supranational level. The results were as decisive as they were unexpected: Plaid Cymru polled 11.7% of the Welsh vote, compared to 8.1% in the general election a few months earlier (see Table 3.1). This was the party's best ever electoral performance. In the words of one senior Plaid Cymru member, 'the loss of the 1975 referendum, loosing ground in the 1979 UK general election, but making significant gains in the European elections, had an important psychological effect on Plaid' (interview, 19 December 2003). At a time when the party was suffering a profound identity crisis, the political effect of such positive results was decisive. This internal momentum in favour of a more favourable attitude towards the EEC was further accelerated by the election of self-confessed Europhile Dafydd Wigley as Plaid Cymru's president in 1981.

A growing tension between opponents and supporters of European integration meant that the European question was one of the most hotly debated issues at Plaid Cymru's annual conference in 1983. A motion put forward by the party's national executive sought to reaffirm the party's opposition to the incorporation of Wales into the EEC as part of the British state, but called for a new relationship between the nations and regions of Europe (*Welsh Nation*, 1983c). In other words, a reaffirmation of the party's Euro-sceptic position since 1975: 'yes' to Europe in principle, but a definite 'no' to the EEC. However, opposition to the motion from a significant number of party members led to a compromise position which, while continuing to condemn the institutional and economic failures of the EEC, called for better representation of Welsh interests within the supranational institutions (Lynch, 1996: 73). Significantly, outright opposition to membership of the EEC was toned down, a small but important concession to the changing attitudes of many of Plaid Cymru's members to European integration. It is also interesting to note that Plaid Cymru's manifesto for the 1984 European Parliament elections was more constructive in tone and content than either the 1983 conference motion or the 1979 European Parliament election manifesto. If the negative evaluation of concrete economic and political opportunities remained, the manifesto framed this critique in a more positive discourse which acknowledged the opportunities offered on the supranational level for achieving certain policy priorities – transport policy, the equal status of women and international peace – which could not be achieved through domestic state channels alone (Plaid Cymru, 1984).

Just as in 1979, a better than average performance in the 1984 European Parliament elections served to reinforce the support for the EEC that had grown gradually within Plaid Cymru's ranks since 1975. As Dafydd Wigley recalls in his autobiography, 'we succeeded in destroying the misconception that had poisoned the mindset of Plaid for over twenty years, that is that the European Community was a threat to our nationalist aspirations. Things changed in light of the 1984 election' (Wigley, 1992: 327). This better than average performance convinced party leaders that European elections operated according to a different logic from that which characterised Westminster elections, and that there were less hurdles in getting the party's message across to Welsh voters.[6]

If a more positive European outlook had gradually taken root among many Plaid Cymru activists by the mid-1980s, at the same time there was a growing realisation on the part of the National Left that they were failing to make any meaningful impact on Welsh and British politics. This reflected the collapse of the left more generally in British politics (Davies, 1996), as the radical socialist agenda failed to provide a coherent and appealing alternative to Thatcher's right-wing free market conservatism. Plaid Cymru's performance at the 1983 general election (see Table 3.2) was very disappointing. The party's new-look radical politics had clearly failed to make any discernible dent in the voting shares commanded by the

Labour Party in South Wales, and the Conservative Party in general. One major problem was that, by throwing its lot in completely with other left-wing groups in resisting Thatcher's socio-economic and industrial reforms, Plaid Cymru was becoming indistinguishable from other social groups and movements in the eyes of its electorate. But the final blow to the National Left's ideological crusade came with the failure of the miners' strike in the spring of 1985. The uncompromising way in which Thatcher dealt with these strikes provided a graphic illustration of the government's determination to confront and defeat any group that questioned the authority of the state (Keating and Jones, 1991: 318). For Plaid Cymru, who had invested heavily in campaigning on behalf of the mining communities directly affected by Thatcher's industrial reforms, this represented the end of utopian beliefs that Plaid Cymru was engaged in a 'national struggle' that would usher in the new Welsh socialist state (Wyn Jones, 2007: 231).

With the strategy of the National Left having failed to provide the direction much needed by Plaid Cymru post-1979, the party was forced once again to rethink its political message and strategy if it was to relaunch itself as a credible political force within Welsh politics. The answer, as many within Plaid Cymru had already come to realise, lay with Europe and the prospects for Welsh self-determination within the framework of a federal European polity.

A new start for Wales: 'full national status' in a 'Europe of the Regions'

If the tension between supporters and opponents of European integration came to the fore from 1983 onwards, by the end of the 1980s a new consensus had emerged on the opportunities for Wales within the EEC. In the end, the reformulation of the party's position on the issue of European integration was a remarkably uncontested process which saw Plaid Cymru avoid the deep internal divisions that have plagued otherwise cohesive political parties in numerous European countries (Hix and Lord, 1997; Gaffney, 1996). Within the space of five years, Plaid Cymru had transformed itself into a zealous Euro-enthusiast, with Europe presented as Wales's only hope for achieving self-government. The party's annual conference in 1988 formally endorsed the EEC for the first time, when a motion was passed supporting the Single European Act (SEA), and which called for reform from within, rather than withdrawal from, the European club. In the 1989 European Parliament elections, the party campaigned under the slogan 'A voice for Wales in Europe' (Plaid Cymru, 1989). These elections became a platform for projecting the party's new Europeanist image, a unique opportunity for situating Wales directly in its broader international context: 'the European campaign has a very important political and ideological significance for Plaid in that it relates Wales directly to the international level outside the British State' (Elis Thomas, 1989).

The 1989 European Parliament election was also notable for two other reasons. Firstly, Plaid Cymru designed its campaign around its association with the EFA, adopting both a common EFA logo and a common election manifesto. This association with other like-minded minority nationalist parties across Europe brought added credibility to a campaign that sought to convince Welsh voters of the opportunities for Wales within the EEC. It did so by linking the specific demands of Welsh nationalism to a broader constituency of actors united in the call for far-reaching reform of Europe's institutions and policies to better accommodate the economic, political and cultural diversity of Europe's small nations and regions. The significance of Plaid Cymru's link with the EFA is discussed in greater detail later in the chapter.

Secondly, the fact that Plaid Cymru's president at the time, Dafydd Elis Thomas – among the most vociferous of opponents to the EEC in the 1970s – decided to stand as a candidate for north Wales reflected the importance the European dimension had acquired in Plaid Cymru's political programme.[7] Once converted to the European cause, Thomas provided arguments in favour of further European integration that were just as passionate as his opposition to the EEC had been ten years earlier. Heading the party list in this way was a tactic for ensuring added exposure for the party's European policy. The fact that the party was also referred to as 'Plaid Cymru – Wales in Europe' on the ballot sheet took the nationalist agenda directly to the electorate, and left no doubt as to the European credentials of the party. Documents discussing the party's strategy in the run-up to the election stated clearly that the aim was to change the party's image away from a focus on Britishness and towards Europeanness, and to do so in such a way that would endure beyond the immediate context of the election (Morgan, 1987; also McAllister, 2001: 171).

Given this tremendous effort to garner support for Plaid Cymru's new Europeanist political programme, the party's eventual electoral performance was highly disappointing. The 12.9% of the vote polled fell far short of the 20% that had been (overenthusiastically) predicted (Wyn Jones, 1996).[8] However, this setback did not dampen Plaid Cymru's new-found enthusiasm for all things European. The party's annual conference in 1990 gave unanimous support to a new constitutional blueprint spelling out how a self-governing Wales would take its place in a wider European community, and which laid down the constitutional framework which would constitute Plaid Cymru's long-term goals until the end of the 1990s. Given that there had been no serious debate about the party's long-term constitutional aims since the 1950s, this was no small achievement. 'Full national status for Wales in Europe' represented Plaid Cymru's answer to the question of Welsh self-government and how to achieve it. With European integration marching ahead with the process of sharing sovereignty between different levels of government, ideas such as that of a Europe of the Regions seemed to offer a feasible way forward for a small nation seeking to free itself from the centre–periphery conflict with the British state, but without having to become a fully independent sovereign state first. 'Full national status for Wales in Europe' would mean Wales would:

> no longer send MPs to Westminster nor would it have a Secretary of State. There would then be a full seat for Wales in the European Council of Ministers … Wales would also have its own commissioner in Brussels. Eventually

we would want to see the diminishing and eclipse of the Council of Ministers, with its replacement coming by way of a second chamber in the European Parliament – a chamber of the regions and nations.

(Plaid Cymru, 1995: 4)

In other words, Wales would be part of 'a system of full self-government within the European Union' (ibid.: 4). The attraction of Europe was unequivocally as an alternative to, rather than coexisting with, the British state. Europe was conceptualised as a way of circumventing the constraining framework of the latter, based on the assumption that the supranational level would be both more receptive to, and considerate of, arguments for Welsh economic, political and cultural specificity. European integration seemed able to resolve key issues about the feasibility and viability of Welsh self-determination, by placing these issues in a framework of supranational authority where full political participation would not come at the price of outright independence.

It was not only the long-term constitutional possibilities for Wales in Europe that fuelled Plaid Cymru's new enthusiasm for Europe. The party also came to more positive conclusions about the concrete opportunities that European integration could offer for achieving shorter-term policy goals that would otherwise be more difficult to meet. Thus, for example, from the mid-1980s onwards, Europe provided the natural framework for the reworking of Plaid Cymru's economic policy. The party's commitments to centralised planning, an expansionist economic policy and higher taxes were gradually replaced by the desire to secure Wales's place within a 'strong economic union based on regional democracies' (Plaid Cymru, 1997: 9). The new regionalist rhetoric adopted by Plaid Cymru took up themes that had characterised the party's economic policy in the 1930s, grounded in the notion of Wales as a 'community of communities' (Saunders Lewis, quoted in Wyn Jones, 2007: 121),[9] where a shared culture and language would provide the basis for a prosperous political and economic order. The party embraced wholeheartedly new regionalist buzzwords such as 'economic regions' and 'growth sectors', based on investment in education, communications and transport infrastructures, and which considered cultural and social vitality as key contributors to economic regeneration. Together, all these factors would contribute to a prosperous Wales able to compete successfully in European and global markets.

Moreover, Europe was presented as an external support structure for facilitating the achievement of other Plaid Cymru policy priorities 'that could not conceivably be maintained by individual countries acting separately, and certainly not countries as small as Wales' (Dafis, 2001). Some policy areas – the environment, social policy, and international peace and security – were by their very nature better dealt with on a supranational level. Environmental policy was the best example of this. There had always been an ecological dimension to Plaid Cymru's nationalism. Over the years, many of the party's campaigns had been motivated by a strong, if romantic, attachment to the land of Wales, and the need to protect communities in rural areas (Lynch, 1995: 203). From the mid-1980s, this developed into a much clearer agenda for protecting and promoting the environment, a process which

Dafis (2005: 206) refers to as the 'greening of Plaid Cymru'. To the extent that, at the same time, a surge in European directives and regulations took on the environmental challenge at the European level, Plaid Cymru's environmental concerns resonated with the policy trend on the European level, and made its arguments much more convincing. The fact that many of the party's other policy priorities – sustainable development, local democracy, social justice, environmental protection, peace and security, and linguistic diversity – were also gaining salience on the supranational level further strengthened the growing support within the party for both the general idea of European integration and its concrete manifestation.

Finally, and in contrast to the conviction in 1975 that Welsh interests would not be adequately represented within the EEC, developments in European integration also promised to open up new avenues of representation for Wales within the European polity. Thus, for example, Plaid Cymru supported the Maastricht Treaty as a 'step in the right direction towards a Europe within which a self-governing Wales could play a full part', despite negative aspects such as the commitment to a European defence policy, the lack of a social policy and the failure to strengthen the role of the European Parliament (Evans, 1997). The treaty's commitment to establishing a Committee of the Regions was interpreted as a first step towards a regional chamber representing the interests of Europe's small nations and regions, and further bolstered Welsh nationalist optimism for the ineluctable emergence of a Europe of the Regions. Moreover, the treaty's formal adoption of the principle of subsidiarity was seen to herald the way for the decentralisation of policy-making competencies to the regional level in accordance with the idea of decision making as close as possible to the people (Plaid Cymru, 1994).

By the mid-1990s, therefore, Plaid Cymru had become a Euro-enthusiastic party. Support for Europe in principle – full national status for Wales in Europe – was combined with a positive evaluation of the economic and political dimensions of European integration up to that point. Despite the novelty of the terminology adopted by Plaid Cymru to describe its long-term constitutional goals, this position remained faithful to Saunders Lewis's ideological Europeanism in important ways. This continuity demonstrated the enduring role of basic party ideology in delineating the basic parameters of a party's attitude towards European integration. In contrast, Plaid Cymru's change of attitude towards the concrete realities of European integration was a result of very different political circumstances in British and European politics by the end of the 1980s. It is to examine these continuities and differences in Plaid Cymru's attitude towards Europe that this chapter now turns.

New terminology, old principle: rethinking Wales as a European nation

The terminology of 'full national status' enabled Plaid Cymru to imagine a very different kind of future Europe where political rights within the European club would be granted, not exclusively to member states who had joined as sovereign entities, but also to other political units possessing extensive political and institutional autonomy. Within such a Europe of the Regions, state sovereignty would mean very little as political authority would be redistributed between the supranational and sub-state levels.

The principles informing Plaid Cymru's Europeanism, however, were wholly consistent with basic ideas formulated seventy years previously by Saunders Lewis: the idea of Welsh self-determination in an international framework, and a commitment to an alternative form of sovereignty falling short of full independent statehood. This was not an unproblematic legacy. Wyn Jones (1999: 178) notes that ever since Lewis's leadership of the party, Plaid Cymru had been trying in vain to translate these abstract principles into concrete political structures. As noted above, over the years, several propositions sought to reconcile Lewis's internationalism and his rejection of absolute sovereignty with a legal and institutional formulation that would allow Wales a large degree of autonomy. In this tradition, the formulation 'full national status' in a 'Europe of the Regions' was simply another attempt at translating Lewis's ideas into constitutional and legal terms that appeared credible and achievable in the political climate of the time.

The extent to which such a formulation successfully achieved this task, however, is debatable. In this respect, Plaid Cymru's notion of full national status for Wales in Europe was also consistent with Lewis's ideas in another, less positive, way. If Lewis's distinction between 'freedom' and 'independence' was more rhetorical than substantive, it was equally unclear how, in its concrete manifestation, 'full national status' would differ from full membership of the European polity as a sovereign member state. Indeed, in Plaid Cymru's description of the rights and benefits that 'full national status' within the EU would grant Wales, it was difficult to grasp how exactly these were different from those accorded to any other member state who had acceded to the EU as a fully sovereign state. Legally and politically, there was – and still is – no such status within the EU that fell short of full member state status but that gave the same rights to non-state entities. In later years, Plaid Cymru's partisan competitors would exploit this inherent vagueness by speculating about the party's true constitutional aspirations within the EU.

Nevertheless, at the time of its adoption, the notion of 'full national status for Wales in Europe' represented a serious attempt by Plaid Cymru to adapt its long-term aims to the changes that were perceived to be taking place on the supranational level. What was most striking about the party's attitude towards Europe from 1985 onwards, therefore, was not the party's position on the basic idea of European integration, but its changing evaluation of the concrete realities of European integration. This change of heart about the nature of the European polity being built was the result of two main factors: (i) a change in the dynamics in party competition in Wales and in the UK by the end of the 1980s; and (ii) significant developments on the supranational level that convinced Plaid Cymru that a new kind of Europe was being built that offered a raft of institutional and policy opportunities for securing self-determination for the Welsh nation. The way in which these factors influenced Plaid Cymru's attitude toward the concrete realities of European integration will be considered in turn.

A new opportunity for progressive Welsh nationalism

From the mid-1980s onwards, the political climate in Welsh politics (and UK politics more generally) was propitious for the re-emergence of Welsh nationalism as an alternative to an increasingly unpopular Tory government. Some of Thatcher's policies, such as the poll tax, were unpopular across the board. But the effects of an economic policy that pursued privatisation as a means to an unregulated free market struck the Welsh economy particularly hard. Moreover, Thatcher's attempts to restore authority in an allegedly ungovernable state, with the net effect of creating a more centralist, authoritarian style of governing, antagonised many voters who resented the concentration of power among governing elites in Westminster. In particular, a belief in individual responsibility, wedded to a strong sense of Britishness, were essentially middle-class English values clearly at odds with the tradition of collective solidarity and community prevalent in the Scottish and Welsh peripheries (Leydier, 1994: 1050). As disaffected voters turned instead to Scottish and Welsh nationalist parties (Keating, 2001: 58), the dwindling Conservative vote in these two parts of the UK exacerbated the perception that policies were imposed from Westminster by a British government which lacked a clear democratic mandate in Scotland and Wales.

In such a context, Plaid Cymru's new president from 1984, Dafydd Elis Thomas, endeavoured to portray Plaid Cymru as 'a responsible constitutional party, and not a pressure group on the margins of the political world' (Dafydd Elis Thomas, quoted in Golwg, 1989: 13). The challenge was to broaden the party's political appeal beyond the 'dry' language of abstract constitutional aims and propose policies that appeared realistic and appropriate (Williams, 1986). Part of this strategy was to link arguments in favour of equality, sustainability and better democracy directly to the issue of Welshness and Welsh identity. Under Thomas's charismatic leadership, Plaid Cymru succeeded in linking the campaign for the future of the language and national self-determination to other salient campaigns against nuclear armament, unemployment and in favour of sexual equality. All these issues were packaged in the terminology of a Europe of the Regions, as the framework within which these socio-economic and cultural policy commitments could be achieved. The result was that Welsh nationalism appeared 'not only relevant, but also progressive' (Wyn Jones, 1996: 49). The party multiplied its contacts with other nationalist parties and social movements, leading to co-operation with the SNP, the Green Party and, on a European level, an intensification of relations with the EFA (Lynch, 1995).

Specifically on the issue of Europe, Plaid Cymru's new support for European integration once more served to distinguish itself clearly from its main competitors for the Welsh vote, the Conservative and Labour parties. Thatcher's uncompromising reassertion of British sovereignty in its relationship with the EEC (Evans, 2004: 82–84) contrasted sharply with Plaid Cymru's calls for greater autonomy for Wales within a European framework that respected linguistic, cultural and political diversity. On the level of pragmatic politics, Plaid Cymru also seized every opportunity to highlight the shortcomings of the British government and assert itself as the only real defender of Welsh interests in Europe. One senior

Plaid Cymru member recalled how, upon the introduction of the EEC's milk quota regime in the mid-1980s, Plaid Cymru organised a deputation to Brussels to meet with the responsible European commissioner and give voice to the grievances of Welsh farmers. The fact that a commission official subsequently visited Wales and declared publicly that at no point had the impact on Welsh agriculture been raised by the Thatcher government in the preceding negotiations, represented a huge political coup for the party, one which translated into notable gains in subsequent elections (interview, 19 December 2003).

For its part, the Labour Party could not offer a convincing alternative European vision, remaining 'hopelessly divided on the issue' (Plaid Cymru, no date). Dafydd Elis Thomas attributed his change of attitude towards Europe during the 1983 general election campaign in part to a tactical move destined to differentiate Plaid Cymru from the Labour Party, which was campaigning for withdrawal from the EEC at the time (Turner, 1998: 115). Under Neil Kinnock the party accepted EEC membership begrudgingly, albeit with the option of future withdrawal, although deep disaffection with it persisted.

There is no doubt that this new agenda of alternative politics, packaged in a progressive European discourse, contributed to a revival in Plaid Cymru's electoral fortunes from the mid-1980s onwards. In statewide general elections, Plaid Cymru's share of the vote in Wales increased in each election, from 7.3% in 1987 to 14.3% in 2001 (see Table 3.2). In European Parliament elections, the party's performance was even more impressive, from polling 12.9% in the 1989 election to an impressive 29.6% in 1999, only marginally behind the Labour Party in Wales, with 31.9% (see Table 3.1).

And yet, an increase in vote share did not translate into an increase in the number of Plaid Cymru representatives returned to either the House of Commons or to the European Parliament. By the end of the 1990s, Plaid Cymru still had only four MPs in the House of Commons. Plaid Cymru's rhetoric and policies may have appealed to an increasing number of the Welsh electorate, but in terms of crossing the threshold of representation, the party had failed to dent the pattern of Labour Party domination that had characterised Welsh politics since 1945 (Wyn Jones and Scully, 2006). The major obstacle faced by the party was the highly disproportional 'first-past-the-post' system used in general elections. This system had the effect of exaggerating electoral swings to the benefit of winning parties while punishing the losers in a 'winner-takes-all' logic. Small parties with territorially concentrated bases of support, like Plaid Cymru, did well in the few seats where such a majority could be secured – the Welsh-speaking heartlands of north-west Wales, for example – but were denied representatives in other seats where party support was not sufficient to challenge Labour Party dominance. The strong centralisation of governmental and bureaucratic power in Westminster and the absence of a sub-state level of directly elected political institutions, meant Plaid Cymru remained confined to the periphery of British and Welsh politics, at least until the establishment of the NAW in 1999.

The party fared little better in crossing the threshold of representation on the European level. In part, this difficulty in crossing the threshold of representation was also attributable to the disadvantageous first-past-the post electoral system which rewarded the larger statewide parties – Labour and, until 1994, the Conservative Party – whose support was more evenly distributed throughout Wales. It is worth noting that only in 1999, when a proportional representation electoral system was introduced for European Parliament elections and an additional constituency was created in Wales (increasing the number of Welsh MEPs from four to five) that Plaid Cymru succeeded in sending MEPs to the European Parliament (see Table 3.1).

European Parliament elections also posed a further dilemma for Plaid Cymru, namely the challenge of getting its message across in an electoral competition that tended to be dominated by domestic, rather than European, issues. The 1989 European Parliament elections provided a clear demonstration of this dynamic at work. Plaid Cymru's below-expectation result also brought home the difficulty of contesting European elections. The tendency for voters to use European elections as an opportunity to pass judgement on the domestic political situation of the day hindered Plaid Cymru from getting its European message across. An internal post-election post-mortem noted that, in a climate of growing discontent with the policies of the Thatcher administration, all political parties had conducted their campaigns on a ticket of opposition to the Conservative government. Moreover, the tendency of the British media to report on the statewide dynamics of party competition rather than focus on the European issues at stake, reinforced the 'domesticisation' of the European electoral campaign (Keelan, 1989). In such a situation, Plaid Cymru's European message had been overshadowed by contiguous political struggles within the domestic political arena.

Despite this difficulty in getting its message across in European elections, Plaid Cymru's arguments in favour of a Europe of the Regions from the mid-1980s onwards made sense, not only in relation to the changing dynamics of party competition at home, but also because they seemed to be tapping into important changes in the trajectory and nature of European integration. If the EEC to which Plaid Cymru objected so strongly in the 1970s was essentially an economic project grounded in the principles of a common market and a free-trade model of competition, it appeared, at least during the 1980s and early 1990s, that a very different kind of Europe was being built, one that, in its policy and institutional manifestations, augured well for the socio-economic, political and cultural well-being of the Welsh nation. Indeed, such was the party's confidence in the transformation of European integration, that it was claimed in 1992 that 'what Plaid Cymru has long demanded is now central to European thinking' (Plaid Cymru, 1992: 46). These concrete developments in European integration throughout the 1980s and 1990s are summarised in the following section.

European integration and the prospects of an emerging multilevel Europe

Firstly, the economic opportunities for Wales in the EEC seemed to be improving. In the early 1980s, the damaging impact of European agricultural policy on the Welsh economy convinced several senior members of the party that there was no longer an alternative to campaigning for Welsh interests within the EEC (Turner, 1998: 113–14). More specifically, the introduction of milk quotas had a devastating effect on the large dairy sector in Wales. This was a bitter pill made even more difficult to swallow by the fact that Ireland's seat at the European negotiating table had allowed it to avoid many of the most damaging effects of the legislation. Having a say in the European policies that affected Wales meant having to accept membership of the EEC.

A few years later, the reform of the European Structural Funds in 1988 was interpreted as a recognition at last of the economic needs of the EEC's poorest regions and small nations, not least because of the significant amounts of money that would be poured into rural and deprived urban areas of Wales. Ireland's phenomenal economic growth from the 1980s onwards provided evidence close to home of what could be done with the efficient use of European monies to create a flourishing economy within a European single market (Turner, 1998: 113–14). Moreover, the new principles governing administration of the funds seemed to constitute a new model for involving sub-state actors in the European policy-making process (Hooge, 1996). The doubling of the financial resources allocated to the European regional policies in 1994 reaffirmed Plaid Cymru's belief in the new importance given to regional politics within the EU.

Secondly, and as noted above, the institutional and legal innovations contained in the Maastricht Treaty of European Union went a long way towards persuading Plaid Cymru that the European context could offer a framework for protecting and promoting the rights of small nations and regions over those of sovereign states. The trend seemed to be towards a redistribution of power both upwards to the European institutions and downwards to the sub-state level: 'Independence appeared to be becoming irrelevant. The member states were beginning to look less and less powerful, and using a term like 'full national status' [for Wales in Europe] left our options open' (interview, 19 March 2003).

Last but by no means least, the supranational level allowed Plaid Cymru to project itself as a political actor in the new European order, and provided a new political space for the articulation of a distinctive nationalist political project. In particular, when it was frustratingly difficult to get the issue of Welsh self-determination onto the political agenda in Britain throughout the 1980s, newly established links with other minority nationalist parties within the framework of the EFA provided an alternative mechanism for articulating the demands of Welsh nationalism directly on the supranational level. Moreover, as a result of the EFA's activism within the European Parliament, Plaid Cymru could claim that, for the first time ever, the interests of the Welsh nation were being articulated and defended directly on the supranational level. The impact of these transnational links on Plaid Cymru's attitude towards European integration merits closer examination.

Representation and co-operation on the supranational level

Plaid Cymru's first contact with other minority nationalist parties in western Europe was through an initiative to establish a Bureau of Unrepresented Nations in

1975, a joint venture between Plaid Cymru, the Breton and Alsace minority nationalist parties and the Partido Nacionalista Vasco (PNV). An office was established in Brussels with three aims: to publicise the policies of the four movements, to act as a pressure group on European institutions, and to gather information on the impact of EEC legislation on the social and economic life of the members (Plaid Cymru, 1975). By 1980, however, the initiative had dwindled due to a lack of financial resources, a weak administrative infrastructure and dwindling political will.

Nevertheless, the political logic that inspired this association would subsequently be given a new channel of expression through the EFA. Plaid Cymru obtained observer status within the association in 1981, and subsequently became a full member in 1984; Plaid Cymru's MEPs, first elected in 1999, form part of the EFA group in the European Parliament. EFA membership was crucial in supporting and reinforcing Plaid Cymru's attempts to make sense of Wales's place within Europe during the 1980s and early 1990s. Firstly, the EFA provided practical resources for articulating and pursuing Plaid Cymru's European agenda. Through organised visits to the European Parliament and regular meetings on developments in European policy making, the EFA was a useful framework within which to develop an understanding of the complex workings of the European institutions. The EFA also constituted a forum for listening to the experiences of other small nations in Europe, and of developing a deeper understanding of the implications of European integration for minority nations. From 1989 onwards, the alliance provided logistical and financial support for Plaid Cymru's campaigns in European Parliament elections. Moreover, with Plaid Cymru without its own MEPs until 1999, the EFA acted as a spokesperson for Welsh nationalist issues within the European Parliament. With the election of two Plaid Cymru MEPs in 1999, the EFA provided a ready-made structure within which these representatives, already well acquainted with the practices of this institution, could be integrated effortlessly.

Secondly, the EFA also provided the terminology to describe the kind of Europe that Plaid Cymru was hankering for. One interviewee recalled a speech given by Jaak Vandemeulebroucke of the Belgian Volksunie, and an EFA MEP since 1979, at a European festival organised by Plaid Cymru in 1988. The speech outlined a vision of the Europe of the Regions that was emerging on the supranational level, and 'as he was describing it, it struck many of us at the same time ... that what he was saying made a lot of sense. It all sounded very neat and promising' (interview, 19 March 2003). This shared language of European regionalism would bring a new credibility to Plaid Cymru's 'Wales in Europe' rhetoric. Presenting Plaid Cymru's project as part of a much broader mobilisation in favour of a Europe of the Regions added legitimacy to the party's European discourse, and portrayed the party as part of a progressive movement demanding the far-reaching reform of the European polity.

From 'full national status' to 'independence' in Europe

The election of two MEPs to the European Parliament was not the only major achievement for Plaid Cymru in 1999. The Labour government elected to Westminster in 1997 embarked upon a programme of devolution that would lead to the most radical constitutional shake-up of the British state since the nineteenth century (Bogdanor, 1999). The Government of Wales Act 1998 created a sixty-member NAW which, although lacking the primary legislative and tax-raising powers granted to a Scottish Parliament, would be responsible for a number of policy areas previously the responsibility of the Secretary of State for Wales in London.[10] The NAW became operational in 1999, creating a democratically elected tier of regional government in Wales for the first time in the nation's history. Given the unitary nature of the British state within which Plaid Cymru had been operating since its establishment some seventy-five years previously, devolution created a major new institutional opportunity structure for Welsh nationalism to pursue and achieve its nation-building project.

Devolution also ushered in a new era in Plaid Cymru's history in another respect. In the first NAW elections in May 1999, Plaid Cymru claimed seventeen out of a total of sixty seats, the party's best ever electoral performance, winning 29.5% of the Welsh vote (in comparison to the 9.9% it polled in the UK general election two years previously; see Tables 3.2 and 3.3). The change in the electoral system to a partially proportional one[11] played no small part in removing the structural hurdle that had constrained the party's ability to send representatives to Westminster for decades. It seemed, in 1999 at least, that Welsh nationalism would be one of the defining forces of Welsh politics at the beginning of the new millennium.

If enthusiasm towards Europe had been a central tenet of the political programme which relaunched Plaid Cymru as a credible political party from the mid-1980s onwards, there was no reason to expect that this would change post-1999. It was a surprise, therefore, that within a few years of the establishment of the NAW, Plaid Cymru was forced to reconsider its position on European integration anew. The most visible outcome of this process was the reformulation of the party's long-term aspirations for Wales within Europe. This process began at Plaid Cymru's annual conference in 2001, when the first serious discussion of the party's long-term constitutional aims since the early 1990s took place. A motion was approved that acknowledged, for the first time, that only 'full member state status of the European Union is most likely to advance [Wales's] national interest'. Previously, the party had always rejected the prospect of becoming a member state of the EU (that is, an independent sovereign state), with 'full national status' implying, as stated above, an intermediate status falling short of full sovereign independence. Despite this acknowledgement, the 2001 annual conference also voted to retain the terminology of 'full national status' as an expression of this constitutional ambition. However, two years later this formulation would be abandoned in favour of a commitment to 'independence in Europe' as the ultimate goal of Welsh nationalism. As the mechanism by which Wales would accede to such a status, the novel term 'internal enlargement' began to appear in the party literature. This process would allow 'those nations and regions which are currently members of the EU through their member states ... to become full members in their own right' (Plaid Cymru, 2003).

To the outside observer, the decision to use the terminology of 'independence in Europe' from 2003 onwards appeared to be a formal recognition by Plaid Cymru of the principle acknowledged in 2001, namely that full membership of the EU could only be countenanced once Wales became an independent sovereign state. If this interpretation were correct, then it was a decision that represented a major U-turn in the party's constitutional policy, given that it was a commitment that seemed to fly in the face of eighty years of strenuous rejection by Plaid Cymru of independence or fully sovereign status as the aim of the Welsh nationalist movement. After all, as declared by the party's president, Dafydd Wigley, in the run up to the May 1999 NAW elections, 'Plaid Cymru has never – ever – stood for independence as our constitutional objective' (Wigley, 2001: 130).

However, in its attempts to elucidate the implications of this change in constitutional aims, Plaid Cymru rejected any claims that the adoption of a commitment to 'independence in Europe' amounted to an abandonment of one of its fundamental political principles. On the contrary, the party sought to stress the continuity with Plaid Cymru's post-sovereigntist legacy by claiming that independence did not, in fact, envisage the creation of a fully sovereign Welsh state and a complete separation from the UK. It was argued, confusingly, that a change in terminology did not equate to a change of the model for Welsh self-government set out in the mid-1990s: 'An independent Wales would be on an equal footing with other small countries – with more seats in the European Parliament, full voting rights in the Council of Ministers and representation in the Commission. Independence would overcome the difficulty of the member states' reluctance to devolve power to the regions' (Thomas, 2003). In other words, if the rights and obligations of an independent Wales within the EU would be those granted to any other member state, Wales would not have to first become a sovereign state as a prerequisite for acquiring these rights and obligations. Just as 'full national status' envisaged full participation within the EU on the basis of some kind of alternative non-state-based membership, Plaid Cymru's conceptualisation of 'independence in Europe' also remained faithful to a post-sovereigntist notion of EU membership. The implication remained that Wales would play an equal role alongside other European member states, but without having to become an internationally recognised sovereign state as a prior condition of membership.

The obvious criticism of Plaid Cymru's constitutional policy was that no such post-sovereigntist class of European membership existed, nor is it likely to exist in the near future. If the terminology of full national status was unclear in its practical implications, then Plaid Cymru's notion of 'independence' was an even greater achievement in conceptual and terminological vagueness. However, Plaid Cymru's nebulous constitutional terminology aside, the fact that the party felt the need to revisit the fundamental tenets of its position on Europe at all, requires explanation. Thus far, this chapter has argued that, in previous years, Plaid Cymru's attitude towards European integration was the product of an attempt to reconcile basic ideological commitments with domestic and European political realities. Plaid Cymru's most recent re-evaluation of its position on Europe can be attributed to a similar motivation. The changing nature of European integration since the late 1990s, combined with the transformation of party competitive dynamics in post-devolution Wales, generated new pressures on Plaid Cymru to rethink the relationship between Welsh self-government and European integration. The terminology of 'independence in Europe', for all the confusion that it generated, represented yet another attempt by Plaid Cymru to translate a basic ideological principle – Wales as a European nation – into a credible political project that made sense in the political climate of the time. The European and domestic political developments that necessitated revisiting Plaid Cymru's long-term goal within the EU merit closer examination.

From a 'Europe of the Regions' to a 'Europe of States'?

If developments in European integration convinced Plaid Cymru of the political value of its Euro-enthusiasm in the 1980s and early 1990s, since then a series of developments had served to highlight the fact that the European polity was not developing along the lines anticipated ten years earlier. On the contrary, it became increasingly clear to Plaid Cymru's keenest EU-watchers that the trajectory of European integration had shifted back in favour of the member states (interview, 16 December 2003). The momentum towards a Europe of the Regions had, it seemed, run out of steam.

This realisation was the culmination of several disappointments for Plaid Cymru over the previous decade. The Committee of the Regions was quickly discovered to be an internally divided and ineffectual body. Similarly, the translation of the principle of subsidiarity into political practice did not result in a significant transfer of competencies downwards to sub-state institutions, but reinforced the two-way dynamic between member states and the European institutions. Furthermore, the limited reform of the European Parliament in the Amsterdam and Nice Treaties, and the successive refusal of national governments to give up their veto rights in certain areas of policy making, further undermined the regionalist momentum that seemed to be gathering pace in the early 1990s. The launching of the euro in 1999 reopened an internal debate within the party – one which had seemingly been resolved by the end of the 1980s – about the costs and benefits of the internal market for an underdeveloped economy like Wales. While Plaid Cymru remained committed in principle to Economic and Monetary Union (EMU) as a necessary step forward for European and Welsh economic competitiveness, some voices within the party expressed fears that economic and monetary integration would only exacerbate regional disparities within the EU. The hypothetical inability of a Welsh – read Plaid Cymru – government to respond to particular economic problems using macroeconomic policy mechanisms, and the undemocratic nature of the European Central Bank, raised new concerns about the fate of the Welsh economy within a European economic and political arena (interview, 26 November 2003).

Enlargement to central and eastern Europe proved similarly problematic for the party. Plaid Cymru supported enlargement for two key reasons. Firstly, it was believed that the greater linguistic and cultural diversity that this would bring to the EU could only reinforce the case for a greater legal and political recognition of *all* such differences – whether state or non-state based. Secondly, the fact that five of the new member states would have a population smaller than Wales would invalidate the argument often made by Plaid Cymru's opponents that Welsh membership of the European club could not be countenanced because of its size.[12] As enlargement to central and eastern Europe became a reality, however, Plaid Cymru's case for greater autonomy within the EU was undermined, rather than bolstered. The fact that these smaller states were to be given full membership rights of the EU without a hint of a similar status being offered to Europe's historic nations only served to frustrate the aspirations of the latter even further. Moreover, the economic consequences of welcoming several very poor countries into the EU created the real prospect that Wales would see a reduction in its eligibility for European agricultural and regional funds in the near future; this could seriously undermine the economic viability of Wales in a competitive European market. Finally, as a result of the redistribution of seats within the European Parliament to accommodate the ten new member states, Wales lost one of its five European seats in the 2004 European Parliament elections. This was one factor that contributed to Plaid Cymru's failure to re-elect its two MEPs in the 2004 European Parliament elections.

The outcome of the Convention on the Future of Europe, launched in December 2001 to consider the future direction of European integration, confounded many of these frustrations. Plaid Cymru was represented on the Convention by the SNP MEP Neil MacCormick, as the nominated representative for the EFA group in the European Parliament. However, the EFA had very limited success in getting the interests of its constituents onto the agenda of the constitutional debate, with only a minimum of its demands being incorporated in the final constitutional document produced in 2003 (McCormick, 2004).[13] In the words of one Plaid Cymru member:

> In the Constitution, it is clear to see that this [Europe] is far from being a Europe of the Regions, but is a Europe of States, and even though there is a recognition of the regional level it doesn't go any further than that. So in a way we're back to the same situation as we were in in the 1980s.
> (Interview, 26 February 2004)

The language of 'full national status' no longer made sense, therefore, in the kind of Europe that had developed since the late 1990s. Reformulating Plaid Cymru's long-term constitutional aims became necessary in order to avoid the accusation that it was a party unwilling or unable to adapt to the changing realities of European integration. However, Plaid Cymru's persistent reluctance to come clean on the full implications of its constitutional aims betrayed a fundamental dilemma faced by the party. The pressure placed by the trajectory of supranational events on Plaid Cymru to recognise the legal reality of membership conditions of the EU was at odds with the party's ideological commitment to a form of self-determination that rejected sovereign statehood fundamentally. Changes in the Welsh political arena from 1999 onwards would make it even more difficult for Plaid Cymru to translate this basic ideological principle into a coherent and credible political project.

Rethinking Welsh nationalism in post-devolution Wales

If the inhospitable climate of British politics after 1979 was the catalyst for Plaid Cymru's growing support for Europe in the 1980s, major changes in the political dynamics of post-devolution Wales exerted new pressures on Plaid Cymru to re-examine its aspirations for Wales within Europe. In the first place, after 1999, Plaid Cymru's new political and media visibility exposed the party to assaults from its political competitors about the nature of its constitutional policy. The deeply ambiguous nature of the terminology of 'full national status', not least the implication noted above that giving Wales a political status equal to that of other small member states within the EU implied Welsh sovereign statehood, was an easy target for Plaid Cymru's partisan rivals. Plaid Cymru's fancy terminology was denounced as a ruse to detract attention from the party's true separatist aspirations. Such was the implication of the 'IQ test' – the 'independence question' – posed for Plaid Cymru by the Liberal Democrat MP for Montgomeryshire, Lembit Opik, where ten questions were posed about the true implications of Plaid Cymru's constitutional policy (*Western Mail*, 2001).

The pressure for a clarification of its constitutional aims became even greater after Plaid Cymru's disappointing performance in the second round of the NAW elections in May 2003. The party's share of the vote was significantly lower than four years previously, and the number of Plaid Cymru seats in the NAW declined from seventeen to twelve (see Table 3.3). This was a major blow to a party aspiring to be the party of government in Wales. The defeat prompted the party's annual conference a few months later to approve the change of aims to that of 'independence in Europe'. In this way, it was hoped that a clarification of its long-term aims would allow the party to 'free ourselves from some of our past defensiveness and step up our campaign significantly' (Thomas, 2003).

This decision was also, however, part of a broader attempt by Plaid Cymru to carve out a new distinctive political agenda in Welsh politics. In their analysis of the reasons for Plaid Cymru's electoral collapse in the May 2003 NAW elections, Wyn Jones and Scully (2004b) argue that one of the major problems faced by Plaid Cymru since devolution was that of maintaining a distinctive policy agenda in the face of the gradual realignment of partisan politics within Wales post-1999. The establishment of the NAW created a new centre of gravity for all political parties in Wales. Statewide parties were forced to discuss regional issues, produce regional solutions and give their programmes a 'Welsh face'. Thus, for example, when Rhodri Morgan replaced Alun Michael as the leader of Welsh Labour in February 2000, one of the first things he did was to order the rebranding of the Labour Party in Wales under the slogan 'Welsh Labour: The true party of Wales'. This was a move clearly aimed at taking on the challenge posed by Plaid Cymru (Osmond, 2000). There had even been voices within the Conservative Party in Wales suggesting that their party should acknowledge that devolution was not necessarily a threat to the historical unity of the British state, and develop a distinctly Welsh Conservative political agenda.[14] In short, if prior to devolution Plaid Cymru could legitimately claim to be the only 'party of

Wales', by 2003 all partisan forces in Wales were laying claim to this title (Wyn Jones and Scully, 2004b: 60).

To what extent would this new commitment to 'independence in Europe' be successful in re-establishing a new support base for Plaid Cymru among the Welsh electorate? Opinion poll data on changing public attitudes in Wales since 1997 suggests that Plaid Cymru's new constitutional formula could have been tapping into changing public attitudes in Wales on the issue of devolution, which were gradually becoming more supportive of greater autonomy for Wales.[15] In the 1979 referendum on devolution for Wales, only 11.8% of the total Welsh electorate voted 'yes'. By 1997, 60.5% of people questioned were in favour of some kind of political autonomy for Wales, with 33.7% of these preferring more powers than were actually given to the NAW in 1999 (that is, either a parliament or independence) (Table 3.4). By 2003, the number in favour of some kind of political autonomy had risen to 78.8%; of these, 51.7% would have liked to see an increase in the NAW's powers. In short, by adopting the language of independence, Plaid Cymru may well have been anticipating a growing sympathy for more radical political solutions to the constitutional future of Wales.

There were, however, also good reasons to doubt whether 'independence in Europe' would be successful in carving out the new political support base craved by Plaid Cymru. For one thing, public opinion surveys also showed that, by 2003, independence remained by far the least popular of the four constitutional options given in the survey by a considerable distance, remaining just as unpopular as it was in 1997, with only around 14% of respondents in favour. Moreover, the language of independence may have been attractive to Plaid Cymru's core electorate, but it also risked frustrating the party's desire to further broaden its electoral appeal beyond its traditional support base in the Welsh-speaking heartlands. These dangers were spelt out bluntly in an internal party document as follows: independence risked becoming a fetish at the expense of concentrating on other aspects of party activities; Plaid Cymru might be seen to live in a fantasy world rather than dealing with the reality and challenges of the present; people who considered themselves Welsh–British and who did not support independence would not vote for the party; and people could be frightened away by the perception that voting for Plaid Cymru equates to voting for independence (Dafis, 2003).

Furthermore, public sympathy for further political autonomy in general may have been increasing, but there was no evidence of a similar trend in support for

Table 3.4 Constitutional preferences in Wales, 1997–2003 (%)

Constitutional preference	1997	1999	2001	2003
Independence	14.1	9.6	12.3	13.9
Parliament	19.6	29.9	38.8	37.8
Assembly	26.8	35.3	25.5	27.1
No elected body	39.5	25.3	24.0	21.2

Sources: Welsh Referendum Study (1997); Welsh Assembly Election Studies (1999, 2003); British Electoral Study (2001).

European integration. On the contrary, one of the biggest problems facing Plaid Cymru was, and continues to be, the increasingly Euro-sceptic climate of Welsh and British politics (interview, 1 December 2003).[16] This makes things much more difficult for any party seeking to gain public approval for closer integration into the EU. This lack of popular support for European integration may well become an even more acute issue for Plaid Cymru in the future, as it has to face up to the possibility that not only is the party facing a general popular disenchantment with European affairs, but that this opposition is particularly strong among some members of its traditional support base. This trend is suggested by the public opinion surveys cited above, which asked respondents about Wales's place within the UK and Europe. In 1999, 8.2% supported Plaid Cymru's constitutional option; that is, for Wales to become independent from the UK but to remain a part of the EU (Table 3.5), declining slightly to 7.8% by 2003. In contrast, support for Welsh independence both from the UK and the EU – the most radical option – more than doubled over the same period of time, from 2.9% in 1999 to 6.3% in 2003. Growing support among Plaid Cymru's hard-line supporters for these two radical options in the future – independence from the UK and the EU – would represent a further challenge to a moderate nationalist agenda firmly rooted in a post-sovereigntist Europeanist vision of Wales's future as an autonomous nation.

The failure of the switch to 'independence in Europe' to reconnect with the Welsh electorate become apparent in electoral contests after 2003. In the 2004 European Parliament elections, the party's share of the vote fell from 29.6% in 1999 to 17.4%. The party also lost one of its two MEPs (see Table 3.1). In the 2005 general election, Plaid Cymru's overall vote in Wales fell from 14.3% in 2001 to 12.6% in 2005, and its number of MPs was reduced from four to three (Table 3.2). Whereas Plaid Cymru's electoral successes from the mid-1980s onwards could be attributed in large part to the appeal of the party's newly formulated 'Wales as a European nation' rhetoric, this could certainly not be said of the party's latest attempt to articulate the party's ideological commitment to Welsh self-determination within a European framework.

Table 3.5 Constitutional preferences for Wales in the UK and Europe, 1999–2003 (%)

Constitutional preference	1999	2003
Wales should become independent, separate from the UK and the European Union	2.9	6.3
Wales should become independent, separate from the UK but part of the European Union	8.2	7.8
Wales should remain part of the UK, with its own elected assembly which has law-making and tax-raising powers	24.8	37.9
Wales should remain part of the UK, with its own elected assembly, which has limited law-making powers only	37.9	26.7
Wales should remain part of the UK without an elected assembly	26.2	21.3

Sources: Welsh Assembly Election Studies (1999, 2003).

This period of electoral decline sparked renewed debate within Plaid Cymru about the party's political image, message and strategy. The party launched a rebranding exercise early in 2006 that saw it change its name and adopt a new logo.[17] A six-month policy consultation process with the people of Wales was launched at the same time, in an attempt to formulate a more appealing political programme for the 2007 elections to the NAW. One of the most striking features of these attempts at renewing Plaid Cymru's electoral appeal was the absence of a European dimension. In contrast to the party's unquenchable European enthusiasm in the early 1990s, the EU was hardly mentioned either as a marker of Plaid Cymru's difference vis-à-vis its political competitors, or as the starting point from whence all other policy concerns departed. References to the party's commitment to 'independence in Europe' were limited to occasions when a general statement of the party's political aspirations was opportune, such as the 2005 general elections (Plaid Cymru, 2005: 8). Otherwise, Plaid Cymru focused exclusively on the bread and butter issues of developing policy for a devolved Wales.

The absence of a European dimension to Plaid Cymru's attempts to relaunch itself as a relevant political party represented a change in focus, rather than a change in policy on Europe. It was a development that signified a change in the prominence of Europe in Plaid Cymru's political programme. The symbolic rhetoric of a Europe of the Regions played well when re-establishing Plaid Cymru's political appeal when the party was marginalised within British politics during the 1980s and early 1990s. However, with such normative demands increasingly out of sync with concrete developments in European integration, and new pressures on Plaid Cymru to adapt to a new political role within the Welsh political arena, such a discourse became increasingly inappropriate. From 1999, Plaid Cymru's priority had become that of influencing policy and securing government office within the NAW. This is not surprising, since 'Plaid Cymru is never going to be in power in Westminster or in Europe ... We're the main opposition party in the Assembly, and only Assembly elections will bring us self-determination' (interview, 1 December 2003). Taking full advantage of these new opportunities, however, forced Plaid Cymru to prioritise its political agenda and focus on policy issues that realistically could be achieved. At the same time, this shift in focus enabled Plaid Cymru to isolate the potentially electorally damaging effects of its ideological commitment to the European project by concentrating instead on developing a distinctive policy agenda for Wales. In this way, the party sought to avoid difficult questions about the future prospects for Wales in the EU.

In the May 2007 NAW elections, Plaid Cymru's efforts to bolster its electoral appeal were partially successful in recuperating some of the votes lost since the 1999 elections (see Table 3.3). The failure of the Labour Party to secure a governing majority created an opportunity for Plaid Cymru to cross the threshold of government for the first time in its history. Plaid Cymru's new status as a partner in regional government will place new pressures on the party to adapt if it is to carry out its new responsibilities effectively. Adapting a new discourse on Europe will be key in this respect. Plaid Cymru's responsibilities for economy and transport, as well as rural affairs, as part of the government within the NAW, will require the party to come to grips with the strong European dimension that is intrinsic to these policy areas. European directives and regulations will constrain Plaid Cymru's freedom to propose policy in these areas. The limited scope for policy innovation may well frustrate party members keen to maximise the party's political impact whilst in office. At the same time, however, government incumbency may open up new channels for Plaid Cymru to represent Welsh interests directly in Brussels, as part of the UK delegation to the Council of Ministers. Given the lack of progress in creating institutional structures that can represent minority nationalist interests directly at the supranational level, representation via the state remains the most realistic channel for Plaid Cymru to shape European decision making. The party can use such opportunities, if they arise, to flaunt its status as a key actor in multilevel European negotiations. It remains to be seen, however, to what extent these intra-state channels of influence are open to Plaid Cymru, since such access depends on the goodwill of UK government actors. The closure of this avenue may lead to a renewed disillusionment within the party with the opportunities for advancing the interests of Wales within the EU.

If government incumbency will demand greater pragmatism in Plaid Cymru's approach to the concrete realities of European integration, it will also enhance the party's pragmatic approach to Europe in another respect. 'Independence in Europe' remains Plaid Cymru's long-term constitutional goal. The prospects of achieving such a goal soon, however, are remote. In contrast, being a party of regional government has bolstered the prospects of increasing Welsh political autonomy substantially, if not as much as Plaid Cymru would ideally like. The coalition agreement signed jointly with the Labour Party included a commitment to explore public support for a referendum on full law-making powers for the NAW (Labour/Plaid Cymru, 2007). Achieving such a referendum will require cultivating the backing of other political parties in Wales and in Westminster. The proposal is highly likely to provoke contentious debate in both political arenas, and so securing such support is by no means a given. However, the simple fact that such a proposal is on the table constitutes a major step towards meeting Plaid Cymru's long-term aspirations for Wales. Ironically, for a party that for twenty years has advocated the demise of the UK state as a prerequisite for securing Welsh self-determination, it is the UK government that is now best placed to deliver on the key issue of constitutional reform for Wales.

Conclusion

This case study of Plaid Cymru has traced the transformation of a long-held philosophical attraction to international solutions for the centre–periphery dilemma, into a substantive constitutional vision that envisaged an economically, politically and culturally vibrant Wales taking her place alongside the other small nations and regions of Europe. Plaid Cymru's support for the basic idea of European co-operation and, by the mid-1990s, the concrete economic, political and cultural manifestations of the EU, saw the party evolve into a highly committed and passionate Euro-enthusiastic political party.

Plaid Cymru's experiences of the supranational level throughout the 1980s and 1990s played no small part in convincing the party of the attractiveness of this European arena both as a general framework for Welsh self-determination, and as a pragmatic opportunity structure for ensuring the economic, political and cultural viability of the Welsh nation. At the same time, however, this strong support both for the idea of Europe and the EU in reality cannot be fully understood without taking the party's ideological values and its domestic political context into account. If a strong ideological tradition made the party instinctively Europeanist in its world view, it was Plaid Cymru's marginalisation within British politics in the early 1980s that served as a catalyst for the party's reassessment of the opportunities for Wales within Europe. It was at this time of domestic political crisis that Plaid Cymru reconsidered the benefits that the EU could bring to the party's quest for greater autonomy for Wales. Imagining a different kind of Europe provided the key tenet of a new party discourse that, it was believed, offered a new and progressive political agenda for Welsh voters.

Plaid Cymru's Euro-enthusiasm by the mid-1990s was in many ways typical of the position usually attributed to minority nationalist parties in the academic literature (see Chapter 1). Such a snapshot does not, however, capture the significant ways in which the party's attitude towards European integration has evolved in more recent years. The confluence of factors that drove Plaid Cymru to fully embrace Europe in the 1980s – developments in European integration and party competitive pressures – were of a very different kind from the late 1990s onwards. In response to developments in European and Welsh politics, Plaid Cymru was forced to search for a new, more appropriate, European discourse. The party's commitment to 'full national status' tapped into what seemed to be moves towards the building of a post-sovereign Europe in the 1990s. By 2003, 'independence in Europe' was seen as a more realistic long-term constitutional aspiration, although the party remained deeply uncomfortable with the sovereigntist implications of this goal. At the same time, however, Plaid Cymru's political and electoral failures within post-devolution Wales prompted the party to reconsider the prominence of Europe in its political programme. The need for political pragmatism and a new prioritisation of party goals led to the downplaying of the party's symbolic Europeanism in favour of an emphasis on the party's policy relevance and credibility within the NAW. The language of 'independence in Europe' will become even less relevant for Plaid Cymru as it seeks to get to grips with the realities of being a party of regional government in Wales. Instead, government incumbency has opened up new opportunities for influencing Welsh, and potentially European, policy making, as well as bolstering Welsh autonomy. With such opportunities not forthcoming at the European level, governing within Wales and negotiating with the UK authorities, rather than the pursuit of independence in Europe, will be the immediate priority for Plaid Cymru.

4 Galicia
The Bloque Nacionalista Galego

The Bloque Nacionalista Galego (BNG) was established in 1982, as an organisational response by Galician nationalists to the new Spanish and Galician institutional framework established as part of Spain's transition to democracy. Over the next twenty-five years, the BNG evolved from being a party that refused to recognise the legitimacy of the new democratic regime established in Spain at the end of the 1970s, to being a party of regional government within Galicia.

This chapter will argue that the transformation of the BNG as a political party holds the key to understanding the party's changing attitude towards European integration over the years. The BNG's early Euro-rejectionism reflected the party's radical Marxist values and anti-system strategy. However, the party's changing aspirations within the Galician political arena by the 1990s generated a significant pressure on the BNG to reconsider its position on the general idea of Europe fundamentally. If the party continued to be highly critical of the concrete realities of European integration, this scepticism was packaged in a more positive symbolic European discourse that linked Galician autonomy to the creation of a Spanish pluri-national state and a 'Europe of the Peoples'. The fact that these two very different positions on European integration were reconciled within the BNG by the end of the 1990s reflected the powerful influence exerted by short-term electoral and political aspirations within the Galician political arena. The electoral decline of the BNG from 2001 onwards triggered new opposition within the party to the 'catch-all' political strategy that had legitimated the party's embracing of a regional Europe in the previous decade. Disappointment with the European Constitution provided further cause for Euro-sceptics within the BNG to voice their opposition to the EU more loudly.

The unexpected success of the BNG in crossing the threshold of government in Galicia in 2005, however, forced the party to adapt its European rhetoric to a very different set of political circumstances. Developments in domestic politics once again trumped deep-rooted ideological values as the principal determinant of the BNG's attitude towards European integration. The precise way in which the BNG adapted its position on Europe revealed a significant change in the status of the European dimension in the party's political programme. The political realities of being a party of regional government led the BNG to minimise the salience of the abstract symbolism of a regional Europe in its political programme. Instead,

Europe was replaced by the Spanish state as the most realistic channel for advancing nationalist goals. This alternative frame of reference for articulating the BNG's political demands was an easy shift for a minority nationalist party that was never completely convinced of the virtues of European integration for the nationalist project.

The origins and development of Galician nationalism

First attempts to mobilise support for an agenda anchored in the notion of galeguismo[1] can be traced back to the 1840s.[2] The origins of the contemporary nationalist movement, however, are much more recent. In the 1950s, with Spain under the rule of General Franco, a clandestine cultural movement led by Ramón Piñeiro aimed to ensure the survival of Galician culture and language, but rejected political activism as an inappropriate strategy given the conditions of the time (Beramendi and Núñez Seixas, 1996: 191–99). However, the dissatisfaction of a new generation of Galician students and intellectuals with these limited cultural aims led to the emergence of several new political formations. Firstly, the Partido Socialista Galego (PSG), established in August 1963, presented itself as a social democratic party within the European tradition. By the mid-1970s, the PSG had developed a more distinctively nationalist and Marxist programme which conceptualised Galicia as an internal colony within Spain, and which defended the right to self-determination within an Iberian federation (Fernández Baz, 2003: 40–43). Secondly, the more radical Unión do Povo Galego (UPG), founded on 25 July 1964, replaced the vocabulary of agrarianism, co-operatism and autonomy which had hitherto characterised the regionalist and nationalist currents of galeguismo, with the terminology of revolution, proletariat and national liberation. A third more conservative tendency was represented by the Partido Galegista (PG), created several years later in June 1978 as a reincarnation of the centrist ideas of an identically named nationalist party from the 1930s, which combined a programme of moderate nationalism with centre–right socio-economic preferences.[3]

On Franco's death in 1975, Spain's transition to democracy led to the fragmentation of the Galician nationalist movement, as different parties reacted more or less positively to the constitutional process set in train, and the new legal and institutional model proposed for the Spanish state. In May 1982, however, discussions began between the UPG, PSG, other smaller groupings[4] and a number of independent activists about the possibility of creating a common nationalist front. The eventual formation of the BNG in September 1982 constituted a collaborative project between the UPG and a number of independent activists directly affiliated to the BNG. In practice, however, the BNG was dominated from the outset by the Marxist UPG, with the latter's influence to be seen clearly in the BNG's political programme, strategy and organisational set-up (Máiz, 2003; Barreiro Rivas, 2003; Vilas Nogueira and Fernández Baz, 2004).[5]

Galician nationalism from 1982 (the creation of the BNG) to the present day has undergone three distinct phases of development. Firstly, from 1982 to 1989, the nationalist spectrum continued to be characterised by the three broad ideological

78 *Galicia: The Bloque Nacionalista Galego*

tendencies evident in the 1970s: the BNG representing the radical left of Galician nationalism, the PSG and EG defining themselves as social democratic,[6] and the conservative tradition upheld by the PG on the right.[7] Secondly, between 1989 and 1994 the nationalist movement underwent a process of rationalisation as the BNG incorporated several smaller nationalist groups into its ranks. These ranged from radical left-wing formations such as Inzar (an amalgamation of Maoist and Trotskyite parties), to the social democratic Unidade Galega (UG)[8] to the more conservative Partido Nacionalista Galego-Partido Galeguista (PNG-PG) and a large number of independent members not aligned to any political group. A further group, Esquerda Nacionalista (EN) was created within the BNG in April 1992, rather than being incorporated from outside.[9] These developments are summarised in Table 4.1.

A third stage, from 1994 (the year of the incorporation of UG, the last party to join the BNG) onwards, was characterised by the consolidation of the BNG as a political organisation in its own right, with legitimacy and authority beyond that of simply being an instrumental coalition or alliance between different sub-parties (Barreiro Rivas, 2003: 233). The implication for the individual sub-parties was a decline in their visibility as ideologically and organisationally distinct entities within the BNG (Gómez-Reino Cachafeiro, 2003), with a corresponding increase in the role played by individual activists in internal deliberative processes. During a lifespan of more than thirty years, therefore, the Galician nationalist movement had been transformed from being composed of small disparate groups unable (or unwilling) to co-operate, into a single political party with broad popular appeal and an increasingly important political force within Galician politics.[10]

The ideological heritage: ambiguity and indifference vis-à-vis Europe

If Plaid Cymru boasted a long legacy of ideological Europeanism, the BNG also laid claim to such an ideological heritage.[11] The nationalist historiography

Table 4.1 Composition of the BNG

Group	Year joined	Ideological tendency	Membership
Independents[a]			8944 (75.6%)
UPG	1982	Marxist-Leninist	1295 (11.6%)
Esquerda Nacionalista	1992	Socialist	595 (5.9%)
Unidade Galega	1994	Left nationalist	565 (4.4%)
Inzar	1993	Post-communist	234 (1.9%)
Colectivo Socialista	1982	Socialist	150 (1.2%)
PNG-PG	1991	Conservative nationalist	132 (1.1%)

Sources: Barreiro Rivas (2003); Gómez-Reino Cachafeiro (2003).

Notes:
a Ever since the BNG's creation, individuals have been able to join the organisation directly as independent members, without having to be a member of any of the BNG's ideologically distinct subgroups. For this reason, no specific joining date or ideological tendency is provided in this table.

of Manuel Murguía in the nineteenth century drew heavily on a Celtic mythology shared by other peripheral regions in western Europe, although not in such a way as to propose any kind of pan-Celtic political or institutional organisation within which the Galician nation would take its place.[12] During the 1930s, the Partido Galeguista demonstrated an awareness of the potential of international co-operation for bringing added legitimacy to Galician claims of nationhood when it requested, in 1933, that the League of Nations formally recognised the territory as a European nation. Several years later, nationalist hero Daniel Castelao also invoked the idea of the Galician nation within a Spanish and European federal system (García Soto, 2000).

These early internationalist and Europeanist proclivities were less salient, however, in the conceptualisations of Galician nationhood proposed by subsequent generations of nationalist activists. A political European dimension emerged in the Galician nationalist discourses of the 1950s, although its significance remained marginal. Piñeiro's cultural galeguismo, for instance, was rooted in the belief that European unity was a necessary development at the time, and would be built upon the existence of cultural communities like Galicia, 'the first pieces of the European puzzle' (Franco Grande, 1985: 151). The establishment of the EEC during this decade was viewed positively as the realisation of these claims (Beramendi and Núñez Seixas, 1996: 201). However, given that Piñeiro's deliberate emphasis was on cultural promotion, rather than political activism, these European federalist ideas were never more than of secondary importance. During the 1960s, the PSG also sought to define itself more clearly as a defender of European federalism (Barreiro Rivas, 2003: 114). However, this self-presentation was abandoned with the adoption of an increasingly radical left-wing programme by the 1970s.

In contrast to these vague yet present affirmations of Galicia's European heritage by Piñeiro's galeguismo and the PSG respectively, no such Europeanism was articulated as part of the UPG's world view. From the very beginning, the UPG's international point of reference was not European, but rather the Third World territories in which post-colonial wars were being waged. As such, much of the UPG's earliest political concepts and vocabulary were inspired by such struggles, in much the same way as the Corsican FLNC in the late 1970s (see Chapter 5). The UPG's ideological stance was radical both on the centre–periphery dimension, and on the left–right dimension. Fashioning itself as a Marxist–Leninist party with Maoist tendencies, 'national liberation' was intrinsically linked to 'social liberation' at the hands of the Galician working class (Barreiro Rivas, 2003: 116–21). For the UPG, Galicia was a colony within a Spanish imperialist state, the latter being held responsible for the region's economic exploitation, cultural oppression and political marginalisation (BN-PG, 1977). On the death of Franco and the beginning of Spain's transition to democracy, the UPG rejected the new Spanish Constitution as being undemocratic and illegitimate due to its failure to recognise Galician historical, cultural and linguistic distinctiveness. The party defended the need for a 'rupture' from the new political institutions being created as the only solution to achieving self-determination and sovereignty within a Spanish federation.

As a result of the UPG's ideological and strategic priorities in its early years, and given the political conditions in Spain at the time, the UPG had very little interest in, or time for, developments in European integration up until the late 1970s. To the extent that the party acknowledged international politics at all, it was to denounce Galicia's 'colonial situation' and the 'appropriation of the Galician economy by the dominant classes of the capitalist countries of Spain and the western world', without any further specification of the agents or implications of this process (BN-PG, 1977: 11). However, several factors would lead the UPG to take European integration much more seriously from the late 1970s onwards. The consolidation of Spain's new constitutional framework and the normalisation of party politics in Galicia forced the UPG to turn its attention to other political developments that the party had hitherto ignored. More specifically, the signing by the Spanish government of an agreement with the EEC in 1978 outlining the terms of future Spanish membership, and the gradual implementation of socio-economic reforms in order to meet the conditions for entry into the EEC, elevated the European question to the top of the party's political agenda. The party's initial disinterest in European integration was be replaced by trenchant opposition both to the principle and concrete reality of supranational co-operation. This Euro-rejectionism would define the parameters of the BNG's position on Europe from 1982 onwards. It is to consider the evolution of the UPG/BNG's Euro-rejectionism that this chapter now turns.

Accepting democracy, rejecting Europe

Máiz (1996, 2003) and others (Lago and Máiz, 2004; Vilas Nogueira and Fernández Baz, 2004) have argued that the collapse of Franco's regime upon his death in 1975, and Spain's subsequent transition to democracy, opened up a new and highly favourable political opportunity structure for Galician nationalism. These opportunities were predominantly institutional, and resulted from: (i) the democratisation of the Spanish state, as enshrined in the 1978 constitution, which facilitated the legalisation of previously clandestine nationalism; and (ii) the creation of a 'state of autonomies' which established seventeen new autonomous communities on the sub-state level and provided new institutional incentives for minority nationalist mobilisation within Spain (Máiz et al., 2002).

As noted above, however, the UPG – the main minority nationalist party at the end of the 1970s – initially rejected these new structures, and campaigned for a complete overhaul of the institutional framework enshrined in the new Spanish Constitution. However, such a strategy became untenable as it became clear that not only was the transition to democracy inevitable, but also that the UPG was failing to mobilise electoral support for the radical political programme it proposed (Barreiro Rivas, 2003: 147–48). In the first democratic elections in Spain in 1977, the UPG polled a meagre 2% of the vote in Galicia, the PSG (in favour of the constitutional process) doing little better (see Table 4.2). Overwhelming approval of both the Spanish Constitution in December 1978 and Galicia's Statute of Autonomy in December 1980, confirmed the reality of this new institutional

Table 4.2 Election results for the Congress of Deputies in Galicia, 1977–2004

Party	1977 %	Seats	1979 %	Seats	1982 %	Seats	1986 %	Seats	1989 %	Seats	1993 %	Seats	1996 %	Seats	2000 %	Seats	2004 %	Seats
UCD	53.76	20	48.18	17	17.71	5	–	–	–	–	–	–	–	–	–	–	–	–
AP/PP	13.13	4	14.19	4	37.60	13	39.19	13	39.02	14	47.12	15	48.31	14	53.99	16	47.15	12
PSOE	15.52	3	17.32	6	32.83	9	35.76	11	34.56	12	35.95	11	33.54	9	23.71	6	37.19	10
CDS	–	–	–	–	2.59	0	8.57	2	7.80	1	1.53	0	–	–	0.10	0	0.14	0
CG	–	–	–	–	–	–	6.24	1	3.44	0	–	–	–	–	–	–	–	–
BN-PG/BNG	2.02	0	5.95	0	2.96[a]	0	2.11	0	3.59	0	8.01	0	12.85	2	18.62	3	11.37	2
PSG	2.41	0	5.43[b]	0	–	–	3.56[c]	0	2.57[c]	0	–	–	–	–	–	–	–	–
EG	–	–	–	–	1.71	0	–	–	–	–	–	–	–	–	–	–	–	–
PNG-PG	–	–	–	–	–	–	–	–	1.09	0	–	–	–	–	–	–	–	–
PCE/EU-IU	3.03	0	4.16	0	1.55	0	1.14	0	3.28	0	4.71	0	3.63	0	1.28	0	1.74	0
Others	10.13	0	4.77	0	3.05	0	3.43	0	4.65	0	2.68	0	1.67	0	2.30	0	2.41	0
Total	100	27	100	27	100	27	100	27	100	27	100	26	100	25	100	25	100	24

Source: Parlamento de Galicia (2005).

Notes:
a BN-PG - PSG coalition.
b As part of the coalition Unidade Galega, along with the PG and POG.
c PSG-EG coalition.

framework.[13] The UPG fared only marginally better in the first Galician autonomous elections in 1981. Although its 4.2% of the vote was better than that achieved by the moderate nationalist party EG (1.4%), it was hardly a challenge to the political hegemony of the two right-wing statewide parties in Galicia, Alianza Popular (AP) and the Unión de Centro Democrático (UCD), who between them gained an impressive 70.4% of all the votes cast by the Galician electorate.

In such circumstances, the decision by the UPG and other nationalist formations and individuals to establish a new organisational front in 1982 – the BNG – was a response to the new institutional opportunities created in Galicia at the beginning of that decade (Vilas Nogueira and Fernández Baz, 2004: 202). The adoption of this new organisational strategy, however, did not change the primary aim of the radical nationalist movement. The BNG, as a 'liberation front', continued to challenge the Spanish and Galician institutional models, and advocated a radical change to the configuration of this new constitutional set-up (Vilas Nogueira and Fernández Baz, 2004: 215). Even if explicit references to Marxism had disappeared in the party statutes that were approved at the BNG's founding assembly in 1982, the party's ideological themes remained the same. As an internal colony, Galicia's economic dependence on the Spanish state could be resolved only by the pursuit of a rupturist strategy as a means of achieving self-determination. Only then could the restructuring of Galician society begin, based on an economic model of nationalisation, co-operatives and family-run enterprises, and the participation of workers in economic and political decision making. In order to achieve these aims, the BNG pursued the 'internal political decolonisation' of Galicia's autonomous institutions, as a means of transforming Galician politics from within (Beiras, in Fernán Vello and Pillado Mayor, 2004: 103).

The BNG's ideological and strategic priorities in post-transition Galician politics had two discernible impacts on the party's attitude towards Europe. Firstly, the party's exclusive concern with overhauling Galician political institutions translated into a strong isolationism and a complete disinterest in state-level or supranational politics (Fernán Vello and Pillado Mayor, 2004: 103). As such, the BNG demonstrated minimal interest in elections to state and European institutions until the mid-1990s. The party also shunned any kind of interaction with statewide parties, those belonging to the liberal bourgeois camp, social democratic parties, and even other minority nationalist parties who did not share its partisan values (Barreiro Rivas, 2003: 133). Secondly, to the limited extent that the BNG was required to state a position on the European issue – particularly as the prospect of Spanish accession to the EEC became a reality – the party's attitude was a natural extension of the UPG's anti-imperialist, anti-capitalist and anti-system values. Antipathy towards the Spanish government and statewide political parties as agents of colonial oppression, and a rejection of the legitimacy of the extant political system, were simply transposed into a European key. As the first expression of the BNG's Euro-rejectionism, the proceedings from the party's founding assembly (26–27 September 1982) stated that 'we are opposed to the EEC and NATO as they are organisations which, on both an economic and politico-military levels, represent the interests of large monopolies and west

European and American imperialism' (BNG, 1982: 2). The linkage of European integration to alien exogenous interests would remain a consistent theme of the BNG's European discourse until well into the 1990s. It is with this vague constituency of all-powerful international capitalists – even more so than the Spanish state – that the blame for Galicia's socio-economic and political misfortunes was squarely and consistently placed. Over the next four years, the BNG also developed remarkably detailed analyses of the negative impact of European integration on the Galician economy and society. These arguments would constitute the basic tenets of the party's opposition to the concrete reality of European integration for the next twenty-five years, and as such, are worth considering in greater detail.

The BNG's rejection of the EEC was grounded, first of all, in the claim that the Spanish governing authorities had deceived the Spanish people about the true nature of Spain's accession to the European club. Official declarations to the effect that accession to the EEC was Spain's destiny and an affirmation of its return to the democratic fold[14] – a powerful argument so soon after the end of forty years of dictatorship – were rejected by the nationalists as demagogic and false. Rather, the real terms of Spain's accession, it was claimed, had been decided on purely economic and political grounds, which in both respects were seriously damaging for Galician society (*A Nosa Terra*, 1985a). Economically, given the terms of accession defined by the *acquis communitaire*, the entry of Spain into the EEC did not affect all its regions equally, but exacerbated economic disparities within the state. In particular, Spanish membership of the EEC would compound Galicia's socio-economic underdevelopment – the product of centuries of neglect by the Spanish authorities – and would increase the region's dependency on the centre (*A Nosa Terra*, 1984). For example, measures to make the Spanish fishing industry more compatible with European interests disguised the fact that 'its disappearance seems to be the pursued aim' (*A Nosa Terra*, 1980d). Similarly, the aim of the CAP was 'the systematic destruction of agricultural smallholdings' and the livestock industry, while wine production would be 'condemned to death' as a result of opening up the sector to competition from the European continent (*A Nosa Terra*, 1980c). The social consequences of such economic measures – unemployment, emigration of labour and increasing class differences – had been completely neglected in the interest of achieving Spanish economic competitiveness within the European common market (*A Nosa Terra*, 1985b). In short, for the BNG 'the principal advantages which are attributed to entry into the EEC are far from clear' (*A Nosa Terra*, 1982).

The BNG also denounced the political manner in which negotiations for Spanish accession to the EEC had been conducted. The deal struck in these negotiations was portrayed as an institutional betrayal – by the left in particular, namely the Partido Socialista Obrero Español (PSOE) and the Partido Comunista de España (PCE) – of the interests of both the Spanish working class and the country's underdeveloped regions (*A Nosa Terra*, 1981). They were negotiations that, furthermore, were defined by the capitalist interests of European monopolies and imposed upon Galicia. Galicia's inability to participate in these negotiations reaffirmed the necessity for national self-determination: 'Our lack of sovereignty to negotiate leaves in foreign hands the right to speculate with our vital interests, making us a sacrificial offering in the interest of protecting the subsistence of other economic sectors favoured by the Spanish state' (*A Nosa Terra*, 1980a).

From the BNG's perspective, joining the EEC was not the only option open to Galicia. Its economic interests would be better served through the pursuit of its own bilateral negotiations with other countries with similar economic interests, with a sovereign Galicia deciding how and with whom to negotiate (*A Nosa Terra*, 1980b, c). Neither was membership of the EEC necessary to ensure the cultural survival of the Galician nation, since the Galician nation was already, historically speaking, a part of Europe.

> Paradoxical as it may seem, Galicia, which economically does not fit with the predominant [EEC] paradigm that is now on offer, is in its essence European from a cultural perspective ... Galicia is the most European – and not the most Latin – of the [Iberian] peninsula's peoples ... And so Galicia's cultural reciprocity and exchanges with other peoples already integrated within the EEC ... does not require [Galicia's] integration into the EEC.
> (*A Nosa Terra*, 1985c)

In contrast to Plaid Cymru, however, this European heritage was not construed as the basis for a future Europe of the Regions; no positive linkage was made between the ongoing process of European integration and the prospects for securing autonomy for Galicia. Rather, the notion of a Europe of the Regions was dismissed as a construct of clandestine nationalism during the Franco regime, when such imagery served the purpose of evoking a democratic alternative when talk of self-determination and national sovereignty incurred political and judicial persecution. While the existence of different European peoples was accepted as a historical fact, such abstract normative posturing had no place in the tough climate that faced the struggling Galician economy at the time (*A Nosa Terra*, 1985b). Picking and choosing what was good and what was bad about Europe was not an option. The BNG's duty, it was claimed, was to assume an unequivocal stance in favour or against the European project as a whole. This stance could only be negative, given the tension between the BNG's pursuit of a progressive alternative for Galicia anchored in traditional socialist values, and the capitalist interests that dominated the EEC. This opposition was expressed succinctly by the BNG's leader at the time, Xosé Manuel Beiras, in the following terms.

> There is an absolute incompatibility between the prospering of the Galician economy through firmly implanted regional initiatives and the strategy of the EEC ... It is not, therefore, a case of discussing whether integration is for better or for worse, more or less favourable, according to a simple cost–benefit macroeconomic analysis of the advantages we would obtain and the disadvantages we would suffer ... because there is an unequivocal and absolute antithesis between the necessities and demands of the Galician economy in the

interest of its own development and the fact of integration as it is understood in the Community strategy.

(Xosé Manuel Beiras, in Fernán Vello and Pillado Mayor, 1989: 343)

The eventual accession of Spain to the EEC on 1 January 1986 forced the BNG to accept the reality of European integration. However, the party's demand for withdrawal from the European club continued to be articulated for several more years. Neither did EEC membership alter the main tenets of the BNG's critique of the European polity as had been formulated up until that point. Economic themes continued to dominate the party's rejection of Europe, as the Galician economy faced the painful realities of adjusting to the European Common Market regime. The party opposed milk quotas, the further reduction of the fishing fleet in response to quotas on fishing, and closures in the shipbuilding industry due to a lack of competitiveness with other communitarian and extra-communitarian countries. With Spain participating in European Parliament elections from 1987 onwards,[15] the BNG acknowledged that representation within the European Parliament would enhance the external representation of Galicia. At the same time, however, it was deemed that such a presence would do little to change the fact that in the decision-making forums that really affected Galician socio-economic and cultural interests – the Council of Ministers – the nation's interests remained unrepresented.

While Plaid Cymru perceived developments in European integration from the mid-1980s onwards to be moving in a direction compatible with the long-term aims of Welsh nationalism, the same developments did little to persuade the BNG that its antipathy towards European integration should be revised. The BNG opposed the SEA in 1987 because 'it signifies the bringing down of all the protectionist barriers put up by the weakest states and creates a vast free market for the benefit of multinational companies' (*A Nosa Terra*, 1987a). Similarly, a doubling of the funds allocated to the EEC's regional policy in 1988 was dismissed as insignificant since 'no regional policy will be able to minimise the inequality caused by the liberation of capital' (*A Nosa Terra*, 1989). If anything, these developments only served to vindicate the party's rejection of the EEC. If the BNG pre-1986 presented itself as the only party warning of the dangers to come, its rhetoric after 1986 became increasingly self-righteous.

> When they put us in the EEC they said that integration would be beneficial for all. And now we see that it was all a lie, that they tricked us deliberately, that they manipulated information, that we were spare change, the price they were willing to pay for other more developed zones and commercial European interests to benefit. Claims that we did not believe and for which we are not willing to pay the price.
>
> (*A Nosa Terra*, 1987a)

In its campaign against the ratification of the TEU in the autumn of 1992, the BNG produced an extensive document setting out its opposition to both the economic and political aspects of the treaty (BNG, 1992). The TEU was judged to contain little promise of any improvement in Galicia's economic fortunes. On the contrary, the European Cohesion Fund, aimed primarily at improving regional disparities, would only 'condemn Galicia and the entire periphery of Europe to be confined to dependency and economic underdevelopment' and would see Galicia '… pass from being a colony controlled by Madrid to being directly an internal colony within a rich Europe' (ibid.: 2). With regard to the political aspects of the treaty, the substance and tone of the analysis were also predictable. Whereas Plaid Cymru saw the TEU as a decisive step in the direction of a Europe of the Regions, the BNG only saw evidence of 'a return to the third Napoleonic Empire, or a revival of the Romano-Germanic Empire or the Fourth Reich' (ibid.: 5). The new institutions established by the TEU were perceived to 'reproduce that obsolete Jacobin institutional model on the supra-state level' while ignoring the social, economic and cultural measures that genuine political integration implied, and which would ultimately recognise the rights of both the working class and the historic nations on Europe's periphery (ibid.: 5). Indeed, the TEU was 'anti-nationalist' since it 'ignores expressly and intentionally the nationalities and identities of the people of Europe' (ibid.: 6). With regard to the Committee of the Regions, the BNG predicted many of the body's eventual weaknesses when it identified in its limited consultative role and heterogeneous composition the ingredients of an institution destined to become, curiously, 'a cage of grasshoppers or a Babel of Lilliputians' (ibid.: 6). The democratic deficit of the European institutions, a repressive justice and home-affairs policy and a xenophobic attitude towards non-Europeans (embodied in the Schengen agreements on the free movement of persons), as well as the TEU's imperial aspirations underlying the proposals to strengthen Europe's security and defence capacities, meant there was very little cause to support the TEU as a step forward for Europe and for Galicia. The only option available for the BNG was thus 'a progressive and systematic campaign that demands the renegotiation of the Spanish Treaty of Accession to the EEC in all areas that affect Galicia' (BNG, 1991: 4).

Europa sí pero non así: from Euro-rejectionism to Euro-scepticism

During the first fifteen years of the BNG's existence, the party's position on the European issue was thus defined by the rejection of the notion that European integration held the potential for resolving the centre–periphery conflict in the long-term, and unrestrained criticism of the way in which the EU was developing in practice. By the end of the 1990s, however, this Euro-rejectionism had given way to a more positive evaluation of the basic linkage between European integration and self-determination. Dissatisfaction with the economic and political benefits accrued from EU membership, however, remained as salient a feature of the party's European discourse as ever. In this respect, the BNG's attitude towards Europe by the end of the 1990s can best be described as Euro-sceptic, according to the typology set out in Chapter 2.

Up until 1998, the BNG's formal declarations on Europe provided no signs that such a change of heart vis-à-vis the basic idea of Europe had taken place. In 1995, for example, Francisco Rodriguez, the leader of the UPG and a senior figure within the BNG, continued to insist that 'we must consider, if things continue in this manner, not only a renegotiation of the [terms of Spain's accession] treaty, but even withdrawing from the EEC' (*A Nosa Terra*, 1995a). The BNG's campaign for both the 1996 general election and the 1997 autonomous elections contained similar pledges. And yet, in its 1998 general assembly, the BNG formally approved a significant reassessment of its position on Europe, acknowledging for the first time that Galician self-determination could be achieved only within a European framework that recognised the rights of small nations to exist within a Europe of the Peoples. The motion approved in the conference accepted the supranational sphere as one in which the BNG was obliged to be active, and as an arena within which the party's long-term constitutional objectives could potentially be resolved.

> [T]he struggle for the national liberation of Galicia is paradoxically embedded in a wider context, full of contradictions, which the Spanish state cannot always control ... Such circumstances demand specific action by Galicia as a nation on the supranational level ... The European Union is, for Galicia, a new and relevant space, a political territory where the Galician nation can also express its desire for self-determination.
> (BNG, 1998: 3)

Gone was the commitment to the renegotiation of the European treaties and Spain's accession treaty, as well as the preference for the pursuit of bilateral alternatives, because:

> the EU is an unavoidable reality; the BNG, as it is with regard to the Spanish state, is obliged to be present in representative European institutions and to use all possible avenues, whether direct or via the Spanish state, which permit the defence of the aspirations and interests of the Galician people, in the political sphere as much as in the economic, linguistic or cultural sphere.
> (ibid.: 16)

Given the uncompromising tone of the BNG's rejection of both the idea of European integration and the EU as a concrete reality for the previous sixteen years, this change of heart was as significant as it was swift. Behind the scenes, however, individual voices had been calling for a change in the BNG's thinking on Europe for some time. As early as November 1992, a representative of the PNG-PG – then newly integrated into the BNG – referred to the BNG's European policy as being 'defensive, closed in the defence of the interests of Galicia, when it should be to the contrary' (Basílio Bembo, writing in *A Nosa Terra*, 1992). In contrast to the BNG's electoral programmes in previous elections, the BNG's campaign for the 1994 European Parliament elections stood out for its more constructive approach to the EU. The party had always accepted the need to pursue representation within the European Parliament as a way of defending Galician interests until a more fundamental reconfiguration of Galicia's relationship with the European polity could be achieved. The manifesto went further, however, because it committed the party to co-operate with likeminded actors within this arena in the pursuit of 'a truly pluri-national, egalitarian Europe, without discriminatory hierarchies' (BNG, 1994: 2). The idea of a Europe of the Peoples was put forward as an alternative to a neo-liberal Europe of States, the former based on the values of democracy, social equality, peace and environmental protection, cultural and linguistic diversity (ibid.: 2). These more positive sentiments were echoed by an editorial in *A Nosa Terra* one year later, to mark the tenth anniversary of the signing of Spain's accession treaty with the EEC. The positive as well as negative implications of European integration for Galicia were pointed out, and the article concluded that 'Europe is, more than anything else, a necessity' (*A Nosa Terra*, 1995b). The decision taken in 1998 to commit the BNG to the pursuit of Galician autonomy within a Europe of the Peoples was, therefore, a formal recognition by the BNG of the gradual change of attitude that had taken place among many within the party over a period of several years.

Importantly, however, the BNG's reconsideration of its support for the basic idea of European integration did not translate into a re-evaluation of the party's 'critical position' (BNG, 2003: 14) vis-à-vis the concrete policy and institutional realities of the EU. Whilst the inevitability of Europe was no longer in question – 'Galician nationalism is inconceivable without Europe' just as much as 'Europe is inconceivable without Galicia' (*A Nosa Terra*, 2004) – the more specific benefits for the Galician nation deriving from EU membership were still perceived to be minimal. The resultant party policy on Europe was characterised by a clear dissonance between normative aspirations for a Europe of the Peoples, and a rejection of European integration and its negative economic, political and cultural implications for Galicia.

In its attitude towards European integration in practice, the BNG remained fundamentally opposed to the EU for much the same reasons as had been articulated during the 1980s and early 1990s. For an underdeveloped economy such as persisted in Galicia the prospects of economic prosperity within the European market remained bleak, since the acceleration of economic integration would only lead to further peripheralisation and the exacerbation of existing regional disparities (*A Nosa Terra*, 2001a). EMU signified the reduction in the scope of national governments to respond to specific economic problems of the kind that Galicia was experiencing (*A Nosa Terra*, 2001b). Policies such as the CAP, fisheries policy and others affecting the industrial base of the Galician economy continued to be just as damaging as they had been on Spain's accession to the EEC in 1986 (BNG, 1999). Moreover, enlargement to central and eastern Europe served only to threaten the region's receipt of regional subsidies, and there was no talk of the positive cultural and political benefits of enlargement as identified by Plaid Cymru (*A Nosa Terra*, 2001c). The party's newly adopted symbolic Europeanist rhetoric aside, the reality of the EU remained for the BNG that of a club of capitalist entrepreneurs, centralising states and ultra-liberalism that had little to offer an underdeveloped Galician economy.

This dissonance within the BNG's attitude towards European integration was revealed, most recently, in the party's campaign for the referendum on the ratification of the European Constitution. Its slogan – 'Europe yes, but not like this' (*Europa sí pero non así*) – resembled that used by Plaid Cymru in the referendum on British membership of the EEC in 1975. A minority within the BNG supported a 'critical yes' vote in recognition of the constitution as a step forward towards a federal Europe, albeit with major deficiencies (interview, 8 November 2004). However, the party's eventual campaign for a 'Europeanist no' vote combined a commitment to Europe in principle with a critique of the constitution's lack of legal or political recognition of nations without states, minority languages, and its failure to move towards greater social cohesion and the protection of workers' rights (BNG, 2004b; interviews, 8 and 16 November 2004). The debates in the run-up to the referendum revealed once again the extent of the discrepancy between the BNG's normative European vision and its scepticism of the EU that was being built. Indeed, there was scant evidence that European integration was even moving in the right direction, either towards satisfying the BNG's long-term aspirations for Galicia or the party's more immediate socio-economic, political and cultural goals. On the contrary, the persistent failure of European integration to respond to the BNG's demands had further galvanised the party's deeply rooted hostility towards supranational co-operation.

This persistent critique of the practical realities of European integration aside, however, the BNG's adoption of the terminology of a 'Europe of the Peoples' from 1998 onwards represented a major change in the party's position on Europe. Such a change cannot be attributed to developments in European integration during the 1990s. As stated above, major steps forward in European integration such as the Maastricht Treaty were greeted with the same hostility as had been consistently expressed towards European integration since the 1970s. Rather, it was the BNG's changing goals within the Galician political arena during the 1980s, and the implications of this for the party's internal composition, ideological profile and political strategy, that played the biggest role in catalysing this major revision in the BNG's general attitude towards Europe. These influences merit a more detail examination in order to fully understand their impact on the BNG's attitude towards European integration.

From ideological purity to the maximisation of votes: the changing goals of the BNG

As noted above, the creation of the BNG constituted a new organisational strategy in the pursuit of ideologically defined goals, namely the national and social liberation of the Galician nation. During the 1980s, however, a strategy of outright confrontation within the Galician Parliament was replaced by an acceptance that electoral competition within this arena was the most effective way of securing greater autonomy for the minority nation (Vilas Nogueira and Fernández Baz, 2004: 214–15). In 1985, a decision was taken to allow the BNG's representatives to sit in the Galician Parliament for the first time, even though the party continued to pursue its oppositional strategy within this institution. Boosting the party's presence within the parliament became the BNG's main priority.

The BNG's new prioritisation of electoral competition began to pay dividends from 1989 onwards. In the 1989 autonomous elections, the party's share of the Galician vote increased from 1.4% in 1985 to 6.7% in 1989 (Table 4.3). The BNG's rejectionist policy on Europe played no small part in contributing to this electoral upturn.[16] In particular, the party's outright opposition to the economic reforms undertaken as part of the readjustment of the Spanish economy to the conditions and requirements of the European Common Market, resonated with a widespread popular antipathy to European integration, based on the personal experiences of large sectors of Galician industry who were suffering as a direct consequence of European imposed rules and regulations. The BNG's opposition to the EEC, and its self-presentation as the only political party which represented the true interests of the Galician workforce – in contrast to the Partido Popular de Galicia (PPdeG) and the Partido Socialista de Galicia (PSdeG-PSOE) who were willing collaborators in the detrimental restructuring policies of the Spanish government – also gave the party new political credibility as an alternative political option to the status quo (Beramendi and Núñez-Seixas, 1996: 295). Playing the anti-European card continued to bring the party electoral benefits in the 1993 autonomous elections, after debates over the ratification of the Maastricht Treaty (Fernán Vello and Pillado Mayor, 2004: 121–23; interviews, 11 and 24 November 2004).

The year 1989 was also a turning point in Galician politics more generally, however. The return of Manuel Fraga Iribarne to Galicia in the late 1980s to lead the newly established PPdeG led to the latter's first of several successive absolute majorities in the Galician Parliament in 1989.[17] This success inaugurated a new period of hegemonic control of the region's political institutions. The socialists and the nationalists were left to fight for second and third place. The dialectical relationship between the BNG and the PSdeG-PSOE, with both competing for votes on the left of the political spectrum, saw a weakly implanted socialist party who had never been able to claim a historically rooted political tradition in the region (Jiménez Sánchez, 2003) loose out to the BNG's growing popularity and appeal. By the 1997 autonomous elections, the BNG's share of the vote reached 24%, making it the second political force in Galicia ahead of the PSdeG-PSOE (although still a long way behind the PPdeG's clear majority of 56%).

Paradoxically, however, while the BNG's Euro-rejectionism was an important factor in contributing to a considerable improvement in its electoral standing from 1989 onwards, electoral success had major repercussions for the party's position on Europe. Firstly, this trend created conditions propitious for the incorporation of several smaller parties into its organisation, some of which espoused more supportive attitudes towards European integration. Secondly, growing electoral success provided a further pressure for ideological moderation that rendered the

Table 4.3 Results of autonomous elections in Galicia, 1981–2005

Party	1981 %	1981 Seats	1985 %	1985 Seats	1989 %	1989 Seats	1993 %	1993 Seats	1997 %	1997 Seats	2001 %	2001 Seats	2005 %	2005 Seats
AP/CP/PP	36.6	26	47.9	34	50.7	38	57.3	43	56.0	42	53.8	41	46.6	37
UCD	33.8	24	–	–	–	–	–	–	–	–	–	–	–	–
CG	–	–	15.5	11	–	2	–	–	–	–	–	–	–	–
PSdeG-PSOE	22.5	16	31.0	22	37.3	28	25.3	19	17.3	13	22.7	17	34.2	25
EU-EG	–	–	–	–	–	–	–	–	2.7	2	–	–	–	–
PCG/EU	1.4	1	–	–	–	–	–	–	–	–	–	–	–	–
UPG/BNG	4.2	3	1.4	1	6.7	5	17.3	13	24.0	18	23.5	17	19.2	13
EG/PSG-EG	1.4	1	4.2	3	2.7	2	–	–	–	–	–	–	–	–
Total	100	71	100	71	100	75	100	75	100	75	100	75	100	75

Sources: Rivera Otero (2003); Parlamento de Galicia (2005).

party's virulent anti-Europeanism ill-suited for a moderate party competing for the political centre ground. Thirdly, the BNG's new electoral priorities required the party to revise its isolationist strategy vis-à-vis state and supranational political arenas if it was to be taken seriously as a potential party of regional government. Together, these developments provided a strong impetus for the BNG to reconsider the potential role of Europe in facilitating the party's long-term aspirations for greater Galician autonomy. They will each be considered in turn.

Changes in the internal dynamics of the BNG

The BNG's electoral success from 1989 onwards provided a set of conditions that were propitious for the coordination and simplification of the nationalist political spectrum (Lago, 2004). Firstly, the BNG's new vote-seeking strategy instigated a drive to moderate the party's image as a radical anti-system party and present itself as a pragmatic political option that could appeal to a broader constituency of Galician voters (Máiz, 2003). The priority became that of developing a broader and more appealing political agenda so that 'people will begin to view the BNG more positively and not only as a force which limits itself to protest' (Beiras, in Fernán Vello and Pillado Mayor, 2004: 122). From such a perspective, the incorporation of other ideologically diverse Galician nationalist formations represented an opportunity for the BNG not only to broaden its support base beyond that of the Galician working class, but also to demonstrate its commitment to pursue a 'common project' composed of nationalists of all colours (BNG, 1989: 9). Secondly, the BNG's electoral growth came at the expense of other nationalist parties who, faced with the prospect of terminal electoral decline, came to the conclusion that there was only one solution if their survival was to be ensured: incorporation into the BNG. In the words of one interviewee, 'there arrived a point when it was clear that from an electoral perspective, support was concentrated in the BNG' (interview, 9 November 2004). The example of PSG-EG/UG is illustrative of this dynamic. After performing badly in the autonomous and European Parliament elections held in 1989, and then failing (as UG) to pass the 5% threshold in the 1994 autonomous elections, joining the BNG was the only option available in order to ensure the party's political survival (interview, 9 November 2004).

It was the successful incorporation of UG into the BNG in 1994, more than that of any other political group, which provided the ideological inspiration and rhetorical substance for the BNG's new commitment to a regional Europe. UG and its antecedents had long proposed a more positive interpretation of European integration and Galicia's future as a self-determined nation within this European framework. The difference with the BNG's position on Europe was not so much in the analysis of the negative impact of economic integration on Galicia, on which UG largely concurred. The deal negotiated by the Spanish government for entry into the EEC was perceived to be prejudicial to Galicia's already weak economic position: 'we always saw that the conditions were not positive and, as such, we were always opposed to them' (Camilo Nogueira, in Toro, 1991: 356). Where

UG differed from the BNG was on the principle of European integration, and on Galicia's place within the European polity that was being constructed: 'one thing is the EEC as a phenomenon of European integration ... [and another is] the EEC as a concrete phenomenon which affects Galicia in a determinate way' (*A Nosa Terra*, 1988). For UG, in principle, European integration was no bad thing, not least because it had the potential to create 'a European confederation of nations, a Europe without frontiers where nations have the right to self-determination' (Camilo Nogueira, in Toro, 1991: 357). UG rejected the BNG's characterisation of the EEC as imperialist, capitalist and dominated by powerful monopolies. While the common market model of the time was far from constituting a Europe of the Peoples, the solution, from UG's perspective, was not to stay outside (as favoured by the BNG throughout the 1980s and early 1990s) but to reform the EU from within. Contrary to the BNG's rejection of the Maastricht Treaty, UG (then called the PSG-EG) supported its ratification as a step in the direction of political union that would create more favourable political and institutional conditions for Galician self-determination.

These ideas, introduced into the BNG by UG, informed the former's reconsideration of its position on the basic values underlying the process of European integration from the mid-1990s onwards. The assumption of senior positions within the BNG by senior members of UG – and Camilo Nogueira in particular – enabled the diffusion of these Europeanist ideas to take place. It was Nogueira who wrote the party's 1994 European Parliament election manifesto which, as noted above, was notably more constructive in tone vis-à-vis the EU than the persistently Euro-rejectionist attitudes of the BNG's leadership. Similarly, it was Nogueira who penned the motion approved in the 1998 general assembly that constituted the formal turning point in the party's principled stance on European integration (interview, 9 November 2004). The BNG's reconsideration of the linkage between the process of European integration and the achievement of Galician self-determination, therefore, was the result of a changing balance of power within the party in the mid-1990s, and the gradual incorporation of UG's long-held ideological Europeanism into formal party statements on the issue of Europe.

One of the most striking features of the BNG's changing attitude towards the idea of European integration was that it did not provoke serious internal divisions or factions within the party. Given the divergence in the ideological positions of the different groups incorporated into the BNG by the mid-1990s, such internal divisions would not have been surprising. And yet, factional tensions did not emerge. The case of UG's incorporation into the BNG is again exemplary. Even though the European dimension constituted one of the major points of contention on UG's entry into the BNG, once the agreement to join forces had been formalised, potential sources of ideological friction simply did not materialise (*A Nosa Terra*, 1994).

Explaining this lack of internal tension over the European issue requires, first of all, an understanding of the role played by the party's organisational structure in mediating potential discord. The BNG's 'frontist' model was rooted in the idea of 'the coming together of parties, groups and individuals who, sharing a common idea, unite in order to achieve certain objectives derived from this common idea' (Fernández Baz, 2003: 31). The BNG's assembly model privileged internal democracy and consensus; all decisions were taken by majority, and all subgroups were represented on the party's executive bodies. Whilst adherence to the BNG required acceptance of certain fundamental principles outlined in the party's founding statutes, each political party was also allowed to maintain its own identity, organisation and right of expression within the BNG. The BNG was also vertically structured through representative fora on the local, county and national (Galician) levels (BNG, 1982: 8). The reconciliation of differences consisted of 'friction and osmosis, of reciprocal contagion and mutual transformation' (Inzar, quoted in Gómez-Reino Cachafeiro, 2003: 17) and a constant search for compromise and consensus, in order to reconcile opposing political cultures within a single partisan framework (Beiras, in Fernán Vello and Pillado Mayor, 2004: 155). In this way, whilst differences on the issue of Europe undoubtedly existed within the BNG in the 1990s, the strong emphasis on deliberation and consultation, and the willingness 'of all sides to make concessions in order to avoid the BNG falling apart' (Beiras, in Fernán Vello and Pillado Mayor, 2004: 83) succeeded in accommodating this diversity.

To this internal organisational factor, a second factor explaining the absence of internal tension vis-à-vis the BNG's change of position on the European issue relates to the pressure for maintaining party unity exerted by electoral competition. Given the BNG's desire to maximise its electoral appeal within Galicia, the existence of ideological differences within the party on European integration became of secondary concern.

> The fundamental objective was to regroup all nationalist forces within the BNG, albeit maintaining ideological autonomy and different positions with regard to certain problems. The overriding priority was this, and differences between us were disregarded ... It was considered, first and foremost, that the most appropriate nationalist strategy was to integrate and not to discuss opposing [ideological] positions.
>
> (Interview, 11 November 2004)

In other words, if intra-party differences over Europe did not materialise within the BNG as a result of incorporating different political groups into its organisation, it is testimony to the powerful unifying effect of electoral competition. Ambitions for continued electoral success subjugated internal ideological heterogeneity, with such differences being resolved via informal reconciliation processes within the party. In subsequent years, as will be argued later in this chapter, a period of electoral decline would undermine this consensus on the party's attitude towards Europe; the internal divisions that were avoided during the mid-1990s would, ten years later, threaten the BNG's ability to articulate a coherent party position on the European issue. At the time, however, the party's vote-seeking goal was highly effective in subjugating potential dissent within the party.

Changing ideological values

The BNG's electoral aspirations also placed a growing pressure on the party to repackage its core ideological beliefs in a more voter-friendly way. This process of moderation had already begun prior to 1989, and made the prospect of incorporation into the BNG more attractive for other nationalist groups (interview, 9 November 2004). From 1989 onwards, however, the BNG's nationalist discourse shifted even further towards the political centre, becoming less explicitly Marxist and more distinctly social democratic in its rhetoric (Barreiro Rivas, 2003: 179). The terminology of colonialism and exploitation was replaced by the softer notions of Galicia's marginalisation and peripheralisation within the Spanish state and within Europe. The agents of nationalist mobilisation were no longer narrowly defined as the Galician working class; a role could also be played by the petit bourgeoisie and the middle classes, these being equally legitimate representatives of a much broader and inclusive notion of the Galician people (Máiz, 2003: 29). Moreover, in an attempt to broaden its political appeal, the BNG increasingly emphasised its commitment to 'new politics' issues such as environment protection, pacifism, and social and gender equality (Van Atta, 2003). Even though these themes had always been detectable in the party's politics, they had hitherto been overshadowed by the party's preoccupation with the 'bigger' problem of economic and social injustice (Beiras, in Fernán Vello and Pillado Mayor, 2004: 73). The BNG's move to the political centre ground was a motive for rediscovering these alternative policy priorities.

Ideological purity was thus compromised for a broader political programme in an attempt to carve out a new political space for minority nationalism within the Galician political arena (Máiz, 2003). In the context of this process of ideological moderation, the BNG's new Europeanist rhetoric complemented the party's attempt to portray itself as more progressive, more constructive and more outward looking than the BNG of the 1980s.

The BNG's changing strategy in a multilevel political system

If party unity was a prerequisite of the BNG's continued electoral ascendancy in the 1990s, the party's change in electoral fortunes also required a reconsideration of the isolationist strategy that had translated into the BNG's exclusive focus on 'open confrontation' within the Galician political arena since the early 1980s (Beiras, in Fernán Vello and Pillado Mayor, 2004: 109–23). Even though the BNG had always competed in electoral competition on the state and supranational levels, gaining representation in these different institutional spheres had not hitherto been a priority for the party. The fact that passing the threshold of representation on both of these territorial levels was particularly difficult (see below) was a further factor that contributed to the relative unimportance of statewide and supranational electoral competition for the BNG in its early years.

With the BNG's change of priorities from the mid-1980s onwards, however, increasing the BNG's presence in these arenas became important since:

the decisions taken by state and European bodies are increasingly numerous, and as such it is indispensable that Galicians take maximum advantage of the political power situated in the parliament and the Galician government, to defend our interests.

(BNG, 1997: 7)

In practice, the BNG's vote-seeking goal required, first and foremost, securing representation at the state and supranational levels; doing so would significantly boost the party's image as a credible and moderate political party. From the perspective of this study, however, it is arguable that once representation had been secured at both these territorial levels, several factors served to reinforce the BNG's formal commitment to a regional Europe. In particular, the new political alliances established by the BNG with other like-minded minority nationalist parties enabled the party to articulate its new commitment to a regional Europe as part of a broader political vision that was gaining currency in territorial peripheries across western Europe. In this way, the BNG sought to present itself as a progressive political party that was part of a new pan-European movement demanding far-reaching constitutional change for the continent's small historic nations.

Representation on the state level and the creation of the Galeusca alliance

Despite the BNG's lack of interest in state affairs for the first fifteen years of its existence, the pattern of increasing electoral support for the BNG in the Galician autonomous elections from 1989 onwards was emulated, albeit in a less pronounced manner, in the party's performance in elections to the Spanish Congress of Deputies (Table 4.2). However, the different nature of these elections made it difficult to translate votes into representatives. The biggest problem faced by the BNG was the strongly bipartisan dynamic of the electoral campaign, which favoured the two main statewide parties, the PP and the PSOE (interview, 11 November 2004). As a result, it took the party until 1996 to achieve representation on the state level, when two deputies were elected to the Congress of Deputies. Since then, the party's representation has been minimal, with three deputies between 2000 and 2004, declining to two in the 2004–2008 legislature.

Despite these difficulties, on crossing the threshold of representation at the state level the BNG undertook to establish contacts with other nationalist parties represented within this arena, namely the Catalan CiU and the Basque PNV. Negotiations between these three parties culminated in the signing of the Declaration of Barcelona on 17 September 1998 and the resurrection of a tripartite alliance under the name of Galeusca.[18] The fact that these were the two parties identified by the BNG as suitable partners for collaboration reflected the extent to which the party had re-evaluated its strategic priorities. Given that, as noted above, the BNG had traditionally eschewed any contact with ideologically diverse political actors, signing up to the Galeusca alliance meant co-operating with two nationalist parties that were very different in their historical origins, their ideological profile and their political aspirations. Not only had these two parties enjoyed greater levels of political success than the BNG at the regional and state level;[19] the PNV and CiU also differed from the BNG in ideological terms, with both being broadly centre–right in their value orientation, in contrast to the BNG's left-wing profile (Perez-Nievas, 2006; Barberà and Barrio, 2006). In short, the formation of the Galeusca alliance represented a major reassessment of the BNG's notion of who did and did not constitute acceptable political and electoral allies.

In order to understand this choice of collaborative partners on the state level, Lago and Máiz (2004) have argued that the signing of the declaration had at least two major attractions for the BNG. Firstly, co-operation with the major Catalan and Basque nationalist parties reinforced the profile and visibility of the BNG on the state level by the clear association made between itself and the more politically heavyweight CiU and PNV. Whereas these two parties had long established themselves as the major governing parties within their respective Catalan and Basque territories, the BNG, by association, could also claim to be a credible political and governing alternative for Galicia. Secondly, the agreement also served to enhance the BNG's profile within its own political territory, namely as a moderate party of the centre in the eyes of the traditionally conservative Galician electorate. Through its alliance with the similarly moderate Catalan and Basque nationalist parties, the BNG's strategic and discursive shift towards the political centre ground was legitimised (Keating, 2000: 40), and provided further evidence of the party's conversion from a radical anti-system party to a nationalist party preparing itself for governmental incumbency.

From the perspective of this study, the participation of the BNG in the Galeusca alliance also had a major impact on the European dimension of the BNG's political programme, in that it enabled the party to showcase its principled support for a regionalist Europe. The PNV and the CiU boasted a much longer Europeanist tradition than the BNG, with both parties proposing a clear linkage between the nationalities question and European integration. Certainly, there were important differences between what exactly these two minority nationalist parties wanted from Europe; while the PNV espoused aspirations for Basque sovereignty within a European framework (Keating, 2001a: 77; Keating and Bray, 2006), the CiU proposed a model of shared sovereignty within a confederal European framework of self-governing nations (Keating, 2001a: 72; Giordano and Roller, 2002). Nevertheless, both these European visions departed from the fundamental idea of a mutually compatible and interdependent relationship between European integration and national self-determination. By aligning itself with parties firmly committed to a European framework for achieving their long-term constitutional goals, the BNG's Europe of the Peoples rhetoric could be presented as part of a broader mobilisation in the Spanish peripheries to challenge the existing state and supranational political and institutional status quo. Such an association further legitimised the BNG's Europeanist turn.

Table 4.4 European Parliament election results for Galicia, 1987–2004 (%)

	1987	1989	1994	1999	2004
PP	41.71	33.48	54.56	49.89	47.72
PSOE	29.61	33.05	24.80	23.62	36.20
CDS	10.25	6.73	–	–	–
BNG	3.70	4.17	11.40	21.98	12.32
PSG-EU[a]	2.93	3.34	–	–	–
EU-IU	1.27	1.99	5.07	1.14	1.53
PNG[b]	1.00	1.38	–	–	–
Others	9.53	15.86	4.17	3.37	2.23
Total	100	100	100	100	100

Source: Parlamento de Galicia (2005).

Notes:
a As a part of the list 'Esquerda dos Pobos'.
b As a part of the list 'Pola Europa dos Pobos'.

The BNG and transnational co-operation

A similar solidarity was derived by the BNG from co-operation with other minority nationalist parties at the supranational level, even though gaining access to this political arena was also problematic for the party. As with statewide elections, even though the BNG experienced growing levels of electoral support in European Parliament elections throughout the 1990s (see Table 4.4), several factors undermined the party's ability to cross the threshold of representation at the supranational level. The polarisation effect evident in statewide elections also disadvantaged the party in European Parliament elections (interview, 9 November 2004). A further complicating factor arose from the fact that the elections for the European Parliament consisted of a single statewide constituency, with representatives being elected from closed party lists using the d'Hondt method of proportional representation with no minimum threshold of representation.[20] Political parties with geographically concentrated support, like the BNG, were forced to compete with statewide parties drawing on support from across the whole state. The fragmentation of the nationalist movement itself also contributed to the failure to return any nationalist representatives to the European Parliament until 1999. Calls for the presentation of a single nationalist list in the 1987 and 1989 European Parliament elections failed, since no agreement could be achieved between different Galician nationalist groups on a common 'lowest denominator' programme on which such a joint candidate could be presented (*A Nosa Terra*, 1987b).[21] In 1994, with the incorporation of these different political formations into the BNG having been achieved, the selection of Carlos Mella to head the BNG's list (an independent individually affiliated to the BNG) was still not enough to overcome the structural obstacles of the European electoral system. Given these various difficulties, it is not surprising that, at least until 1999 when there was a realistic chance that the BNG would poll enough votes to return an MEP to the European Parliament, the BNG viewed European Parliament election campaigns 'simply as an informational and propaganda campaign, without it ever being a real possibility that we would gain a seat' (Beiras, in Fernán Vello and Pillado Mayor, 2004: 108). European Parliament elections certainly did not serve as a platform for communicating the BNG's Europeanist credentials, as they did for Plaid Cymru in Wales.

Against this background, the election of the BNG's Camilo Nogueira to the European Parliament in 1999 represented a major breakthrough for the party. The result had several important implications. Firstly, it brought the BNG new political credibility since it enhanced its image as a party capable of winning elections. The failure to keep this seat in the next round of European Parliament elections in 2004 was, in contrast, seen as a major blow to the party's image, since 'society views it as a political failure' (interview, 8 November 2004). Secondly, having an MEP also meant that, at last, Galician interests and preferences would be represented directly in Europe. This was no small achievement given the long-lamented lack of representation of such interests within Galician, Spanish and European decision-making fora (Nogueira, 2006: 294). Most of all, however, the single fact of gaining representation in the European Parliament in 1999 provided the forum for the elaboration of the BNG's hitherto abstract Europe of the Peoples rhetoric. Xosé Manuel Beiras (in Fernán Velo and Pillado Mayor, 2004: 283) noted that the European dimension to the party's activities 'made a qualitative jump forward ... in 1999 with the representation of the BNG in the European Parliament, where ... Camilo Nogueira undertook an intensive and creative programme of activities ... encompassing all the themes salient in international politics, European issues as well as global ones'.

This substantive boost to the BNG's Europeanist discourse was in no small part due to the party's membership of the EFA. Again, for reasons noted above, the BNG did not have a history of pursuing such transnational links prior to the mid-1990s. In its campaign for the 1985 autonomous elections, the BNG announced its intention to 'reinforce its collaborative links with nationalist organisations in Europe and within the [Spanish] state, within a mutual respect for the methods used by each one in combating the oppression of their respective peoples' (BNG, 1985: 4). In practice, however, this translated into loose and infrequent contacts with certain radical nationalist parties within the framework of the Conference of Nations without a State in Western Europe (CONSEO), including the forerunner to the Basque party Herri Batasuna (HB),[22] the Catalan ERC, the Irish Sinn Fein (SF) and the public fronts of the Corsican FLNC (see Chapter 5). However, significant differences in strategies and objectives between the participants served to limit the degree of co-operation possible between these groups. CONSEO provided more of a symbolic platform for demonstrating solidarity rather than an institutionalised framework for concrete co-operation of the kind that would later develop under the auspices of the EFA.

The BNG initiated contact with the EFA upon the incorporation of UG into the party in 1994. Between 1994 and 1999, and without a direct voice within the European Parliament to represent Galician interests, the EFA group assumed this representative role. The most significant impact of EFA membership on the BNG's European discourse, however, was witnessed from 1999 onwards, after Camilo Nogueira took up his seat in the European Parliament. In the broadest sense, membership of the EFA group within the European Parliament both encouraged and legitimated the BNG's new symbolic Europeanism. Of course, the EFA structure provided a ready-made framework which facilitated the BNG's adaptation to the procedures and processes of the European Parliament; this forum also facilitated the exchange of information and experiences between like-minded actors. Most importantly, however, co-operation within this transnational alliance provided the BNG with the vocabulary and substantive detail to go beyond the vague rhetoric of a Europe of the Peoples in order to express its long-term constitutional aspirations more coherently. Thus, for example, it is no coincidence that the notion of 'internal expansion' used by Plaid Cymru from 1999 onwards also crops up frequently in Camilo Nogueira's declarations on Europe, to express the mechanism through which small nations such as Galicia would take their place within a federal Europe (interview, 9 November 2004). The BNG also adopted other, more sophisticated, arguments in favour of such a federal Europe of Nations and Peoples that echoed those put forward by other adherents to the EFA group. In this way, the BNG adopted the themes developed by the EFA and utilised them to further legitimise the party's specific demands for Galician autonomy. As with the BNG's strategy of alliances at the state level, the fact that these demands were presented as part of a much broader and more far-reaching process of minority nationalist mobilisation added weight to the BNG's arguments in favour of further European integration.

The impact of EFA membership on the BNG's European discourse was not limited to the contextualisation of the party's long-term constitutional aims. The institutional and material resources provided by the EFA for its members enabled the BNG to develop a sophisticated European vision notable for its breadth of substantive policy positions, from classic nationalist concerns for economic, political, cultural and linguistic policy, to other aspects of the BNG's model of society, including health and public services, environment protection, and social and gender equality (interview, 9 November 2004). Taken together, these policy alternatives proposed a new image of Galicia as a European nation which, alongside other European nations and peoples, was leading the drive to build a Europe of economic stability, social well-being, and linguistic and cultural preservation, as well as the fundamental pursuit of adequate political recognition and representation: 'a Europe of the Peoples, which recognises Galicia's rights as a nation. A European Union that is political, social and cultural, and not only economic and monetary' (BNG, 2004a). Initiatives instigated by the BNG, such as the establishment of the Inter-group of Nations without States within the European Parliament, sought to link the BNG's nationalist project with a more global struggle for the recognition of the economic, political and cultural rights of minority nations, with a view to presenting Galician autonomy within a European framework as both a credible and sustainable project (interviews, 5 and 8 November 2004).

The limitations of the BNG's turn towards Europe

Thus far, this chapter has argued that the BNG's re-evaluation of the potential of European integration to resolve the centre–periphery cleavage can be attributed to the changing aspirations of the BNG within the Galician political arena from the mid-1980s onwards. This had significant knock-on effects on the internal composition of the BNG and the party's strategy vis-à-vis different territorial levels of political representation which, in turn, impacted upon the party's position on Europe. But to what extent did these instrumental discursive and strategic changes represent a change in the BNG's ideological position on the issue of Europe?

There is good reason to argue that the 1998 resolution that saw the BNG formally adopt a commitment to purse a Europe of the Peoples as its long-term constitutional goal did not mean that the fundamental attitudes of the majority within the party had changed. Many of the party's members and senior figures retained deeply ambivalent views on the virtues of European integration. The scepticism still espoused by many within the BNG was summarised by the following dilemma that, according to one senior party member, the party still had not fully resolved.

> On the one hand, deciding if we should openly support these processes of economic integration, in the confidence that we will be able to act in Europe as a nation, institutionalised in such a way that would allow us to bypass the Spanish state. On the other hand, not confiding too much in a process which may well be seriously eroding the power of the states, but which may also be even more erosive ... for national formations that today lack adequate institutional protection ... From my point of view, Galician nationalism should undoubtedly opt for the second option.
>
> (Interview, 11 November 2004)

Further evidence that the BNG's formal support for the process of European integration had not taken root in the mindset of the party as a whole was provided by the party's general lack of engagement with European affairs beyond the core economic issues that directly impacted upon the Galician economy. It is telling that, the party's literature and activities for the European Parliament elections aside, the European dimension hardly featured at all on the BNG's political agenda from 1998 onwards. Indeed, the referendum on the European Constitution in February 2005 prompted the first serious debate within the BNG on its position towards European integration since the party's formal decision was taken to support a Europe of the Peoples. During the intervening years, no time or effort was invested by the BNG in considering questions such as what exactly this constitutional blueprint would mean for Galicia and for Europe, and what rights the former would have within such a European polity. This was in stark contrast to the considerable effort expended by Plaid Cymru in spelling out the different stages by which Wales would achieve full national status within the EU.

Neither did the BNG's formal commitment to a regional Europe lead the party to incorporate a European dimension into its broader policy programme, in the sense of exploring the extent to which the EU could help achieve domestic policy objectives. Whilst issues such as the normalisation and promotion of the Galician language and culture remained key priorities for the BNG, there was no recognition that European initiatives in this area could facilitate the achievement of such goals. Similarly, in the achievement of the party's new politics agenda, there was no attempt to link these policy goals with allied supranational initiatives in the same direction, as a means of facilitating the resolution of problems that were inherently transnational and would benefit from international co-operation. In short, a repackaging of the BNG's long-term constitutional goals in a more attractive Europeanist language did not alter the fact that the sphere of reference for the BNG's policy proposals still remained, first and foremost, Galicia. For most people within the BNG, the European issue remained unimportant from the mid-1990s onwards, despite the party's formal adherence to a symbolic Europeanist discourse that linked Galician autonomy with the future development of European integration. Indeed, the limited engagement of the BNG as a whole with the issue of Europe revealed the extent to which not only was there a dissonance between the party's position on the different facets of European integration, but that this discursive differentiation was a reflection of an organisational differentiation within the party. In other words, the BNG's turn towards Europe during the mid-1990s was driven, first and foremost, by the activism of a small number of committed Europeanists within the party, whilst the vast majority of party activists remained unconvinced by, and unconcerned with, the European dimension to the BNG's nation-building project.

It is not only with regard to the issue of Europe that the ideological moderation of the BNG was limited. Once one begins to scratch beyond the surface of the BNG's social democratic rhetoric, it is not difficult to find evidence of the party's radical ideational origins, a testimony to the resilience of core values and their enduring influence in shaping a party's response to different policy issues. The BNG's basic economic, political and cultural values remained essentially unchanged, albeit repackaged within a more politically acceptable global discourse which presented itself as being both progressive and relevant to Galicia's needs as a nation. In its economic model for society, the BNG combined new regionalist themes such as endogenous sustainable development based on education, innovation and competitiveness – ideas long espoused by EG/UG (Barreiro Rivas, 2003: 181) – with old commitments to the nationalisation of key industries within the framework of a planned Galician economy. A European model based on free trade and a common market remained incompatible with such (de-)centralised economic planning. The BNG as a whole may have voted to accept the adoption of a commitment to a Europe of the Peoples in 1998 for the instrumental reasons identified above. But the endurance of other long-held values in shaping the BNG's political programme still nourished a strong scepticism of the concrete benefits of European integration for the Galician nation.

Reconsidering Europe: a revival of the BNG's Euro-rejectionism?

The dissonance in the BNG's position on Europe – between formal support for a regional Europe and criticism of the EU as a concrete reality – did not lead to intra-party conflict during the 1990s due to the pressures exerted by party competition and the success of the BNG in meeting its electoral goals. However, a decline in the party's electoral fortunes from 2001 onwards threatened the BNG's compromise position on the European issue. New tensions between Euro-enthusiasts and Euro-rejectionists forced the party to reconsider its position on the European question. These tensions were symptomatic of a bigger challenge faced by the BNG, of adapting to a new political context within Galicia.

Two events in particular served to demonstrate the difficulties of reconciling the Europeanist values of a minority within the BNG, with the deep-rooted hostility of the party's rank and file towards European integration. Firstly, the BNG competed in the European Parliament elections in June 2004 on a joint list with its Galeusca partners. This was the first time the Galeusca coalition had been put to the electoral test. It was a tactical decision forced upon the BNG by the political conditions in which the election took place. In addition to the difficulties allied with European Parliament elections identified above, the number of Spanish seats within the European Parliament had been reduced since 1999; this, combined with the BNG's electoral decline since 2001, made it unlikely that the party would cross the threshold of representation by presenting its own electoral list. In the event, the Galeusca list proved an electoral liability for the BNG. The BNG's share of the Galician vote fell substantially from 22% in 1999 to 13% (Table 4.4). Camilo Nogueira, third on the Galeusca list, was not re-elected to the European Parliament.

The BNG's immediate reaction to this disastrous electoral performance was to blame discrepancies in the counting of votes for 'robbing' Camilo Nogueira of his seat by a mere 162 votes (*La Voz de Galicia*, 2004). The real reason for the collapse of the BNG's vote, however, lay in the party's failure to convince its core electorate of the virtues both of collaboration with Catalan and Basque nationalist parties and, more fundamentally, of a moderated Europeanist programme anchored in the notion of a Europe of the Peoples. The BNG's electorate rejected the tripartite Galeusca alliance because of the perception that the CiU and PNV were very different from the BNG in terms of their historical development and political ideology: 'many sectors of the BNG and the BNG's voters did not understand, or disagreed with, this decision which we took, and maybe this explains in large part the decline [in votes] that we experienced' (interview, 9 November 2004). At the same time, however, the rejection of the BNG's political alliances also constituted a rejection of the broader programmatic orientation that underpinned this co-operation, in particular the symbolic Europeanism that the adherents of the Galeusca alliance professed to share. What the Catalan and Basque nationalist parties wanted from Europe had for years been denounced by the BNG as unacceptable for Galicia, as expressed by the latter's persistent opposition to the concrete realities of the EU. In the words of one interviewee:

> The PNV and CiU ..., as representatives of communities which are economically much more advanced than Galicia, hold more favourable views of the process of European integration which are more free-market orientated.

> Everything associated with European integration, the dilution of the Spanish state [is good] ... because as a result of these changes, we will be able to participate directly in Europe, and so we will support this process. Within the BNG, this is not a view we share ... States maintain important competencies that they have no intention of delegating to us. As such, we think a critical position of European integration is necessary because the protagonist continues to be the state.
>
> (Interview, 24 November 2004)

The Galeusca alliance presented to the electorate in June 2004 played down such a critical position in favour of the symbolic Europeanist themes that were shared with the BNG's Basque and Catalan counterparts. However, an electoral campaign designed to highlight shared values and aspirations was clearly out of sync with the ideological and strategic preferences of the BNG's supporters, who were unsympathetic to both the party's choice of electoral partners as well as the political message articulated.

Secondly, the debate within the BNG, ahead of the referendum on the European Constitution in February 2005, revealed similar tensions between different groups within the party on the European issue. Discussions on the position to be advocated in the referendum did not revolve around the actual content of the constitutional text, on which there was broad agreement as to its strengths and weaknesses. Rather, disagreement related to the most appropriate tactics to adopt, and can be summarised as follows.

> If we separate the [constitutional] text from the problem of the referendum, the question is a very different one. Within the BNG, there has been ... a debate ... and I think there was a broad agreement on the positive and negative aspects of the treaty ... What makes our position more difficult is the fact that there is a referendum, and the necessity of adopting a public position as a party ... There are individuals within the BNG who are of the opinion that the BNG should favour a 'yes' vote ... that this would be more profitable for the party in the actual political situation [in Galicia], and not so much to do with the text itself ... , since there are autonomous elections in a few months' time, and [voting 'no'] could be harmful to the BNG's electoral appeal ... I am of the opinion that ... the BNG cannot be supportive because it would be very difficult for a certain sector of society to accept, since we have always assumed the position of condemning European integration, and this would not be consistent ... There would be too much difference between our 'yes' and the Partido Popular's 'yes'.
>
> (Interview, 11 November 2004)

That these internal divisions on Europe did not lead to open confrontation between the BNG's different subgroups was again largely due to the role of the party's internal deliberative mechanisms in mediating political conflicts.[23] However, it was a debate that once more brought the BNG's aspirations for regional government into direct conflict with the need to remain faithful to the party's core ideological values. On the one hand, a rejectionist attitude towards European integration was no longer befitting of a party anxious to portray itself as an important player in Galician – as well as Spanish and European – political arenas. On the other hand, this shift towards the political centre risked alienating the party faithful even further. This, in turn, could provide new opportunities for other minor nationalist parties on the BNG's left flank who competed on a more radical ticket of complete withdrawal from the EU – for example, Frente Popular Galega and Nós-Unidade Popular (Nós-UP) – to flourish.

The need to shore up support from its core electorate, and fend off the challenge from radical nationalist groups, may have provided the BNG with good reason to reassert its opposition to Europe, rather than emphasise its Europeanist credentials. However, doing so would jeopardise the BNG's chances of appealing to the median voter courted by the party since the 1990s. The overwhelming rejection of the BNG's position in the referendum on the European Constitution demonstrated that even a compromise 'Europeanist non' position was out of touch with a largely pro-European Galician electorate in favour of further integration.[24] Recent survey data reveal the extent of this support for the EU. Questions in surveys conducted by the Observatório Político Autonómico from 2002 to 2005 asked respondents in Galicia whether they considered European integration to be beneficial or prejudicial for the autonomous community. The results are shown in Table 4.5. The majority of respondents declared European integration to be beneficial for Galicia, with only a very slight decline in support over the four-year period (from 59.6% to 57.1%). A second question asked respondents to evaluate Spain's membership of the EU (Table 4.6). The number of respondents perceiving this as something good remained very high over the four-year period, peaking at 81.2% in 2003; only 5.4% of Galician respondents on average perceived EU membership as something bad. Faced with such a pro-European electorate, reverting to the Euro-rejectionism of the 1980s would risk alienating the BNG from the Galician voting public.

The previous chapter argued that Plaid Cymru's recent difficulties in articulating a coherent position on the European question represented more fundamental problems faced by the party in adjusting to the new political context of post-devolution Wales. The tensions within the BNG on the party's attitude towards Europe were similarly indicative of more general challenges facing the party

Table 4.5 Do you consider European integration to be beneficial or prejudicial for your autonomous community (Galicia)? (%)

	2002	2003	2004	2005
Beneficial	59.6	65.1	53.7	57.1
Neither beneficial nor prejudicial	20.3	22.0	25.3	22.9
Prejudicial	12.4	9.3	15.9	14.1
Don't know/No answer	7.6	3.7	5.2	6.0

Source: Observatório Político Autonómico (2005).

Table 4.6 How do you evaluate Spain's membership of the EU?

	2002	2003	2004	2005
Something good	75.5	81.2	71.2	74.1
Neither good nor bad	14.0	13.8	17.0	14.7
Something bad	4.9	3.5	6.6	6.5
Don't know/No answer	5.6	1.5	5.2	4.7

Source: Observatório Político Autonómico (2005).

arising from the problem of demarcating a clear nationalist political space within the Galician political arena. The BNG was not the only party to adapt its strategy and policies to the new institutional opportunity structure created in Galicia in 1981. Máiz (2003: 22–24) notes that one of the consequences of the creation of a 'state of autonomies' was that statewide parties like the PPdeG and the PSdeG-PSOE also modified their political programmes to take on a distinctly Galician appeal, not least in an attempt to undermine the electoral growth of the BNG (see Lagares Díez (2003) and Jiménez Sánchez (2003)). In particular, the rejuvenation of the PSdeG-PSOE since the late 1990s saw the latter compete directly with the BNG for votes on the left of the political spectrum. In 2005, PSdeG-PSOE succeeded in dislodging the BNG from its much-valued status as Galicia's second political force.

The BNG's electoral decline from 2001 onwards plunged the BNG into a period of deep crisis. Modernisers within the party advocated the continued pursuit of the electoral avenue, accompanied by major organisational and ideological changes in order to prepare the BNG for the challenges of being a party of regional government. Party traditionalists opposed such a strategy, and argued in favour of defending the BNG's radical ideological tradition and organisational distinctiveness (Beiras, in Fernán Vello and Pillado Mayor, 2004: 84–100). The tension between these two factions resulted in an acrimonious leadership contest in 2001, which saw the independent Anxo Quintana replace the historical figure Xosé Manuel Beiras as the BNG's spokesperson. Over the next four years, the BNG's new leader oversaw the replacement of many of the party's historical figures with a new generation of activists. The party's organisational model was also modified to make the BNG more responsive to the demands of representative politics (Gómez-Reino, 2006). Opposition to these reforms led two of the major figures of Galician nationalism since the 1970s – Camilo Nogueira[25] and Xosé Manuel Beiras – to withdraw from active politics within the party. The departure of the former represented the withdrawal of the principle architect and promoter of the BNG's principled Europeanism since the mid-1990s.

By 2005, therefore, the internal organisational changes and domestic political pressures that pushed the BNG to commit to a Europe of the Peoples ten years earlier, had disappeared. The party's disappointing performance in the 2005 autonomous elections threatened to exacerbate internal tensions within the BNG. With mounting pressure from within the party to return to a more confrontational style of politics that remained faithful to the BNG's radical origins, the conditions were propitious for the BNG's retreat to a position on Europe akin to the Euro-rejectionism espoused by the party until the mid-1990s. This did not happen, however, because of the unexpected success in agreeing a coalition deal with the PSdeG-PSOE to govern in Galicia. This development placed the BNG in a novel political situation that required the party to adapt its political discourse and strategy in a very different way. As for Plaid Cymru, rethinking the party's position on Europe was one of the many challenges that faced the BNG as a result of passing the threshold of government.

During the BNG's first two years in office, what the party had to say about Europe evolved in two ways. Firstly, the BNG substituted its long-held opposition to the policy realities of the EU with a more pragmatic focus on the particular European policy areas that had a direct impact on the Galician economy and society. This was particularly the case in the areas of agricultural and fishing policies, and economic and industrial regeneration. Whereas supranational intervention in these policy areas was historically the target of the BNG's most vitriolic anti-Europeanism, these areas now fell within the BNG's ministerial portfolio within the Galician government.[26] The toning down of the party's oppositional rhetoric in office, combined with the limited scope for policy innovation in these areas, could easily have generated a new rift between the party in public office and a persistently Euro-sceptical party membership. At the time of writing, however, no such tension had emerged. This was partly because of the way in which the BNG's representatives dealt with the European dimension to their governing portfolio. The party played the blame game masterfully, to dissolve itself of any responsibility for the limited scope for reforming the Galician agricultural, fishing and industrial sectors. The Spanish government, and to a lesser extent the EU, were designated as the guilty parties for failing to put in place a regulatory and financial framework sensitive to the real needs of the Galician economy (*BeNeGa*, 2006a). For the same reason, the BNG also argued repeatedly that its hands were tied with regard to the planning and administration of European regional fund monies in Galicia. These arguments were usually accompanied with the claim that only by granting Galicia greater political autonomy can this situation be remedied.[27] By linking the specific constraints imposed by European policies with the fundamental issue of constitutional reform, the BNG successfully maintained the party's traditional self-image as an opponent to the statewide and supranational status quo.

A further explanation for the lack of tension within the BNG over the party's approach to Europe since being in office lies in the fact that European issues have largely been overshadowed by other policy debates. In particular, negotiations over the reform of Galicia's Statute of Autonomy have dominated the Galician political agenda since 2005. These negotiations revealed a second important evolution in the BNG's European discourse. Early on in this debate, the BNG reaffirmed its commitment to securing Galician autonomy within a pluri-national Spain and a Europe of the Peoples. This symbolic European rhetoric was invoked as a marker of the progressive nationalism espoused by the BNG and the other historic nationalities within Spain. Demands for greater autonomy were justified as a reasoned response to the changing conditions imposed by globalisation and

European integration, changes that defenders of Spain as a homogenous nation-state had chosen to ignore (BNG, 2007). As negotiations on the details of a new Statute of Autonomy for Galicia progressed, however, this European dimension gradually disappeared from the BNG's political discourse. Instead, the bilateral distribution of political power between the Spanish state and Galician political institutions became the predominant frame of reference for the party's arguments in favour of greater political autonomy. This two-level dynamic was reinforced as negotiations between Catalonia and the Spanish government progressed with regard to a new Catalan Statute of Autonomy. The BNG's draft Statute of Autonomy for Galicia reaffirmed this new territorial orientation. The document proposed a division of policy competencies exclusively between the state and the Galician levels; demands for a better representation of Galician interests within the EU were proposed via state channels, rather than directly on the supranational arena (BNG, 2005). This pragmatic attempt to define a new autonomist deal for Galicia thus privileged negotiation at the level of the Spanish state as the only realistic channel for the advancement of nationalist demands. The symbolic politics of a Europe of the Peoples brought very little added value to this search for a political compromise on the issue of the territorial redistribution of power within Spain. First attempts at agreeing a new Statute of Autonomy for Galicia failed due to the failure of achieving sufficient cross-party support for the proposed reforms. However, the fact that the European arena has nothing better to offer with regard to the long-term aspirations of Galician nationalism means that the state will remain the privileged partner in future attempts to increase Galician autonomy.

Conclusion

This chapter has traced the evolution of the BNG from being a Euro-rejectionist party for the first fifteen years of its existence, to being a Euro-sceptic party from the mid-1990s onwards. The party's changing attitude towards Europe was of a very different nature to that of Plaid Cymru. In contrast to the latter, it was not the result of a re-evaluation of the socio-economic, political and cultural benefits derived by the Galician nation from the European polity. One of the most striking features of the BNG's position on Europe is the remarkable consistency of its hostility towards the way in which European integration has proceeded in practice. Rather, the BNG's change of attitude on the issue of Europe related to the second dimension defined in Chapter 2, namely support for the general idea of European integration. The BNG energetically rejected any association between Galician autonomy and the process of European integration for the first fifteen years of its existence. From 1998 onwards, however, securing political autonomy for Galicia was intrinsically linked to the construction of a very different kind of European polity, a Europe of the Peoples that recognised the national specificities of small historic nations like Galicia. The party's continued scepticism of the concrete realities of European integration led the party to adopt the slogan 'Europe yes, but not like this' in an attempt to reconcile these two very different attitudes towards European integration within a single European discourse.

The BNG's attitude towards European integration over the years was the result of the combined effect of two factors: basic party ideology and the changing dynamics of domestic politics. This case study provides strong evidence of the enduring impact of ideology on the BNG's understanding of, and response to, developments on the supranational level. A long history of ideological opposition to supranational co-operation continues to generate scepticism of European integration among the BNG's rank and file. Nevertheless, the changing dynamics of party competition within Galicia during the 1990s prompted a major revision of the party's stance on the basic principle of European integration. The BNG's desire to move from the margins of the political system towards the political centre ground triggered processes of organisational and programmatic change that pulled the BNG in a very different direction on the European issue. The dissonance between support for the principle of European integration for short-term electoral gain, and an enduring ideological opposition to Europe, did not generate tension within the BNG thanks to the party's electoral growth throughout the 1990s. The reversal of this electoral trend from 2001 onwards, however, threatened this compromise position on Europe. A downturn in electoral fortunes, combined with the repeated failures of European integration to advance in the building of a regional Europe, fuelled a resurgence of anti-Europeanism within the BNG at the turn of the century.

Once again, however, changes in domestic politics – this time the BNG's entry into coalition government in 2005 – overrode basic ideological values in shaping the way in which the party has dealt with European issues in recent years. There is no doubt that the BNG's membership remains fundamentally unconvinced by the benefits of European integration for Galicia. However, a very different set of political circumstances since 2005 placed new constraints on the positions the BNG could adopt towards the EU. The new pragmatism that office incumbency has demanded of the BNG has led the party to downplay its Euro-scepticism. Instead, the party has articulated its opposition to the EU via a more moderate critique of the extant statewide and supranational policy framework for dealing with specific socio-economic policy problems in Galicia. At the same time, a change in priorities switched the party's focus away from the symbolic politics of a regional Europe, to the pursuit of more promising opportunities for increasing the political autonomy of Galicia via state channels. Just as for Plaid Cymru, the BNG's support for the basic idea of European integration has been eclipsed by the pursuit of other more promising channels for meeting nationalist goals. The declining salience of this symbolic European dimension reflected the party's adaptation to a very different set of political circumstances. At the same time, these new opportunities for pursuing nationalist goals via a two-way negotiation between the central state and Galicia gave welcome cause for the BNG to shift its focus away from a European arena which was never fully or easily integrated into the party's mindset. In this respect, and despite the party's formal declarations to the contrary, the 'Europeanisation' of the BNG has been limited.

5 Corsica
A comparison of moderate and radical Corsican nationalist parties

Since the late 1950s, minority nationalist parties have steadily grown in political and electoral salience in Corsica. By the early 1990s, the minority nationalist movement had established itself as the second political force in Corsican politics. There are several reasons to expect these actors to have been highly aware of developments in European integration, and to have embraced the opportunities provided by this supranational arena for the pursuit of nationalist demands. Firstly, the geographical location of the island of Corsica within the Mediterranean Sea – the heart of Europe in historical terms – may well have imbued political actors with a deep-rooted sense of belonging to Europe. Secondly, with France being a founding member of the EEC, the evolution of the Corsican minority nationalist movement has paralleled the evolution of the process of European integration. The confrontation between the Corsican periphery and the central state thus originated and evolved in the broader context of French membership of the European club. Thirdly, the French Jacobin state tradition has given rise to an ideological antipathy to the recognition of cultural and linguistic differences within the state's territory. In such a context, minority nationalist parties may reasonably be expected to have turned to Europe as a way of bypassing a hostile state, in search of more promising ways of achieving their nationalist goals.

This chapter will argue, however, that far from being overwhelmingly supportive of Europe, Corsican minority nationalist parties have adopted a range of positions on Europe ranging from Euro-rejectionism to Euro-enthusiasm. On the one hand, moderate Corsican nationalists have long sympathised with the idea of a Europe of the Regions, and have supported European integration because of its potential to act as an external pressure for the internal constitutional reform of the centralised French state. On the other hand, radical nationalists vacillated between outright opposition to European integration during the 1980s to begrudgingly adopting the goal of 'independence in Europe' in recent years. These formal positions on Europe, however, belie a nationalist movement which has never seriously engaged with the detailed implications of European integration for the Corsican nation. European integration remains largely unimportant for Corsican minority nationalist parties, regardless of their ideological predilections. The chronic instability of the nationalist movement, and the powerful effects of a clientelistic political culture, have mediated and limited the degree to which Corsican minority nationalist parties have engaged with, and adapted their political programmes to, European integration.

The origins and development of the Corsican nationalist movement

The origins of the contemporary nationalist movement in Corsica can be traced back to the 1950s. Even though nascent nationalist sentiment was expressed during the interwar period,[1] its impact on the Corsican political arena was minimal (Pomponi, 1977). The sympathies of the protagonists of this first wave of nationalist mobilisation with the irredentist ideas put forward by Mussolini – that is, the reunification of Corsica with the Italian state[2] – saw the nationalist cause being discredited completely after the Second World War (Loughlin, 1989). Moreover, the revival of feelings of patriotic allegiance to the French Republic after the liberation of Corsica from Italian and German occupation – the first part of France to be so – saw any persistent nationalist sentiment disappear definitively in the immediate post-1945 period (Molas, 2000: 8–9).

From the 1950s onwards, a programme of economic modernisation of an underdeveloped and traditional society, designed and administered unilaterally by the French government, led to a period of dramatic economic growth in Corsica (Loughlin, 1989: 138–45). However, these reforms also created the conditions for the re-emergence of nationalist contestation on the island. The economic benefits of modernisation were perceived to be distributed unequally, with 'continental' (that is, mainland French) financial and professional interests profiting at the expense of the island's inhabitants. The environmental fallout of economic modernisation, and a complete disregard for the island's natural resources, further fuelled nationalist resentment towards the French authorities (Poggioli, 1996: 31; Crettiez, 1999: 164–67). The process of decolonisation in northern Africa during this period exacerbated many of these latent frustrations, since repatriated French citizens were given privileged access to the new economic and occupational opportunities being created on the island.[3] The negative implications of such socio-economic development and ecological exploitation for Corsican identity were made explicit by a government-sponsored report on the future of the island,[4] and provided a further catalyst to Corsican nationalist mobilisation (Simeoni, 1995: 51).

Motivated by these disadvantageous socio-economic reforms, in 1959 the Movement du 29 Novembre organised a number of public protests against the high cost of living on the island and the underdeveloped transport and communications infrastructure (Briquet, 1997: 243). A few years later, the Fronte Régionaliste Corse (FRC) put forward a more distinctive Marxist analysis of a situation of 'internal colonialism'. However, differences of opinion over ideology and strategy within the FRC led some of its activists to create the Action Régionaliste Corse (ARC) in 1967. The ARC proposed a much less radical and more pragmatic analysis of the status quo, a distinctly 'regionalist' interpretation which emphasised economic reform as the central tenet of a programme for indigenous economic development.

112 *Corsica: Moderate and radical nationalists*

The events of Aleria in 1975 – a small town on the east coast of Corsica – constituted a decisive turning point in the nature and direction of the contemporary Corsican nationalist movement: 'nothing would be the same as before' (UPC, 1991: 43). Members of the ARC occupied the property of an Alerian wine producer of Algerian origin, with the aim of drawing attention to the economic disadvantages faced by locals (Simeoni, 1995: 29–30). The result, however, was a fatal stand-off between the nationalists and a disproportionately large and heavily armed police presence (Lefevre, 2000). The clear demonstration of the intransigence of the French authorities vis-à-vis nationalist concerns had a major impact on the Corsican nationalist movement. The ARC was officially proscribed by the French authorities, and replaced by the Associu di u Patriotti Corsi (APC) in January 1976 (later to become the Unione di u Populu Corsu (UPC) in July 1977). A more radical nationalist tendency was also created on 5 May 1976, called the Front de Libération Nationale de la Corse (FLNC). Cuncolta di i Cumitati Naziunalisti (CCN), established in 1980, became the public face of the clandestine FLNC.[5] With the creation of the FLNC, 'les problèmes corse' – economic, social and cultural – would become 'le problème corse', namely the use of political violence as a strategy in the pursuit of national self-determination (Crettiez, 1999: 44).

From 1976 to the present day, these two tendencies – moderate and radical – have defined the parameters of the nationalist political space in Corsica, although their evolution can hardly have been more different. Under the charismatic leadership of the brothers Edmond and Max Simeoni, the UPC was, until recently, the main representative of moderate Corsican nationalism. The UPC merged with a smaller moderate group, Scelta Nova, in November 2000 (Scelta Nova-UPC), and was later dissolved to create the Parti National de la Corse (PNC) in December 2002 (Dominici, 2004). However, this name changing was a repackaging, rather than a reformulation, of the UPC's moderate nationalist agenda. As will become clear in the analysis that follows, this ideological and strategic continuity was reflected in the consistency of moderate nationalist attitudes towards European integration over the thirty-year period covered by this study.[6]

In contrast, the FLNC was riven by factional rivalry for most of the 1980s. Internal differences over the FLNC's political strategy and a struggle over the control of its organisational apparatus (Crettiez, 1999: 124; Crettiez and Sommier, 2002: 30–31) led to an implosion of the military structure at the end of the 1980s, and a series of splits which complicated the radical nationalist panorama considerably. One-time leader of the FLNC, Pierre Poggioli, resigned from the movement's political front A Cuncolta Naziunalista (aCN) in 1989 to form his own party, Accolta Naziunale Corsa (ANC), with links to its own clandestine group Resistenza. The FLNC split again at the end of 1990, to create the FLNC 'canal habituel' with its new public front, Movimentu pà l'Autoderminazione (MPA),[7] and the FLNC 'canal historique', whose public front remained aCN. An electoral alliance between moderate and radical nationalist groups formed in 1992, under the name Corsica Nazione, brought together the UPC, ANC, aCN and the Greens. However, the refusal of some of the adherents (aCN) to renounce the use of violence, ultimately led to the withdrawal of the UPC, the ANC and the Greens.

Corsica Nazione thus became the electoral front of radical nationalism, with close links to the FLNC 'canal historique' and the aNC. The aNC would change its name to Cuncolta Indipendenza in 1998, and then again to Indipendenza upon its fusion with Corsica Viva and other smaller radical groups in 2001. The close but opaque relationship between Indipendenza and Corsica Nazione has recently been formalised by a further name change to Indipendenza-Corsica Nazione.

On 6 February 1998, the assassination of the French Prefect in Corsica, Claude Erignac, by a previously unheard of nationalist militant group provided the catalyst for a third phase in the evolution of the Corsican nationalist movement, one which Crettiez and Sommier (2002: 31) have referred to as 'the politics of reconciliation'. By the end of 1999, eight of the thirteen known legal nationalist groups had come together to form an electoral alliance called Unità.[8] The various clandestine groups followed suit shortly after by establishing FLNC 'Union des combattants'.[9] Both of these attempts at consolidating the Corsican nationalist movement were short-lived, however; strategic disagreements between both moderate and radical nationalist groups gave way to yet another wave of scissions, name changing and the creation of new groups in the years following 1999. The most recent attempt at unity was the formation of yet another nationalist alliance – Unione Naziunale – for the March 2004 regional elections, again bringing together radical and moderate nationalists.[10] However, despite this renewed attempt at defining a common nationalist programme, the simple observation that eighteen different nationalist groups contested these elections – on three separate lists – demonstrated the degree to which division, and not reconciliation, continued to define nationalist contestation in Corsica (Roux, 2005b). By the summer of 2007, the survival of the alliance Unione Naziunale was under threat as different groups wrestled to gain control of leadership of the Corsican nationalist movement.

It is impossible for this chapter to analyse the positions of all these different groups on the issue of Europe. The focus, therefore, is on the main partisan groups that have represented moderate and radical nationalist tendencies within the Corsican nationalist movement since the 1970s. The chapter thus examines the European attitudes of the ARC and its successors (the UPC and, from 2002 onwards, the PNC), and the FLNC in its various manifestations, including Corsica Nazione from 1992 onwards, as the main mouthpiece of radical nationalism.

The ideological heritage: a Corsican nationalist movement divided over Europe

Despite France having been a founding member of the EEC, in the early years of nationalist mobilisation in Corsica, there were varying levels of interest on the part of different nationalist groups in the process of European integration. This section begins by summarising the European attitudes of moderate and radical nationalist groups in turn, before proceeding to analyse the factors that gave rise to these positions on Europe.

For the different parties that belonged to the moderate nationalist tradition during the 1970s and early 1980s (ARC, APC and later UPC), taking up a position on Europe did *not* mean expressing an opinion on the process of economic integration. Whereas the other minority nationalist parties included in this study vehemently rejected the European free-market project during this period, the UPC had little interest in debating the costs and benefits of this process for Corsica. In part, this was due to the limited impact that such a European free market was thought to have on Corsica. The UPC argued that economic integration would do little to undermine the stranglehold of the French state on economic decision making on the island. In contrast to other European regions in charge of their own infrastructure and resources, and who were thus in a position to benefit from access to the European common market, Corsica, 'at the extreme end of her umbilical cord ... remains isolated from the network of market transactions' (*Arritti*, 1972). Engaging in an evaluation of the pros and cons of economic integration, therefore, was a futile exercise since these were developments that would have little concrete impact on the island's underdeveloped economy.

Rather, for moderate Corsican nationalism, European integration was important because it promised to bring new pressure on the French state to undertake constitutional and institutional reforms that would grant new autonomy to Corsica (*Arritti*, 1977b). According to the UPC, the European arena served to highlight the increasingly anachronistic approach of the French state to the treatment of cultural and linguistic minorities within its territorial borders. This would be achieved by contrasting the 'colonialist' French approach to other European states' more progressive attitudes towards national diversity. European integration, therefore, was conceptualised as a valuable resource in the confrontation between the Corsican people and its French colonial masters. A growing concern with protecting human and minority rights – initially as much on the international[11] as on the European level – convinced moderate Corsican nationalists that European integration would generate a new top-down pressure on the French state to adapt its internal structures in recognition of the rights of cultural and linguistic minorities. Informed by this pragmatic conceptualisation of the value of European integration, in 1977 the UPC launched an initiative aiming at the 'internationalisation' of the Corsican problem. This represented 'the most efficient type of action ... in order to push the French state to begin a dialogue, to admit the right of our people to existence' (*Arritti*, 1977a). It was a strategy that entailed establishing contacts and arranging interviews, exchanges and seminars with international organisations concerned with the respect of fundamental human rights. Gradually, however, a generic strategy of internationalisation took on a more specifically European guise, with the European arena established as the sphere most likely to be receptive to the UPC's nationalist demands.

The UPC's pragmatic approach to European integration quickly evolved into a principled linkage between supranational co-operation and the achievement of Corsican autonomy. In 1978, for the first time the UPC linked its long-term constitutional goals to the future evolution of the European polity. The party declared its intention to pursue 'an internal statute of autonomy' as the constitutional solution to the centre–periphery problem, as part of a 'democratic and progressive Europe of the Peoples' (*Arritti*, 1978). This basic principle would constitute the key theme of the party's constitutional aspirations for the next twenty-five years. The UPC also further developed its activities in pursuit of such an aim by establishing contacts with other minority nationalist parties across western Europe. Indeed, the UPC was a key actor in propelling the creation of the EFA, with the inaugural meeting of the EFA taking place in Bastia (Corsica's second largest city) in 1979 (Lynch, 1998: 192).

In contrast to moderate nationalism's principled support for European integration, radical Corsican nationalism vacillated between disinterest in, and outright opposition to, the European project during the latter half of the 1970s. References to the supranational arena in the FLNC's early literature and declarations were few and far between. On the rare occasions that European integration was referred to, it was presented as one example of a more general phenomenon to be overcome, namely global capitalism and imperialism (Hermant, 1992). Attempts by the French authorities to portray the European project as a way forward for solving the Corsican predicament were dismissed as nothing more than 'incredible French propaganda' (*U Ribombu*, 1979b), a convenient way for the French government to wash its hands of all responsibility for the island's problems. However, these demonstrations of anti-Europeanism, although scathing, were not a salient theme in the FLNC's political programme in its early years.

By the beginning of the 1980s, therefore, the principled support of moderate Corsican nationalists for the process of European integration contrasted starkly with the sporadic but vitriolic Euro-rejectionism of their radical nationalist counterparts. These contrasting attitudes towards Europe resulted from the differential influence of key variables outlined in Chapter 2, namely party ideology and political opportunities within the French and Corsican political arenas.

In the first place, divergent attitudes towards Europe reflected the different ideological lenses through which different nationalist groups viewed European affairs. The support of various moderate Corsican nationalist parties for European integration drew on a deep-rooted and instinctive Europeanism. The island's geographical location within the Mediterranean and its historical experience as the hub of Mediterranean traffic, imbued the UPC and its forerunners with a deeply rooted philosophical attachment to Europe – 'we are European by default' (interview, 16 March 2004). These parties were also motivated exclusively by centre–periphery goals, and did not complement this core business with other ideological left–right or new politics values. Indeed, the UPC explicitly refused to define itself in left–right terms. In this respect, the UPC remained faithful to the principles established by the ARC in the early 1970s, to the effect that:

> The ARC ... is neither a part of the centre or of the margins. It does not situate itself 'between' right and left ... Insular politics have nothing to do with right or left, liberalism or socialism, capitalism or Marxism, but only regionalisation against centralisation ... We are regionalist. The others – all the others – are centralists.
>
> (Interview, 4 March 2004)

116   *Corsica: Moderate and radical nationalists*

The movement's sole concern, therefore, was to challenge the entire system of centralised politics, as represented both by other Corsican political groups and the French authorities. For this reason, moderate Corsican nationalists were unconcerned with any aspect of European integration that did not relate to the pursuit of territorial autonomy or the protection of the nation's cultural and linguistic specificities. Aspects of European integration that elicited the antipathy of minority nationalist parties in Wales and Galicia during the 1970s, such as the capitalist-driven process of economic integration, received no noteworthy reaction from the UPC or its predecessors.

The FLNC, on the other hand, espoused radical ideological positions on both the centre–periphery dimension and the left–right dimension. Just as for the UPG in Galicia during the 1970s, the FLNC's world view was influenced from the outset by national liberation struggles against colonialism in several Third World countries at the time. Sympathy with these international struggles was expressed through the terminology, symbolism and ideas espoused by the FLNC. The use of the language of 'national liberation struggle', as well as the acronym 'Front de Libération National', were references drawn directly from the colonial struggle in Algeria. The FLNC's monthly newspaper, *U Ribombu*, even suggested that 'the chain which attaches Bastia and Ajaccio [in Corsica] to Paris is the same as that which attaches Hanoi or Algiers to the French capital' (*U Ribombu*, 1979a). Ideologically, the FLNC promoted the idea of a revolutionary struggle against colonialism. The party aimed to create a new model of society inspired by 'original socialism, defined during the struggle and by every moment in the struggle, [and which] draws its force from its historical rootedness in the memory of "A terra di u Cumunu" and the independent nation of Pascal Paoli' (*U Ribombu*, 1989). This goal envisaged a complete breaking away from the French state as the only way of securing self-determination for the Corsican nation. In order to achieve these aims, the FLNC identified its own role as being 'that of a "direction politique" which assumed responsibility for propaganda, offering the struggle a political perspective, and taking charge of "military" activities' (*U Ribombu*, 1980). Importantly, however, it was not the task of the national liberation struggle to propose a detailed blueprint of what would replace the status quo. Rather, the FLNC's role was limited to putting in place the conditions that would enable such a process of self-determination to take place (FLNC, 1977).

These radical ideological values, and the strategies they inspired, had a number of implications for the way in which the FLNC responded to developments in European integration during the late 1970s. The FLNC's antipathy towards capitalism and imperialism in all its forms translated into a vehement rejection of a process of European integration which was perceived to be driven by the very forces that the FLNC had mobilised against. In this sense, the EEC represented one manifestation of a much bigger enemy to be overcome. The fact that the FLNC did not propose an alternative, more sympathetic, model of European polity reflected the party's own conceptualisation of its role in the political struggle, as outlined above. It was simply not the business of the FLNC to propose alternatives to the status quo. Such alternatives, it was argued, would only be formulated once the existing power structures had been removed.

Basic party ideology, therefore, defined the parameters of the attitudes of different minority nationalist parties towards European integration until the end of the 1970s. These ideological preferences, however, were themselves intrinsically shaped by the nature of the political system within which Corsican minority nationalist parties mobilised during the 1960s and 1970s. Two features of this domestic context were particularly important: France's Jacobin state tradition and an insular political culture characterised by clientelism.

France has long been considered one of the most centralised states in Europe, a 'one and indivisible Republic' premised on the principle of the equal treatment of citizens as well as territory within the boundaries of the state (Loughlin and Seiler, 2001). Even if in practice France has always been characterised by more cultural and linguistic diversity than is acknowledged by this principle, the state has rejected giving formal or legal recognition to these markers of ethnic difference. This, combined with the concentration of political and bureaucratic authority in Paris, with no regional tier of government between local and state levels until the early 1980s, designated the French Parliament the only political arena within which Corsican nationalist demands could be articulated. In practice, however, passing the threshold of representation on the state level was a Herculean task. With a majoritarian electoral system in use for elections to the French Parliament, the two Corsican constituencies in these elections overlay the territorial organisation of the island's two political clans.[12] These clans' monopoly of the political arena in Corsica (of which more is said below) made it impossible for any Corsican nationalist party to muster a sufficient majority to return representatives to the French Parliament. As an arena within which the demands of Corsican nationalism could be pursued via democratic electoral means, the state level was, and remains, closed to these actors. For this reason, Corsican minority nationalist parties have only ever participated in statewide elections for symbolic purposes, with no realistic prospects of gaining representation within the French Parliament.

Within Corsica itself, the mediation between the state and the citizens historically took place via certain 'political' families, a system of clan politics that continues to shape the island's political culture and practices (Briquet, 1997). This particular form of socio-political organisation derived its political authority from the distribution of scarce material resources – for example, employment and financial support – in return for political patronage (Briquet, 1998: 27). Such clientilistic practices were sustained by a hierarchical political structure from the chief of the clan, down to the mayors of local communities. Over several centuries, these structures have constituted the key mechanism by which insular politics has been conducted. The persistence of clan-based politics in Corsica is evidence of the success of the clans in adapting themselves to the needs and demands of modern politics (Briquet, 1997). For non-clanist political actors, however, the persistence of such a system meant the closure of the political process on the island, with no opportunity for articulating grievances through normal democratic and electoral processes.

The lack of access to decision-making spheres on the state level, combined with the stranglehold of the clans on the political channels and material resources between Corsica and the state, provided the context in which the Corsican nationalist movement mobilised during the 1960s and 1970s. Nationalist responses to this political and institutional closure, however, were very different. For moderate nationalists, the failure to make inroads via electoral means on either the state-wide or regional levels designated the European arena the only one available for the articulation of its nationalist demands. Europe represented an external support structure for a nationalist movement with nowhere else to turn. In the words of one senior UPC member at the time:

> We quickly came to realise that we were in a sterile confrontation between a state that was closed to all ideas of institutional evolution, and a Europe that was being designed as a new, and more favourable, political force.
> (Interview, 23 April 2004)

Radical nationalists, on the other hand, came to very different conclusions about the best way to gain access to Corsican and French decision-making arenas. Whilst the UPC turned towards Europe in search of a solution to the centre–periphery *impasse,* the FLNC turned towards the national liberation struggles of the Third World for its ideological and strategic inspiration. The FLNC's ideology of 'rupture' and 'decolonialisation' represented a calculated attempt to break the mould of traditional non-ideological Corsican politics through the introduction of radical ideological values, as summarised above. This ideological radicality was complimented by a strategy of targeted violence for political ends. The use of violence was thus an explicitly instrumental strategy for negotiating entry into a closed political arena (Simeoni, 1995: 28–29; Crettiez, 1999: 67). It was to be the politics of violence, more than anything else, which was to offer Corsican nationalism a hitherto unparalleled political visibility within French and Corsican politics (Crettiez, 1999: 77).

Institutional change and changing party attitudes towards Europe

In 1982, a directly elected regional tier of government was established in Corsica. The newly elected French president, François Mitterand, passed a 'statut particulier' which established a Corsican Assembly to be elected by proportional representation,[13] with responsibilities for administering the social, cultural and economic affairs of the island (Loughlin, 1985). A second statute – the Statut Joxe, named after the interior minister Pierre Joxe who was the architect of the proposals – came into force in 1991, and enlarged the competencies of the rechristened Collectivité Territoriale de la Corse and reformed all electoral lists.[14]

Given the Corsican clans' monopoly of the island's political system prior to 1982, these two developments created a major new opportunity structure for minority nationalist parties to pursue their constitutional demands via democratic electoral channels at the regional level. If the closure of the Corsican political arena pre-1982 drove the externalisation of the nationalist struggle (towards Europe for the UPC and towards the Third World for the FLNC), after 1982 minority nationalist parties of all ideological persuasions turned their attentions to securing representation within the new regional institutions. Moderate nationalists had always accepted the principle of electoral participation, and the UPC competed in the very first elections to the Corsican Assembly in 1982. The FLNC refused to participate in these first elections since 'in the shadow of the "statut particulier", colonialism is still at work' (*U Ribombu*, 1982),[15] although it abandoned its anti-system strategy in favour of electoral participation ahead of the 1984 regional elections. Over the period 1984 to 1992, the Corsican nationalist movement, considered collectively, enjoyed growing levels of electoral popularity in regional elections (see Table 5.1). The electoral success of the minority nationalist movement peaked at 24.9% of the insular vote in 1992, making them the second political force on the island.

Despite the electoral growth of the Corsican nationalist movement as a whole during this ten-year period, however, all minority nationalist parties did not enjoy equal amounts of electoral success. Whilst the UPC's vote declined from the first elections in 1982, the FLNC's successive political fronts benefited from growing levels of political support among the Corsican electorate. The BNG's experience of a similar competition within the nationalist camp led to the consolidation and simplification of the nationalist movement by the beginning of the 1990s. As demonstrated in Chapter 4, this process was the catalyst of significant changes in the BNG's attitude towards European integration. However, no such development took place among the different nationalist parties represented within the Corsican Assembly from 1984 onwards. Even though an electoral alliance was formed under the name Unita Naziunale for the 1985 regional elections, this was abandoned two years later because of the FLNC's refusal to denounce its strategy of political violence (*Arritti*, 1987b). Rather, for most of the 1980s, there were no major changes in the basic attitudes of moderate and radical nationalists towards Europe beyond a moderation of tone or change of emphasis. It is to examine this broad continuity in party attitudes towards Europe that this chapter now turns.

Moderate nationalism: Euro-enthusiasm from the political margins

As far as the moderate nationalists were concerned, given the UPC's electoral decline throughout the 1980s and its increasing marginalisation within the Corsican political system, it would have been reasonable to expect the party to adopt a more critical position on Europe, as part of a more general oppositional strategy vis-à-vis political parties occupying the centre ground. As noted in Chapter 2, peripherality within a party system often leads to Euro-scepticism, as opposition to European integration is adopted as an expression of a more general critique of the political system. However, there is no evidence of Euro-scepticism on the part of the UPC during this decade. On the contrary, the UPC was remarkably

Table 5.1 Results of Corsican regional elections, 1982–2004 (%)[a]

Party	1982		1984		1986[b]		1992			1998[c]			1999			2004		
	%	Seat	%	Seat	%	Seat	1st round %	2nd round %	Seat	1st round %	2nd round %	Seat	1st round %	2nd round %	Seat	1st round %	2nd round %	Seat
Left	–	23	–	25	–	25	–	–	9	–	–	20	–	–	19	–	–	24
Nationalist	12.70	9	11.40	9	8.97[e]	6	21.08	24.85	13	17.37	9.90	5	22.78	16.80	8	14.91[g]	17.30	8
UPC	10.61	7	5.21	3	–	–	–	–	–	4.97	–	–	3.85	–	–	–	–	–
PPC	2.40	1	0.96[d]	–	–	–	–	–	–	–	–	–	–	–	–	–	–	–
MCS	2.11	1	–	–	–	–	–	–	–	–	–	–	–	–	–	–	–	–
FLNC/Corsica-Nazione	–	–	5.22	3	–	–	13.66[f]	16.85	9	5.22	9.90	5	10.41	16.80	8	12.14	17.30	8
MPA	–	–	–	–	–	–	7.42	8.00	4	3.41	–	–	–	–	–	–	–	–
RN	–	–	–	–	–	–	–	–	–	–	–	–	4.43	–	–	2.19	–	–
Others	–	–	–	–	–	–	–	–	–	3.77	–	–	4.09	–	–	0.58	–	–
Right	–	29	–	24	–	28	–	–	29	–	–	26	–	–	24	–	–	19
Extreme right	–	–	–	6	–	2	–	–	–	–	–	–	–	–	–	–	–	–
Total	–	61	–	61	–	61	–	–	51	–	–	51	–	–	51	–	–	51

Sources: Roux (2005a), Ministère de l'Intérieur (2004).

Notes:
a The unavailability of a full set of data for all parties for all elections means that for right, left and extreme right parties, only the number of seats won is provided. For the nationalists, data on vote share and number of seats is provided. This information is given as an aggregate for the nationalist movement as a whole, as well as broken down by party (as shown in the shaded area).
b The results for the Department of Haute Corse were declared void; these elections were re-held in 1987. In the second round of elections for the department, the left and right political groups both lost one seat, whilst the extreme right Front National gained two seats. The number of seats won by the nationalist alliance within the Corsican Assembly did not alter.
c The 1998 regional elections were declared void after the UPC, who narrowly failed to pass the 5% barrier in the first round of the elections, protested against apparent irregularities in the voting. Elections were re-held in March 1999.
d PPC-MCS alliance.
e UPC and MPA joint list (Unita Naziunale).
f 'Corsica Nazione' alliance between aCN, UPC, ANC and I Verdi Corsi.
g 'Unione Naziunale' alliance between Indipendenza-Corsica Nazione, PNC, A Chjama, ANC and PSI.

consistent in its attitude towards European integration, with the party elaborating upon the key Europeanist themes articulated prior to 1982. In particular, the notion of a Europe of the Peoples as the only legitimate alternative to 'a Europe of States that is no more than a Europe of markets', was developed as a key tenet of the party's political programme (*Arritti*, 1984b). The party bought fully into the idea of the inevitability of such a development – 'Europe cannot avoid it; Europe will become a Europe of the Peoples and the Regions' (*Arritti*, 1991a) – and believed that only such a federal Europe would 'give full rights to all cultures and to all nations, by proposing the free association of all within a common political framework', as a basis for 'a new political ethics which will banish cultural and colonial domination' (*Arritti*, 1987a). Importantly, a 'Europe of the Peoples and Regions' did not envisage a severing of Corsica's link with the French state. In this respect, the UPC's vision of a regional Europe differed significantly from, for example, Plaid Cymru's post-sovereigntist Europeanist rhetoric. As argued in Chapter 3, for Plaid Cymru such a regional Europe implied the eclipsing of state sovereignty and the dispersal of political authority across the supranational and the 'national' (that is, sub-state) levels. Rather, constitutional reform within the French state and the EU was the aim of the UPC.

> Autonomy provides the means to allow us to adapt to the European continental and economic context. Autonomy is not meant to satisfy a desire for an independent Corsican state. It is a necessity in order to survive in, and adapt to, a world that is constantly moving and changing. The UPC ... is not in favour of either the disappearance of the state or its substitution by the regions. We want a federation of states, but one that takes the regions, peoples and nationalities that compose it, into account.
>
> (*Arritti*, 1996b)

In part, independence for Corsica – the preferred constitutional option of the FLNC – was rejected because it was both unrealistic and against the wishes of the Corsican people (*Arritti*, 1996a). This position also, however, reflected the UPC's basic understanding of the nature of Corsica's problems on the French periphery and how they should be resolved. The French state was designated as the agent of colonial repression, but was also deemed responsible for remedying the problems of contemporary Corsican society. Just as Corsica's history had been tied up with the history of French exploitation, so its future was also intrinsically linked to France. The only solution, therefore, was a limited degree of political autonomy through an internal reform of the French state. Introducing Europe into this equation did not change the basic outcome for the island: 'The internal autonomy of the Corsican nation within the framework of the French Constitution and the Europe under construction ... That is the solution' (*Arritti*, 1990).

The UPC's reaffirmation and elaboration of the linkage between European integration and the achievement of Corsican autonomy was the result of two developments during the 1980s. Firstly, just as was the case for Plaid Cymru (see Chapter 3), developments in European integration throughout the 1980s and early 1990s boosted the UPC's confidence that a Europe of the Peoples was becoming a reality at the supranational level. The EEC's growing financial commitment to redress regional disparities and facilitate economic competitiveness, a nascent legal framework for protecting minority rights, the formal adoption of the principle of subsidiarity as the basis for devolving decision making to the sub-state level, and the creation of new institutional arenas for representing nationalist demands, were all cited as evidence that European integration was creating a federal supranational framework within which greater Corsican autonomy would be safeguarded. In the French referendum on the ratification of the Maastricht Treaty held on 20 September 1992, the UPC campaigned in favour of abstention in order not to jeopardise its electoral alliance with its Euro-rejectionist partners; in private, however, the party fully supported the Maastricht Treaty as an important step forward toward creating a federal Europe of the Regions (interview, 13 April 2004).

Secondly, at a time when the UPC was increasingly marginalised within the Corsican political arena, the European arena provided an alternative platform for articulating the party's nationalist demands. Despite the UPC's attempts to 'internationalise' awareness of the Corsican situation since the 1970s, until the late 1980s the party had no direct voice at the supranational level. Even though elections to the European Parliament were introduced in 1979, getting a nationalist MEP elected was extremely difficult. Just as in Spain, a single statewide constituency for European Parliament elections until 1999 constituted a major obstacle for small parties with a territorially concentrated support base to get representatives elected. In part for this reason, radical Corsican nationalist parties never contested European Parliament elections. The UPC, for its part, called for its supporters to abstain in both the 1979 and 1984 European Parliament elections in protest at an electoral system which was undemocratic, prejudicial towards small parties, and constituted nothing more than an opportunity for the government to gage the state of domestic public opinion between French presidential and/or legislative elections (*Arritti*, 1984a).

In the 1989 European Parliament elections, however, the UPC crossed the threshold of representation at the European level for the first and only time in its history. In order to overcome the constraints imposed by the electoral system, the UPC contested the elections in co-operation with several other minority nationalist parties from Alsace, Brittany, Occitania and Corsica, and the French Green Party. The list built upon the co-operation of Green and regionalist parties in the European Parliament under the auspices of the Rainbow Group, and the joint election programme adopted reflected the main interests of the participants: ecological protection and the promotion of national diversity (Lynch, 1998). The strategy of co-operation was successful, and Max Simeoni, leader of the UPC, became the Corsican nationalist movement's first MEP in the European Parliament.

Given the UPC's lack of political space within the Corsican political system during the 1980s, the symbolic importance of having a Corsican nationalist MEP should not be underestimated (Lefébvre, 1992: 4). Presence within the European Parliament provided the party with a political platform that was not available within Corsica itself. Within the European Parliament, the UPC joined the EFA parliamentary group. Since the party's involvement in the setting up of the EFA at the end of the 1970s, the UPC had been a regular participant in EFA meetings.[16] Even before having a directly elected European parliamentarian, the EFA served as a mouthpiece for the Corsican nationalist movement, putting down specific questions relating to Corsica and defending its interests when necessary (interview, 16 March 2004). But finally joining the EFA parliamentary group in 1989 had similar reinforcing and deepening effects on the UPC's Europeanist discourse as was the case for Plaid Cymru and the BNG. The benefits of membership of the EFA group derived in part from the better understanding facilitated by EFA membership of the workings of the European institutions and the implications of European policies for Corsica. This alliance also, however, bestowed a new legitimacy on the UPC's Europe of the Peoples rhetoric: '[Membership of the EFA] showed us that what we were demanding for Corsica was not exceptional or unique' (interview, 13 April 2004). The UPC readily took up the arguments articulated by other EFA members in favour of a regional Europe, and deployed these in its critique of the peripherality of Corsica within the French state. By linking the general theme of European regionalism to the particular problem of Corsican self-determination, the UPC sought to generate a top-down pressure for the internal reform of the French state. In this respect, the UPC's conceptualisation of European integration as an external resource for achieving Corsican autonomy was once again in evidence.

Despite the unprecedented visibility enjoyed by the UPC as a result of being represented in the European Parliament, Max Simeoni failed to be re-elected in the 1994 European Parliament elections. Internal divisions within the French Green Party prohibited the re-presentation of a Green–nationalist list, and although an all-minority nationalist list under the name 'Régions et Peuples Solidaires'[17] was put forward to contest the election, this did not attract sufficient votes to pass the threshold of representation. The abandonment of the single statewide constituency in favour of eight European constituencies in 1999 – with Corsica falling within the South-East France constituency – did not significantly improve the chances for Corsican minority nationalists to pass this threshold of representation once again. A joint Green–nationalist list was once again presented for the 2004 European Parliament elections, although it did not attract sufficient support to send a Corsican nationalist to the European Parliament. The small number of Corsican voters as a percentage of the constituency as a whole, the fragmentation of the minority nationalist movement, the historical absence of contacts with other minority nationalist parties on the French continent as a basis for joint electoral lists[18] and the statecentric bias of the French media are factors that have continued to constrain the ability of these parties to secure representation directly on the supranational level (see Table 5.2).

Radical nationalism: between disinterest and opposition to Europe

In contrast to the UPC's sustained enthusiasm for Europe throughout the 1980s, the FLNC and its various political fronts remained largely disinterested in European

Table 5.2 European Parliament election results for Corsica, 1984–2004 (%)[a]

Party	1984	1989	1994	1999[b]	2004
Left					
PCF	15.9	10.8	7.7	10.0	5.2
PS	14.9	19.5	7.4	20.0	28.9
MRG	–	–	16.1	–	1.4
Other left	–	1.0	1.0	6.0	–
Right					
UDF/RPR	42.8	36.5	36.5	25.2	26.0
UDF	–	2.8	–	4.2	5.6
Other right	–	–	8.9	13.0	9.2
Extreme right	13.2	10.9	6.2	5.4	10.1
Ecologist	11.4	–	1.6	1.5	1.0
Nationalists	–	15.5[c]	10.9	–	7.4[d]
Others	1.8	3.0	3.7	14.7	5.2

Source: Observatoire Interrégional du Politique (2005).

Notes:
a Results for 1979 not available.
b From 1999 onwards, Corsica has formed part of the 'South-East France' constituency.
c Nationalists participated in a list with the Green Party, headed by Antoine Wechter.
d As part of a joint list with the Green Party, headed by Jean-Luc Bennahmias.

affairs. Events such as European Parliament elections required the radical nationalist movement to state formally its position on European integration, and on these occasions the FLNC reiterated its outright opposition to European integration in all its forms. Meetings with like-minded nationalist groups from across western Europe also provided a public opportunity to make formal statements rejecting Europe. During the 1980s, the FLNC participated in CONSEO alongside the BNG and other radical nationalist parties. However, as noted in Chapter 4, beyond a common ideological sympathy motivated by opposition to 'repressive states', the aims and achievements of CONSEO were limited from the outset by the different conceptualisations of the liberation struggle put forward by the organisation's adherents (Lefébvre, 1992: 4; Crettiez, 1999: 162). As such, contacts with these other radical groups never constituted a real coalition of shared political interest. Rather, the usefulness of such symbolic alliances related exclusively to domestic propaganda. For example, the FLNC organised the annual Journées Internationales de Corte, where the party was joined by representatives from other radical nationalist movements from Europe and further afield (interview, 7 April 2004). The international dimension to this event provided a platform for decrying the ills of European integration. However, Crettiez (1999: 162) notes that the annual event was 'more than anything an occasion for a show of force by the radical branch of Corsican nationalism, anxious to reaffirm its predominance in the nationalist political sphere'.

On these occasions, the EEC was rejected on the same grounds as had been set out during the late 1970s, albeit in a tone which notably lacked the radical revolutionary zeal of the FLNC's earliest declarations on Europe. The general process of economic integration was denounced as detrimental for Corsican society, since it was a process that served only to aggravate the ills already inflicted upon the island by the colonial French state, and augmented the politics of austerity and exploitation through a restructuring of international capitalism (*U Ribombu*, 1984). The capitalist logic of the EEC and the privileging of the economic interests of states and multinationals not only endangered the viability of Corsica's insular economy on the periphery of Europe, but also its cultural and social survival. Important developments in European integration during the 1980s, if they could not be ignored, certainly did not inspire confidence that the EEC was evolving into something apart from a capitalist club. For example, the signing of the SEA in 1987 and its commitment to the creation of a free market by 1992 was denounced on the grounds that it would only reinforce and perpetuate Corsica's economic, cultural and social decline (*U Ribombu*, 1987). Just as for the BNG, developments in European integration during the 1980s did little to persuade radical Corsican nationalists of the economic, political and cultural benefits for Corsica of French membership of the EEC.

This hostility to concrete developments in European integration was accompanied by a complete disregard for 'the "federalist type" solutions supported by certain parties', a mildly disguised attack on the UPC's notion of a Europe of the Peoples (U Ribombu, 1986). The UPC's Europeanist rhetoric was denounced as a ruse to 'camouflage the dominant political system with new political and administrative divisions' (ibid., 1986). As for its own conceptualisation of an international framework for Corsican self-determination, an alternative political, cultural and social European space, founded on the basic rights of the different 'peoples' of Europe, was cited sporadically. However, the FLNC's idea of a 'Europe of Nations without States' was neither a salient nor a recurring theme in the party's nationalist discourse. There was certainly no principled commitment on the part of the FLNC to the idea that the process of European integration could facilitate the achievement of Corsican self-determination.

In short, by the end of the 1980s, there was little evidence to suggest that the experience of electoral participation and political representation within the Corsican political arena had had a direct impact on the substance of the attitudes of radical nationalist groups towards European integration. As noted above, the only change of note in the FLNC's position on Europe was a moderation in the tone with which this Euro-rejectionism was articulated. This change of tone was attributable to two developments during this decade. On the one hand, broader global changes led to the questioning of the continued legitimacy of the FLNC's radical Marxist ideology. Many of the FLNC's early utopian ideas had originally been inspired by the 'cliché of 1968' and the 'romanticism' of young Corsicans in exile on the French mainland in the 1970s (Poggioli, 1996: 21). However, events throughout the 1980s, such as the collapse of communism in central and eastern Europe, made such an ideology appear increasingly irrelevant and anachronistic. The failure of specific attempts to put these utopian ideas into practice 'on the ground'[19] further contributed to a realisation by the movement's leaders that such ideas had little relevance for the specific conditions of Corsican economic and cultural underdevelopment (Poggioli, 1996: 44, 97). On the other hand, the FLNC's ideological radicalism had also been deliberately exaggerated in its early years, for the particular political purpose of forcing nationalist concerns onto the Corsican and French political agenda in the late 1970s (Crettiez, 1999: 199). However, with access to the Corsican political arena having being secured by the end of the 1980s, ideological radicalisation was no longer a strategic necessity. The FLNC continued to talk of 'rupture' with the French state, and defined its struggle as one for the 'national liberation of Corsica'. Apart from this radical terminology, however, there was very little detailed substance to the FLNC's political programme. The movement adhered to a very abstract commitment to a form of 'original socialism' inspired by the communitarian spirit of Corsican society in the past (*U Ribombu*, 1983). The FLNC's 'Projet de société', published in 1989, simply committed the party to a model of society that would be elaborated by the conditions of the liberation struggle itself (*U Ribombu*, 1990).[20] The FLNC's views on Europe thus reflected a principled disinterest in pragmatic political details, and a commitment to abstract ideological goals that were articulated in a less radical tone throughout the 1980s.

This abstract Euro-rejectionism should not, however, detract from the fact that, on the whole, the FLNC remained largely disinterested in European affairs during this decade. During the late 1970s, this could be explained as a consequence of the movement's alternative ideological world view (see above). During the 1980s, in contrast, disinterest was more the result of the internal problems suffered by the radical nationalist movement. Disagreements within the FLNC related to the organisation of military activities, the restructuring of the FLNC after successive police raids and arrests (Crettiez, 1999), and the acceptability of illegal activities in order to finance the movement, including the imposition of a 'revolutionary tax', money laundering and investment in black-market trading (Poggioli, 1996; Lefevre, 2000: 35–50). Tensions also escalated between those who favoured a gradual abandonment of the violence strategy in favour of pursuing the democratic channel of institutional representation and those who remained faithful to the FLNC's original 'logique de guerre' strategy. These divisions over the most appropriate way to conduct the nationalist struggle had the effect of directing energies and attention inwards onto the movement itself rather than outwards towards political developments elsewhere. International affairs, and European affairs in particular, were of secondary importance. In the words of a senior FLNC member at that time:

> Our international interests ... only accounted for a very small part of our political activities. We devoted some importance to such issues, but not very much; we were too concerned with our own internal problems.
> (Interview, 7 April 2004)

These internal tensions resulted in the implosion of the FLNC between 1989 and 1991. As noted at the beginning of this chapter, new political groups were formed with very different ideological values and strategic goals. This was particularly evident with regard to party attitudes towards European integration (Lefébvre, 1992).

The diversity of the positions adopted by the political groups that emerged out of the FLNC was in full evidence during the French referendum campaign on the ratification of the Maastricht Treaty in September 1992. The ANC was established as a scission from the FLNC in 1989. The party declared itself in favour of a 'no' vote in the referendum, since the crippling costs of economic integration as managed by states and transnational business outweighed the as yet unsubstantial opportunities for the reassertion of national self-determination. As an alternative to Europe, closer co-operation between the Mediterranean islands was advocated as a more favourable context for Corsican independence.[21] In 1991, more of the FLNC's leadership split from the movement over disagreements about ideology, objectives and strategy. They established the FLNC 'canal habituel' (with the MPA as its public front), notable for a position on Europe more akin to that of the UPC than the FLNC of the 1980s. In the referendum on the Maastricht Treaty, the MPA voted in favour of ratification. The party argued that the treaty constituted a major step forward in the ineluctable march towards a federal Europe that heralded the disappearance of the nation-state and the legal and institutional recognition of national identities (interview, 7 April 2004). The public front of the FLNC 'canal historique', meanwhile, informally rejected the Maastricht Treaty because of its damaging implications for Corsican interests. This position was justified by the claim that 'an analysis of the treaty shows clearly that no derogations have been given to Corsica, either in the cultural, fiscal or political domains' (La Corse, quoted in Lefébvre, 1992: 3). However, the party's membership of the coalition Corsica Nazione, and the resultant requirement to find a consensus with the ideological Europeanism of the UPC, saw it campaign for abstention in the referendum.

The reconfiguration of the radical nationalist panorama between 1989 and 1991 led to new attempts to establish electoral alliances between moderate and radical nationalist parties. The failure of these attempts, however, led to a renewed period of instability within the Corsican nationalist movement, and the eventual emergence of a new dominant nationalist actor, namely Corsica Nazione (with close links to the FLNC 'canal historique'). It is to consider the implications of these developments for party attitudes towards Europe that the next section now turns.

The 1990s: continuities and changes in Corsican nationalist positions on Europe

During the 1990s, the European issue continued to have very low salience on the political agendas of both moderate and radical nationalist parties. This lack of interest in Europe was attributable in part to the continued instability of the Corsican nationalist movement during this decade. Between 1989 and 1996, twenty-six different nationalist organisations could be identified within the nationalist movement, most of them having no more than ten or twelve adherents (Crettiez, 1999: 128). The radical nationalist movement was riven by partisan rivalry between different groups who disagreed over political goals and the most appropriate strategies for achieving them. A civil war erupted between the FLNC's 'canal habituel' and 'canal historique' in the mid-1990s, resulting in the death of around thirty nationalist activists (Crettiez, 1999: 243). The effect of this conflict was not only to preoccupy the nationalist groups directly implicated, but also moderate nationalists who feared for their safety. Lefevre (2000: 61) even argues that the entire political process was effectively suspended in Corsica, given the high social tensions and widespread fear of blind retaliation. The disappearance of the European dimension from the nationalist agenda during these years was hardly surprising. The assassination of the French Prefect in Corsica, Claude Erignac, in 1998 by a previously unknown nationalist group in protest at the electoral and institutional priorities of the main political parties within the radical nationalist camp, was further evidence of the internal divisions within the nationalist camp over ideology and strategy (Dominici, 2002: 136). Successive attempts at co-operation between moderate and radical groups failed because of the refusal of the latter to denounce formally the use of violent means in the nationalist struggle. Just as in previous decades, nationalist preoccupations with these internal affairs severely constrained these actors' interest in, and engagement with, European affairs.

Just as in previous years, minority nationalist parties in Corsica formally stated their positions on Europe only when political circumstances required them to do so. On these occasions, continuities and differences were evident in the European attitudes of different moderate and radical nationalist parties. The UPC continued to advocate the pursuit of Corsican autonomy within a Europe of the Peoples. The seductiveness of the idea of a Europe of the Peoples continued to lie in the prospect that 'the Europe that is being constructed will apply pressure on the Jacobin state. [Europe] will bring to the fore its internal contradictions and will force it to transform itself' (*Arritti*, 1991b). This symbolic rhetoric aside, however, the UPC's engagement with concrete developments in European integration remained minimal. The party continued to stress the value of European regional funds in redressing Corsica's economic problems, and defended the pursuit of political representation within the European Parliament as a means of publicising the Corsican question. The UPC also made much of the Charter on Regional or Minority Languages, adopted in 1992 under the auspices of the Council of Europe. This initiative was lauded as a positive initiative for the protection of linguistic diversity, and provided a further opportunity to expose the backwardness of the French state in refusing to sign up to the charter (*Arritti*, 1994). Beyond these token regionalist issues, however, there was no detailed substantive discussion of the concrete costs and benefits of European integration for the Corsican nation.

In contrast, Corsica Nazione – the main mouthpiece for radical nationalism during this decade – undertook to revise its position on Europe in important ways. Significantly, the party abandoned the Euro-rejectionism that had been espoused by the FLNC during the 1980s, and accepted the EU as an entity that had to be acknowledged. Corsica Nazione undertook to adapt the party's long-term constitutional goals to reflect the reality of Corsica's situation as a Mediterranean island within the European sphere of influence. The party experimented with several different formulations for defining the linkage between Corsica and Europe. By the mid-1990s, Corsica Nazione was calling for a 'Statut de Territoire d'Outre Mer'[22] for the island. Such a statute would not require Corsica to become a full member state of the EU. Rather, a bilateral convention was envisaged that would allow the island to 'benefit from Community funds while escaping the destructive effects of the CAP and its system of quotas, taking part in Europe while preserving the derogations – fiscal or otherwise – that are indispensable for our development' (*U Ribombu*, 1994). A limited but profitable association, therefore, that would allow Corsica to benefit financially without having to be formally a part of a European polity that was still viewed with considerable scepticism. This proposal was replaced in 1998 by the argument that 'independence in Europe' was the only political solution that could bring the exploitation and domination of the Corsican people by the French state to an end.

> We do not in any way intend to secede from the rest of the world; on the contrary, we want to establish Corsica within a framework that is the most appropriate – Europe – since we believe that it is more useful for Corsica to be a region within Europe than to be the twenty-second region within France.
> (*U Ribombu*, 1998)

By the end of the 1990s, therefore, the EU had replaced revolutionary colonial struggles as Corsica Nazione's main international reference. The party had formally abandoned the principled opposition of radical nationalism to the European project, in favour of a more constructive conceptualisation of the relationship between European integration and Corsican self-determination. However, the significance of this new professed pro-Europeanism should not be overstated. The commitment to 'independence in Europe' was, more than anything, a slogan that served as a marker of Corsica Nazione's continued radicalism on occasions that demanded that the party state its long-term political and constitutional ambitions. The party certainly did not pay any heed to the constitutional, political and legal ramifications of independence within the European polity. Neither were the pragmatic implications of such a constitutional goal examined in any detail.

Corsica Nazione's engagement with specific developments in European integration throughout the 1990s was also limited. The party's interest in the concrete reality of European integration was entirely instrumental, and driven by utilitarian economic and political imperatives. As such, European integration was only ever invoked either to serve insular political ends, or in opposition to the French state (Lefébvre, 1992: 7). The party was concerned exclusively with two aspects of European integration during this period. Firstly, the party's analysis of the benefits forthcoming to Corsica from the supranational arena focused on the receipt of European funds. European integration provided important financial resources for an underdeveloped Corsican economy; Corsica Nazione's support for further integration rested on the continued receipt of these European monies. Secondly, Corsica Nazione used European integration to attempt to breach the stronghold of the French state on the island's decision-making structures. Just as for moderate Corsican nationalist parties during the 1970s, the EU constituted a useful stick with which to beat French and Corsican authorities, and to highlight the deficiencies in their treatment of the island's socio-economic, political and cultural problems. The issue of the representation of Corsican interests in Brussels provides a good example of the instrumentalisation of Europe by Corsica Nazione. The party successfully campaigned for the creation of a new Commission for European Affairs within the Corsican Assembly in 1999. Corsica Nazione's leader – Jean-Guy Talamoni – was appointed president of this commission. The party extracted significant political capital from being able to go directly to Brussels to defend Corsican interests where French and Corsican political authorities had allegedly failed to do so.

How can moderate and radical nationalist party attitudes towards European integration during the 1990s be explained? To begin with, the limited engagement of moderate nationalists with European integration throughout the 1990s was attributable in part to the continued marginality of these actors within Corsican politics. During this period, the UPC struggled to compete electorally with Corsica Nazione, whilst the European arena as a platform for articulating nationalist was closed off due to the difficulties of passing the threshold of representation for the European Parliament. The symbolic rhetoric of a Europe of the Peoples continued to be articulated as a marker of the UPC's more moderate political agenda, but the party's focus was on establishing collaboration with other nationalist parties as a means of retaining a presence within the Corsican political arena. In such a situation, engaging with the concrete realities of European integration was not a priority for a party struggling to retain a political voice at the regional level.

The factors shaping the changing attitudes of Corsica Nazione towards European integration were considerably more complex. Firstly, Corsica Nazione's changing political aspirations throughout the 1990s had a crucial impact on the party's attitude towards European integration. Just as was the case for the BNG, Corsica Nazione's electoral consolidation throughout the 1990s generated new ambitions to be a party of government at the regional level. Outright opposition to the EU became an unattractive policy position for a political party keen to present itself as a moderate and credible governing option. The instrumentality of Corsica Nazione's rhetorical turn towards Europe is betrayed by the fact that the party's attempts to define a new, more Europeanist policy position, took place in the immediate run-up to regional electoral contests, in 1994 and 1998 respectively. The eventual adoption of the terminology of 'independence in Europe' was thus a direct response to the pressures of party competition emanating from the Corsican political arena. The party's ideological heritage was still evident in the manner in which the party conceptualised the linkage between Corsica and the EU, with the idea of 'independence' being defended as the end result of the 'rupture' from the French state long demanded by Corsica Nazione's partisan predecessors. By the mid-1990s, however, core ideological values had been adapted to fit a political discourse that was more befitting of Corsica Nazione's new political status within Corsican politics.

At the same time, however, ideology ceased to be a factor shaping Corsica Nazione's attitude towards the concrete realities of European integration. The FLNC's opposition to economic integration on the grounds that it was incompatible with its socialist values was replaced by a much more pragmatic evaluation of the costs and benefits of European integration for Corsica. Such an utilitarian approach to Europe, as outlined above, was a response to a Corsican political culture that prioritised personality and pragmatism over traditional values and ideas as the basis of political authority. Within such a clientelistic system, the political process was represented by the figure of the single individual as the giver of material resources and the receiver of political patronage. Ideas, in contrast, were completely alien to the everyday conduct of politics: 'partisan affiliation, a vote based on political ideas, ideological references, and abstract conflicts of values always arouse suspicions, and are seen as deliberate attempts to mystify, or as phenomena which have been imported from elsewhere and which cannot be understood by [the ordinary Corsican voter]' (Briquet, 1997: 30). If traditional clans formally adopted the left–right trappings of a modern party competitive system (Briquet, 1997, 1998),[23] in practice this has very little meaning since it is impossible to distinguish between a left-leaning clan and a right-leaning one on the basis of policy preferences.

The declining salience of the revolutionary Marxism of radical Corsican nationalist groups was thus the result of adaptation to an insular political culture where the pragmatic requirements of maintaining political patronage took precedence over abstract ideas and values. This process of de-ideologicalisation was not confined to radical nationalist parties. As noted above, moderate nationalist groups also refused to define themselves in traditional left–right terms. Research by Molas (2000) on the ideological orientation of nationalist voters in Corsica confirms the absence of traditional ideological cleavages among this sector of the Corsican electorate. The electoral success of radical Corsican nationalism, however, created the conditions for the acceleration of this process of de-ideologicalisation. Lefevre (2000) has argued that the party's electoral growth was based on the nurturing of its own clientelistic political constituency, based on the exchange of material rewards for political patronage. Adopting such practices was a prerequisite to electoral success in a political system that, as argued above, ascribed little value to political ideas as the basis for voting behaviour. Just like the traditional clans, therefore, Corsica Nazione developed its own geographically concentrated communities of support whose votes were rewarded by concrete goods and resources of direct benefit to the community.

Much of the financial resources at the heart of this relationship were derived from illegal activities such as the collection of the revolutionary tax, the illegal extortion of money and other illegal activities. Such practices had long been associated with radical Corsican nationalist groups.[24] During the 1990s, however, the significant increase in the transfer of European monies to the island provided additional resources for developing these clientelistic networks even further.[25] Lefevre (2000: 270) has argued that it was no coincidence that Corsica Nazione's revisions of its Euro-rejectionism throughout the 1990s corresponded to a massive influx of European regional funds into the insular economy. Both Giudici (1997) and Crettiez (1999) found evidence of European funds being used by radical nationalists to fund such clientelistic practices. Corsica Nazione was not the only political party to take advantage of European monies in this way. A European Commission inquiry into the spending of CAP subventions aimed at the milk sector in 1994 discovered a system of institutionalised fraud by the Corsican authorities on the basis of claims for non-existent cattle (Crettiez, 1999: 59). In this respect, Corsica Nazione's instrumental interest in European regional funds was a symptom of the party's adaptation to the rules of the political game in Corsica. It is ironic that a movement still intent on proclaiming its radicalism operated, in practice, according to the clanist dynamics that were routinely denounced as being at the root of all Corsica's troubles.

Corsica Nazione's electoral consolidation throughout the 1990s had a second ironic effect on the party's attitude towards European integration. Despite Corsica Nazione's formal commitment to independence from the French state, during this decade the party developed ever-closer links with the French authorities. Electoral success bestowed upon Corsica Nazione a new political legitimacy in the eyes of the Parisian political elite. If the French state traditionally used the traditional clans as its mediators on the island, Corsica Nazione established itself as the new privileged interlocutor between the centre and Corsican citizens on the periphery (Lefevre, 2000). Representatives of the nationalist movement were included in negotiations on institutional reforms in 1991, and again in 1999 as part of the so-called 'process Matignon' that proposed a more far-reaching programme of decentralisation. This rapprochement also enabled Corsica Nazione to use access to European decision-making arenas to score valuable political points at home. The fact that Jean-Guy Talamoni, leader of Corsica Nazione, was often present in French delegations to the European Commission was portrayed in the Corsican public arena as a demonstration of the status of the party as a major political actor in Corsican politics. The rhetoric of 'rupture' with the state was sharply at odds with a political party who unashamedly exploited state channels to bolster its political image in the eyes of Corsican voters. Such an utilitarian use of the European arena befitted a party interested, first and foremost, in reasserting its political weight within the Corsican political arena.

Unity among nationalists, united in support of Europe?

A third wave of institutional reform in Corsica launched by the socialist prime minister Lionel Jospin in 1999 ultimately failed to deliver a significant increase in the political autonomy of Corsica's regional political institutions. In January 2002, proposals to give the Corsican Assembly greater political power and a limited right to pass its own laws were declared to be in breach of the principle of national unity by the French Constitutional Court. Upon being re-elected French President on 28 April 2002, Jacques Chirac abandoned other controversial aspects of the proposed reforms.[26] A referendum subsequently called on 6 July 2003 asked Corsicans to decide in favour or against the abolition of the two electoral constituencies on the island, to be replaced by a single constituency consisting of the island as a whole. Corsican voters rejected the proposal by the narrowest of margins (51% against, 49% in favour).

This defeat was a heavy blow for the Corsican nationalist movement, which had supported these proposals as a step towards greater Corsican political autonomy. However, the failure had the unintended consequence of prompting a new attempt at co-operation among Corsican nationalist groups. The formation of the alliance Unione Naziunale for the March 2004 regional elections was driven by the shared desire to demonstrate the political strength of a nationalist movement that demanded further policy and institutional concessions from the French state. One of the key points of agreement noted in the founding document of Unione Naziunale was the necessity of defending Corsica's receipt of European regional funds, and securing a better representation of the island's interests in French and European policy making (Unione Nazionale, 2004). The document deliberately avoided references to the long-term nationalist aspirations for Corsica within Europe, on which key differences continued to distinguish moderate 'autonomist' nationalists from their more radical 'independentist' counterparts. Nevertheless, over the next two and a half years, several declarations with a clear European dimension were formulated with the aim of highlighting the intransigence of the French state vis-à-vis the Corsican question. Developments such as enlargement to central and eastern Europe – and the accession of countries with a smaller population than Corsica to the EU, such as Malta – were cited as evidence of the progress made on the European level towards the recognition of the rights of small nations (*U Ribombu*, 2006). Unione Naziunale partners also participated in several meetings with representatives from other minority nations from across western Europe. On these occasions, the examples of the suspension of political violence in Northern Ireland and the Basque Country were employed to demonstrate the progress made elsewhere in addressing the issue of peripheral nationalities (Corsica Nazione Independente, 2006; PNC, 2006). These initiatives were conceived as part of a strategy to 'put the French state on trial, and to respond to European and international opinion' (*U Ribombu*, 2006). Just as for moderate nationalist groups in the 1970s and 1980s, references to Europe were employed as rhetorical ammunition in the confrontation between the Corsican nationalist movement and the French state.

This new but limited interest in European affairs among moderate and radical Corsican nationalist parties did not mean that the parties had abandoned their different conceptualisations of Corsica's future role within the future European polity. These differences came to the fore during the referendum on the European Constitution in France, held on 29 May 2005. Defending a 'yes' vote, both the PNC and La Chjama saw in the European Constitution a step forward towards the creation of a Europe of the Peoples. The PNC applauded the constitution's commitments to protect minority languages and improve democracy as positive advances, and believed the document would weaken the legitimacy of the centralised French state (*Arritti*, 2005; *Corsica*, 2005). A divided Indipendenza-Corsica Nazione, on the other hand, did not adopt a formal position for or against the European Constitution and allowed its members to vote freely. In spite of a broad agreement on the shortcomings of the proposed European Constitution, the party was divided on the position that should be adopted for the referendum campaign. Disagreements echoed those within the BNG on the same issue. Backers of a 'yes' vote argued that this would reinforce the party's image as a moderate political party. Others favoured rejecting the constitution due to its failure to recognise the rights of Europe's minority nations; moreover, anything other than a 'no' vote also ran the risk of alienating the party's core supporters, who remained deeply hostile to the process of European integration. Other smaller nationalist groups outside the Unione Naziunale alliance campaigned to reject the constitution. These included ANC, PSI, Voce Popular, U Rinnovu, Partitu di a Chjama and the 'inorganisés'. Their rejection was based on the undemocratic nature of the constitutional process, the lack of representation given to Europe's 'nations without states', and the excessive liberalism of economic integration.

The European Constitution was rejected by 56.9% of Corsican voters, slightly higher than the average French rejection of 54.6%. These results reflected the trend seen during the referendum on the Maastricht Treaty in 1992, with Corsican voters demonstrating higher levels of opposition to European integration than elsewhere in France.[27] In the absence of survey data on the European attitudes of the Corsican population, these results provide the best indicators of Corsican public opinion towards Europe. This trend of popular opposition towards European integration poses a difficulty for minority nationalist parties who are in favour of European integration in principle. This problem is greatest for moderate nationalist parties who have long defended European integration on the basis of its potential for advancing nationalist interests. The challenge for radical Corsican nationalist parties is slightly different. The referendum on the European Constitution highlighted the dilemma faced by Indipendenza-Corsica Nazione between adjusting its position on Europe to reflect its status as an aspiring party of regional government within the Corsican political system, and rejecting European integration on the basis of voter preferences. Whilst the pressures of party competitive dynamics pulled the party in one direction on Europe, the ideological antipathy of many party members and voters to the European project pushed the party in an opposing direction.

Indipendenza-Corsica Nazione faces a further challenge with respect to the popular appeal of its goal of 'independence in Europe'. The limited public opinion data available on attitudes towards constitutional change in Corsica point to a population with little enthusiasm for such far-reaching constitutional change. A survey conducted in 1991 suggested that only 6% of respondents favoured independence, with the majority – 44% – in favour of greater autonomy, while 33% preferred the status quo.[28] By 1998, a slightly different question asked respondents whether or not they supported independence. Only 10% said 'yes', whilst an overwhelming 80% said they did not (with 10% saying they did not know).[29] The fact that the referendum in 2003 on further institutional reform was narrowly rejected provided further evidence of the disinterest of voters in the radical transformation of Corsica's institutional and political status.

It is not only the lack of public support for Europe and institutional/constitutional change within a European framework that has undermined the ability of Corsican nationalist parties to mobilise popular support for their respective political agendas. The positions adopted by these parties – especially Indipendenza-Corsica

Nazione – vis-à-vis the concrete realities of European integration has also been increasingly difficult to defend. As noted above, the receipt of European structural funds constituted a major impetus for the party's growing support for European integration during the 1990s. However, minority nationalist parties were not alone in taking advantage of these financial transfers for political gain. The traditional clans have also seized upon this alternative revenue source for their own instrumental advantage. If historically the clans relied on resources from the French state for the maintenance of clientelistic networks, since the 1990s these actors have also utilised European funds as a means of sustaining the system of political patronage on the island. This instrumental use of European monies was accompanied by a Europeanisation of these actors' political rhetoric. The majority of Corsican political actors, whatever their formal party allegiance, began to demand a special financial status for Corsica within the EU to take account of the underdevelopment of the insular economy (Lefevre, 2000: 308). Jean Baggioni, a senior figure in the traditional RPR clan was instrumental in the creation of the Îles de la Méditerranée Occidentale (IMEDOC) network in May 1995, to lobby for privileged economic recognition on the European level.[30] Similarly, a Europe of the Regions discourse become an integral theme in the programmes of both Jose Rossi's Unione pour la Démocratie Française (UDF) and Paul Natali's RPR group in the north of the island. The latter was even known as 'le petit européen' in reference to his interest in, and involvement in, projects linked to the EU (Lefevre, 2000: 182).

As a result of cross-party adaptation to developments in European integration, both moderate and radical Corsican nationalists have been forced to relinquish political space on the European issue. For the former, a commitment to a regional Europe no longer serves to distinguish their political programme from those espoused by the clanist parties who, prior to the 1990s, showed little interest in European affairs. Radical Corsican nationalist parties, on the other hand, have faced direct competition for access to European regional funds, as well as for the political credit for defending Corsican interests within an ever-expanding EU. With Corsica's Objective 1 status expiring at the end of the European budgetary period (31 December 2006), the prospect of a significant decline of European funds mobilised both nationalists and traditional clans to campaign in Paris and Brussels for continued financial aid from the EU. However, with a right-wing government in Paris since 2002 – significantly more hostile to nationalist demands than the previous socialist government – Corsican nationalists were no longer the partners of choice for French–Corsican delegations to Brussels. Due to the changed political panorama within France, Indipendenza-Corsica Nazione was unable to extract political advantage from the fact of having direct access to negotiations at the heart of the EU.[31] Given that the party's support for European integration since the 1990s had been based in no small part on this instrumental use of the European dimension, the basis for continued support for the concrete realities of European integration had been removed.

Together, one would expect these three factors – unsympathetic public opinion, partisan competition on the European issue and the decline in the amount of

136 *Corsica: Moderate and radical nationalists*

European regional funds received by Corsica – to have led minority nationalist parties to adopt more Euro-sceptical positions. As yet, however, there is little evidence that any changes in party attitudes towards European integration have occurred. Two reasons can be put forward for this lack of party responsiveness.

Firstly, there are overriding factors that have made minority nationalist parties stick to their lines on Europe. For the PNC – the ideological descendant of the UPC – a principled commitment to Europe as the framework for securing Corsican autonomy continues to indelibly shape the party's position on European integration. The remarkable continuity of this fundamental idea, in spite of the political and electoral marginality of successive moderate nationalist parties, attests the strength of this basic value in shaping these parties' world view. For Indipendenza-Corsica Nazione, it is the pressure of party competition that has limited the degree to which the party has been able to adopt a more sceptical attitude towards the EU. Indipendenza-Corsica Nazione faces a dilemma that is not dissimilar to that faced by the BNG in Galicia, between maintaining a moderate European discourse that befits a party that is competing for the political centre ground, and espousing a more critical position more in keeping with the deep-rooted anti-Europeanism of the party's core support base. Other smaller radical nationalist parties who remain electorally and politically marginal within Corsican politics are unconstrained by these pressures, and remain free to adhere to the Euro-rejectionism long-associated with this branch of the Corsican nationalist movement.

Secondly, the European dimension remains largely unimportant for Corsican nationalist parties. From time to time, parties declare their support for a 'Europe of the Peoples, or a 'Europe of Nations without States'. But these are political gestures aimed at a domestic audience rather than the articulation of a serious and well thought-out constitutional programme. The naive Europeanist rhetoric expounded periodically by both moderate and radical nationalist parties belies a nationalist movement that, in practice, continues to have only a marginal interest in the ways in which European integration impacts upon the Corsican nation, its economy and society. In part, the superficiality of these European positions can be attributed to the fact that neither moderate nor radical nationalist parties had ever been in the position of having to get to grips with how the existing European polity actually works, and what the costs and benefits of European integration a for Corsica. Unlike Plaid Cymru and the BNG, neither the PNC nor Indipendenza-Corsica Nazione had ever had direct experience of engaging with the realities of the EU, either within the European Parliament, the Committee of the Regions, or as parties of regional government. These parties have thus avoided the specific pressures to acknowledge the realities of European policy making that come with these different political responsibilities. In other words, there is no reason for the time being for these parties to reconsider or adapt the abstract symbolism of a regional Europe which serves as a demarcator of their long-term aspirations for their nation.

The limited engagement of these parties with Europe is also, however, a strong reflection of the political context in which these parties have evolved. A clanist political culture combined with a highly unstable nationalist movement has given moderate and radical nationalist parties an instinctively introspective approach to politics. The complexities and peculiarities of Corsican politics has significantly constrained the degree to which these parties have taken Europe seriously, beyond the easy rhetoric of a regional Europe. The result is that, in contrast to Plaid Cymru and the BNG, there is little incentive for the PNC and Indipendenza-Corsica Nazione to adapt their European discourses in response to the kind of short-term pressures that shaped changing nationalist attitudes toward Europe in Wales and Galicia.

This limited interest in European affairs is likely to decline even further in the near future as a result of renewed tensions within the Corsican nationalist movement. Several developments since the latter half of 2006 have generated new pressures on the Unione Nazionale alliance. The alliance was increasingly criticised for its lack of policy impact within the Corsican Assembly. There were also growing fears among radical Corsican nationalist activists that the movement's ideological and strategic profile was being overly watered down within the alliance. The resumption of violence by the FLNC 'Union des combattants' – thus breaking the ceasefire established in 2004 as a gesture of support for the Unione Nazionale initiative – and the refusal of Indipendenza-Corsica Nazione to condemn political violence, placed further stress on the relationship between moderate and radical nationalist groups (*Corsica*, 2007a, b). Finally, the election of Nicolas Sarkozy in May 2007 created a new political climate for bilateral negotiations between Corsica and France. A press conference soon after by the FLNC urging Indipendenza-Corsica Nazione to take the lead in restarting negotiations of constitutional reform was taken as a sign of the final breakdown of relations between the adherents to Unione Naziunale. The reinforcing of the statist orientation of radical Corsican nationalist parties paves the way for a new period of instability within the Corsican nationalist movement. Both these developments will contribute to the continuing disinterest of Corsican minority nationalist parties in either the basic idea, or the concrete realities, of European integration.

Conclusion

In Corsica, different minority nationalist parties have come to different conclusions about the implications of European integration for the pursuit of national self-determination. The fundamental ideological differences between moderate and radical nationalist parties defined the parameters of basic party attitudes towards European integration until the 1990s. The UPC's instinctive Europeanism contrasted starkly with the virulent Euro-rejectionism of the FLNC and its successive political fronts.

The principled support of moderate Corsican nationalism for the basic idea of European integration remained remarkably constant over the thirty-year period which this chapter has covered. This is despite the repeated failure of these parties to make any significant electoral breakthrough within the Corsican political arena. Given this political marginality at home, the UPC's success in electing an MEP to the European Parliament provided a crucial – and unique – platform for highlighting the party's Europeanist credentials to a largely disengaged Corsican electorate. Apart from this one-off success, however, direct European representation within the European arena was closed off to moderate nationalist parties because of the difficulties of passing the threshold of representation. As a result, neither the dynamics of party competition at home nor the experience of supranational representation exerted a sustained pressure on moderate nationalist parties to modify or elaborate upon its enthusiastic yet abstract commitment to a Europe of the Peoples.

The European arena was also closed off to radical nationalist parties, but through choice as well as due to structural constraints. Instead, it was the electoral success of these parties during the 1980s and 1990s that exposed them to very different influences on party attitudes towards European integration. The pressure of party competition was especially salient in the case of Corsica Nazione. On the one hand, the party's vote-seeking aspirations constrained what the party could say on the basic idea of European integration. The commitment to 'independence in Europe' was adopted in response to the need to appear as a moderate and progressive party of potential regional government. The BNG in Galicia undertook a similar programmatic revision as it sought to move from the margins of the political system towards the political centre ground. For both parties, formal declarations in support of European integration belied a deep-rooted hostility to Europe amidst party members. On the other hand, Corsica Nazione's electoral rise exposed the party to a very different kind of pressure when it came to responding to the realities of the EU. The impact of a clanist political culture that emphasised patronage as the basis of politics was expressed in a limited but highly instrumental interpretation of the benefits forthcoming to Corsica from the supranational level.

This analysis of the European attitudes of Corsican minority nationalist parties has also revealed, however, that the European dimension remains of marginal significance in the day-to-day political agendas of these parties. At the beginning of the 1990s, Lefébvre (1992) analysed the salience of European issues in nationalist politics in Corsica. He concluded that 'the European dimension external to Corsica is far from being a major preoccupation for Corsican nationalist organisations, who have done very little to adapt in this respect' (ibid.: 4). This conclusion remains valid fifteen years later. There are several reasons that explain this lack of engagement with, or interest in, European affairs among Corsican nationalists. Firstly, structural constraints – the impossibility of gaining access to political arenas at the state or supranational levels – has rendered the Corsican political arena the only one within which these parties can realistically compete electorally and achieve political influence. Secondly, Corsica's clanist political culture has indirectly affected the nature and degree of minority nationalist party engagement with Europe. The ideas and preferences of these actors have gradually been adapted to the prevailing way of 'doing politics' on the island, with the result that engagement with the EU in practice has meant a focus on exploiting any financial resources for clientelistic purposes. Finally, the chronic instability of the Corsican nationalist movement has undermined the ability of different nationalist parties to engage seriously with the political process within Corsica, at the state level as well as within the EU. The most recent developments within the Corsican nationalist movement will continue to mitigate the degree to which Corsican minority nationalist parties take European integration seriously.

6 Conclusions

A comparative analysis of minority nationalist party attitudes towards European integration

The last three chapters have provided a detailed account of the European attitudes of minority nationalist parties in three different contexts. The aim of this final chapter is to draw on this empirical data in order to answer the two research questions formulated in Chapter 1: How have minority nationalist parties interpreted and responded to European integration? and What factors have shaped the European attitudes adopted by these actors?

Before proceeding to this task, however, it is useful to begin by restating briefly the conventional scholarly account of minority nationalist party attitudes towards European integration as outlined in Chapter 1. Such accounts posit that the key to understanding these parties' attitudes towards European integration lies in the impact the latter has had on the centre–periphery cleavage around which minority nationalist parties mobilised historically. As a result of European integration, the bilateral confrontation between the centre and the periphery has been reconfigured, with actors representing the periphery no longer 'locked in' by the territorial, functional, social, political and cultural boundaries of the state (Bartolini, 2005: 276–78). European integration has provided sub-state actors with access to external extra-state financial resources and new market opportunities that potentially loosen the economic ties that bind the region/minority nation to the state. Moreover, new institutional opportunities have been created to articulate peripheral grievances within alternative supranational arenas, and to form transnational alliances in pursuit of shared constitutional and functional goals. The fact that European integration has also undermined the congruence between territory, political authority and identity that defined the sovereign state system, has also encouraged minority nationalist parties to imagine alternative non-state based configurations of political authority, with the minority nation as a central unit within any future European polity. As a result of these transformations wrought by European integration, it has often been argued, minority nationalist parties have been overwhelmingly supportive of European integration, since this process has redefined the axis of political contestation that defines their *raison d'être*.

The findings of this study demonstrate, however, that minority nationalist party responses to European integration are significantly more complex than is suggested by their frequent portrayal as enthusiastic backers of the European project.

		Support for the idea of Europe	
		Strong	Weak
Support for Europe as a concrete reality	Strong	Euro-enthusiasts Plaid Cymru (mid-1980s – late 1990s) UPC/PNC	Euro-pragmatists Corsica Nazione (from mid-1990s)
	Weak	Euro-sceptics BNG (from mid-1990s) Plaid Cymru (until mid-1980s; again from late1990s)	Euro-rejects BNG (until mid-1990s) FLNC (until mid-1990s)

Figure 6.1 Typology of minority nationalist party attitudes towards European integration.

The next section maps the general attitudinal patterns among the minority nationalist parties studied in the preceding case studies. The positions taken up by these actors on Europe are demonstrated to be far more diverse and changeable than is acknowledged in the existing scholarly literature. The following section evaluates the significance of different factors in shaping minority nationalist party attitudes towards European integration. Party attitudes are shown to be influenced by the enduring effects of party ideology, but are also contingent upon the ever-changing realities of domestic and supranational politics. The chapter concludes by reflecting on the continuous challenge that minority nationalist parties face in reconciling a normative aspiration for a regional Europe with the opportunities and constraints for articulating such an aspiration within domestic and supranational political arenas.

Mapping the changing European attitudes of minority nationalist parties

Chapter 2 proposed a fourfold typology for categorising minority nationalist party attitudes towards European integration, based on a distinction between two dimensions: Europe as a basic idea and Europe as a concrete reality. Drawing on the empirical data provided in the preceding three chapters, Figure 6.1 summarises the range of positions adopted by minority nationalist parties along these two dimensions. This fourfold typology enables a first categorisation to be made of the range of positions assumed by individual parties towards Europe over time. Thus, for example, the BNG in the early 1980s typified a Euro-rejectionist party that was not supportive either of the general idea of Europe or of the opportunities offered by Europe (the EEC) as it actually existed at the time. At the other extreme, Plaid Cymru by the late 1990s epitomised a Euro-enthusiastic party; the party combined zealous support for a European framework for Welsh self-determination with a positive evaluation of the economic, political and cultural opportunities for Wales within the EU. Moderate Corsican nationalist parties espoused a similar position, albeit based on a less thorough evaluation of the concrete realities of Europe. In between, Corsica Nazione during the 1990s displayed several of the features of pragmatic Europeanism, with its opportunistic emphasis on the financial benefits of integration for Corsica. In contrast, Plaid Cymru in the late 1970s, and the BNG from the mid-1990s onwards, adopted Euro-sceptic positions. Both parties were firmly committed to the basic idea that European integration held the potential for resolving the nationalities question, but were also highly critical of the way in which the European polity had developed up until that point.

This typology is not without its shortcomings, however. Two major limitations must be noted. Firstly, it is difficult to identify general patterns of attitudinal change from Figure 6.1, because of the static categorisation of party positions that is presented. Secondly, the small number of categories means that whilst parties that share broad attitudinal traits are categorised together, they may differ significantly in the detail of what they have to say about Europe. The categorisation of Plaid Cymru and moderate Corsican nationalist parties as Euro-enthusiasts demonstrates this problem. Whilst both parties were ardent supporters of both the idea and the concrete reality of Europe from the mid-1980s to the late-1990s, Chapters 3 and 5 showed that the basis of this support was clearly different. Plaid Cymru was highly attuned to developments in European integration and sought to develop a detailed political programme which spelt out the ways in which key territorial and policy goals would be achieved within a regional Europe. In contrast, Europe was an abstract slogan for moderate Corsican nationalists, a theme that remained tangential to the everyday political priorities of the UPC and its successor parties. These different degrees of engagement with Europe cannot be grasped from Figure 6.1.

These limitations can be partially redressed by situating minority nationalist parties in a two-dimensional space rather than four discrete categories. Figure 6.2 therefore plots the shifts in minority nationalist party positions on Europe along the same two analytical dimensions at the beginning and end of the time period covered by this study (from the mid-1970s to 2007). This alternative representation of minority nationalist party attitudes allows several further observations to be made about the nature of, and changes in, minority nationalist party attitudes towards Europe.

Firstly, the general attitudinal trend evident in Figure 6.2 is that of growing principled support among minority nationalist parties for Europe over time. All

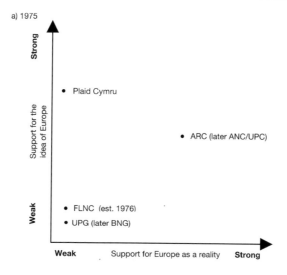

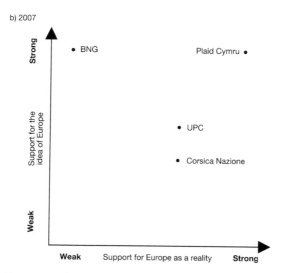

Figure 6.2 The European attitudes of minority nationalist parties: (a) 1975 and (b) 2007.

the minority nationalist parties included in this study have at some point come to the conclusion that European integration facilitates the achievement of national self-determination. Minority nationalist parties in Wales, Galicia and Corsica adopted different versions of the Europe of the Regions narrative to express this perceived linkage between territorial restructuring and European integration. Even those most strongly opposed to Europe in all its manifestations during the 1970s and 1980s modified their long-term constitutional goals to reflect this basic conviction. Thus, whereas in 1975 two parties can be categorised as being Euro-rejects, none fall into this category by 2007. At the end of the 1970s, the UPG (forerunner to the BNG) and the FLNC opposed both the idea and reality of European integration on similar anti-colonialist, anti-capitalist grounds. By the mid-1990s, however, the BNG had reformulated its long-term nationalist aspirations within the context of a Spanish pluri-national state and a 'Europe of the Peoples'; Corsica Nazione, meanwhile, adopted the idea of 'independence in Europe' and re-evaluated the pragmatic benefits forthcoming for Corsica within the European polity. Over the same period of time, Plaid Cymru evolved from a party ideologically committed to the notion of Wales as a European nation but opposed to the concrete policy implications of the EEC, to a party strongly favourable towards both the principle and reality of European integration. Strikingly, only the UPC/PNC did not show any significant change in its position vis-à-vis Europe over this thirty-year period; these parties were always, and remain, enthusiastic supporters of the European project and the reasons for this attitudinal stability are set out in the next section. What is important to note here is that none of the minority nationalist parties studied have made significant shifts in the other direction, that is, to become less supportive of the basic idea of European integration. This remains true in spite of the fact that some minority nationalist parties (such as Plaid Cymru) have become more sceptical of developments in European integration in recent years. The findings of this study thus confirm what has often been asserted in the academic literature: minority nationalist parties have been, and continue to be, supportive of European integration in principle because of the potential of this process to offer new and more satisfactory ways of organising political authority than has hitherto been possible within the framework of the sovereign state.

Secondly, however, growing support for Europe in principle has not been accompanied by similar support for the concrete realities of European integration. On the contrary, Figure 6.2 points to the degree to which minority nationalist parties have disagreed on the implications of actually-existing Europe for their respective national communities. A comparison of the changing European attitudes of Plaid Cymru and the BNG illustrates this point clearly. Both parties were formally supportive of the long-term goal of creating a regional Europe by the mid-1990s, and co-operated closely within the EFA to advance this agenda on the supranational level. However, Plaid Cymru and the BNG followed different trajectories to arrive at this shared vision of a future European polity. Plaid Cymru had a long pedigree of ideological Europeanism which predisposed the party to the idea of supranational co-operation as a framework for achieving political autonomy for Wales; it was a re-evaluation of the costs and benefits of the EEC for Wales during the 1980s that constituted the most significant modification of the party's stance on Europe. In contrast, the BNG's position on the implications of actually-existing Europe remained consistently negative throughout the 1980s and 1990s. Instead, it was the party's position on the fundamental linkage between securing Galician autonomy and the future direction on European integration that had changed by the late 1990s. Corsica Nazione's trajectory of attitudinal change differed again. Just like the BNG, Corsica Nazione came to be supportive of the basic idea of Europe by the late 1990s, but the party's response to the concrete realities of European integration was more positive than the former's, albeit more narrowly focused on the new financial opportunities for Corsica from European regional monies.

Examining party attitudes towards the concrete realities of European integration also helps to make sense of the tendency identified in Chapter 1, namely for some minority nationalist parties to combine formal support for European integration with hostility towards the European polity in practice. The preceding case studies demonstrated clearly that, as posited in Chapter 2, minority nationalist parties have evaluated different aspects of European integration in very different ways, based on the different effects that this process has on their interests and goals. As a result, some minority nationalist parties have reconciled support in principle for European integration with much less positive evaluations of the concrete implications of this process for the minority nation in question. The most striking case of this is the BNG, which has espoused such a Euro-sceptic position since the 1990s. More recently, other parties such as Plaid Cymru have also become more critical of developments in European integration, although the party has not abandoned 'independence in Europe' as its long-term constitutional goal. This evidence suggests that the nature of minority nationalist party support for Europe is changing. Whilst minority nationalist parties remain formally committed to a European framework for national self-determination, those that are aware of concrete developments on the supranational level are increasingly questioning the current direction in which European integration is moving. There is a growing dissonance between the normative ideal of a regional Europe and the realities of a European polity that has repeatedly failed to enhance the status of minority nations within the EU's institutional and legal structures. This is particularly clear to see in the cases of Plaid Cymru and the BNG. In recent years, these parties have sought to manage this tension by shifting attention away from the European issue, to focus on other domestic policy priorities. This strategy has thus far been successful in enabling these parties to avoid difficult questions about the growing gap between their long-term Europeanist goals and the current state of European politics. This emergent Euro-scepticism among some minority nationalist parties reveals the limits of any account of minority nationalist party attitudes towards Europe that insists on these actors being Europeanists *par excellence.* Such accounts overlook how minority nationalist parties perceive and engage with the concrete realities of European integration, realities that may not necessarily sit comfortably with these actors' normative aspirations for a regional Europe.

Mapping minority nationalist party attitudes within a two-dimensional space is thus useful for illustrating broad changes in party attitudes over time, as well for understanding the different facets of Europe that these actors respond to. However, mapping party attitudes in this way comes at the expense of losing considerable detail about what these parties have to say about Europe. The broad attitudinal trends summarised thus far in this section belie a huge diversity of ways in which individual minority nationalist parties have understood and responded to Europe.

146 *Conclusions*

The empirical analyses in Chapters 3, 4 and 5 showed this diversity to exist in several respects: in party understandings of the place of the minority nation within a future European polity; in evaluations of the costs and benefits for the minority nation from European integration; and in the importance of the European dimension in these actors' nationalist programmes.

Firstly, there is no consensus among minority nationalist parties about what role minority nations should play in a future European polity. Parties have opted for a range of labels to represent their shared desire for the territorial reorganisation of political authority within Europe: a 'Europe of the Regions' for Plaid Cymru, a 'Europe of the Peoples' for the BNG and parties on the moderate wing of Corsican nationalism, and a 'Europe of Nations without States' for radical Corsican nationalists in the 1980s. Beyond the fact that all parties employ some version of a regional European rhetoric, there is no agreement on how this alternative European political order should be organised, or what the relationship should be between the minority nation, the state and the European institutions. At one extreme, only Corsica Nazione has adopted the rhetoric of full-blown independence and traditional statehood for Corsica within the EU (although the fact that the party does not spell out in any detail its long-term constitutional plans makes its precise ambitions impossible to grasp). At the other extreme, Plaid Cymru for a long time aspired to a post-sovereigntist Europe where being a sovereign state would no longer be the only criterion for acceding to a full political role within the European polity. Even though the party recently committed itself to the pursuit of 'independence in Europe', it was reluctant to recognise that this implied the prior creation of a fully sovereign Welsh state. This attempt to re-conceptualise conventional understandings of concepts such as independence and sovereignty suggests that Plaid Cymru's understanding of 'independence in Europe' remains distinct from Corsica Nazione's understanding of the same goal, even if it is not clear what, in practice, either objective would mean. The UPC/PNC and the BNG envisaged a less zero-sum solution that did not anticipate the disappearance of states as a prerequisite for minority nations to gain a greater stake in European decision making. Rather, a reorganisation of the internal political structure of the state would be paralleled by enhanced opportunities for representing nationalist interests on the supranational level.

Secondly, and as argued above, minority nationalist parties have disagreed on the concrete costs and benefits of European integration for their respective minority nations. Parties have also focused on different aspects of the European reality, with some focusing (exclusively or predominantly) on economic issues (Corsica Nazione and the BNG), whilst others have also been concerned with the political and cultural implications of European integration for the minority nation (Plaid Cymru). The implications of economic integration, for instance, were interpreted differently by different parties at different points in time. At the end of the 1970s, all parties except the Corsican UPC decried the negative impact of an integration process defined and driven by the interests of states and transnational capital on peripheral economies. By 2004, only the BNG persisted in rejecting the economic opportunities for Galicia within a European common market and a system of monetary union. Corsica Nazione replaced the FLNC's anti-EEC rhetoric with a very narrow focus on the benefits to the Corsican economy of large financial transfers under the guise of EU Structural Funds. Plaid Cymru's re-evaluation of the economic opportunities for Wales within the EU led the party to adopt a very different position. It was argued that the opening up of the European market offered a favourable set of conditions for an innovative and sustainable regional economy to compete successfully and prosper within European and global markets.

The political and cultural implications of European integration have also been evaluated differently by different parties. As noted above, successive radical nationalist groups in Corsica simply ignored the political and cultural dimensions of the European opportunity structure. The BNG recognised the virtues of having direct representation in the European Parliament, although this and other political channels for interest representation have been largely closed off to the party. The BNG was always – and remains – highly sceptical of supranational opportunities for solving cultural and linguistic issues. In contrast, both Plaid Cymru and (to a lesser extent) moderate Corsican nationalist parties perceived concrete developments in European policy making and institution building as an external support structure for building the nation as a viable political and cultural entity. The expansion of the powers of the European Parliament and the creation of a Committee of the Regions were perceived to be major steps towards building a regionalised Europe. Similarly positive evaluations were made of the EU's growing activism in the area of human and minority rights in general, and more specifically with regard to the protection of minority languages and cultural diversity. In recent years, however, these two parties have disagreed on the progress made by European integration in providing a framework for protecting and promoting minority nationalist issues. The PNC's unqualified support for the European Constitution contrasted with Plaid Cymru's disappointment with the document's lack of recognition of the rights and interests of Europe's historic nations and regions.

The contrasting evaluations offered by Plaid Cymru and the PNC of the European Constitution reflected the different degrees of engagement of these parties with European integration and the concrete realities of the EU. This observation points to a third way in which minority nationalist parties have differed in their responses to European integration, namely in the salience of the European dimension for different minority nationalist parties at different points in time. The interest of radical Corsican nationalist parties in Europe has always been minimal. Corsica Nazione's 'independence in Europe' rhetoric, for example, has always been confined to occasions when the party is forced to state its broad political goals; otherwise, Europe does not feature in the party's programme beyond a narrow concern with European regional policy spending in Corsica. The salience of the European dimension in the BNG's nationalist agenda has also varied, both within the party and over time. The party's formal declarations in support of a Europe of the Peoples from the mid-1990s onwards belied a party membership that remained uninterested in European affairs; the European dimension has declined even further in salience in the party's programme since it entered regional government in 2005. Whilst the discourse of a Europe of the Regions was a defining theme of Plaid Cymru's politics throughout the 1990s, in recent years the party has also played down its Europeanist credentials.

148 *Conclusions*

The issue of Europe is no longer given as much prominence as a defining feature of Plaid Cymru's political agenda within post-devolution Wales.

These observations demonstrate that whilst minority nationalist parties have mobilised around the centre–periphery cleavage, and even though European integration has challenged the way in which this cleavage has been historically defined within the context of the state, Europe is not always a primary concern for these actors. European integration has undoubtedly provided a powerful impetus for minority nationalist parties to rethink their long-term constitutional goals. This study has also demonstrated, however, that minority nationalist support for Europe and these parties' interest in and engagement with European integration can also wax and wane. This is a significant finding that qualifies the scholarly tendency to assume that European integration, because of its potential to resolve the key territorial issues that constitute the *raison d'être* of the minority nationalist party family, is a central and constant feature of minority nationalist politics.

The above observations demonstrate that minority nationalist party attitudes towards Europe are considerably more complex than has hitherto been posited in the academic literature. Portrayals of minority nationalist parties as Europeanists *par excellence* overlook the highly diverse ways in which these actors have perceived and responded to European integration. The next section examines the different factors that have given rise to such a heterogeneity of positions on Europe.

Explaining the changing European attitudes of minority nationalist parties

The fact that the positions assumed by minority nationalist parties on the European issue have differed both within individual parties over time and between parties is the result of a confluence of different factors that have come to bear on each individual party. It is the complex interaction between different types of factor, which have varied in their strength and timing, that explains the diversity of attitudes adopted by these actors. Minority nationalist party responses to European integration are thus highly actor and context specific. Nevertheless, it is possible to identify a number of factors that are present in each case and which have exerted comparable influences on what these actors have had to say about Europe.

Factors from within the party

The influence of basic party ideology

This study reinforces the findings from other empirical work that has examined the attitudes of political parties vis-à-vis Europe, and that has found European integration to be assimilated into a party's pre-existing ideological value set. The two value dimensions that are the most important for minority nationalist parties are the centre–periphery dimension and the left–right dimension. Further values may also come into play for individual parties, especially 'new politics' values. Some parties included in this study, such as Plaid Cymru and the BNG, espoused green–ecological values from the late 1980s onwards. However, on the whole these values were not determinant in shaping party attitudes towards Europe because they were less central than the centre–periphery and left–right dimensions in these parties' political programmes. The way in which minority nationalist parties combined these two sets of values – centre–periphery and left–right – differed from case to case, but together they constituted an enduring influence on the basic attitudinal orientation of individual minority nationalist parties towards Europe. This does not mean that ideology is immutable. Ideas are liable to a certain degree of reinterpretation and repackaging when it is politically or strategically beneficial to do so. The case studies show very clearly how adept these parties have been at adapting their core values to changing circumstances; this is particularly the case as minority nationalist parties have moved from the margins towards the centre of the political system, and have moderated their political programmes in order to maximise their voter appeal. However, even when such ideological modification or moderation took place, on no occasion did this alter the fundamental thrust of party preferences towards Europe. Basic ideological values continued to determine the broad parameters of party attitudes towards Europe even if, as will be argued below, such values were at times downplayed in response to short-term political pressures.

Minority nationalist party attitudes towards Europe have been shaped primarily by their rootedness in the historically defined centre–periphery cleavage. Party attitudes have thus been filtered through the party's experiences of, and struggle against, the central state. Minority nationalist party support for European integration in principle has been driven by the basic conviction that European integration brings something new to the territorial conflict that constitutes the *raison d'être* of these parties. Minority nationalist parties have always had a vested interest in a process that alters the nature and function of the state, not least because the latter has constrained the ability of minority nations to take control of their own destinies. At the same time, European integration has encouraged minority nationalist parties to imagine a new form of European polity within which nationalist demands would be satisfied. The exact configuration of such an alternative Europe reflected the different ideological profiles of individual parties. Plaid Cymru's post-sovereigntist heritage inextricably informed the party's conceptualisation of a future Europe of the Regions within which sovereign states would disappear. The radical ideological heritage of Corsica Nazione, in contrast, informed the party's preference for a complete rupture from the French state and independence for Corsica within the EU. The more reformist European imagery adopted by the BNG and moderate Corsican nationalists was also a product of these parties' specific understanding of the nature of the centre–periphery conflict, and how best to resolve it. For the latter, for example, the switch from demanding internal autonomy within the French state to the internal constitutional reform of the state within a broader federal European framework was an easy and consistent transposition to make.

At the same time, however, party responses to the concrete realities of European integration have also been shaped by the left–right ideological values that complete the ideological repertoire of minority nationalist parties. All the parties included in this study, except the UPC (neither left nor right), can be situated on the left side of

150 *Conclusions*

the ideological spectrum. At the end of the 1970s, there was very little to distinguish between Plaid Cymru, the BNG and the FLNC in their opposition to European integration in the 1970s; opposition to the EEC was motivated by a socialist-inspired rejection of the capitalist system being developed on the supranational level. In two of these three cases – Plaid Cymru and the BNG – the radicalism of this left-wing anti-Europeanism declined over time, and was replaced by more moderate social democratic values. This moderation was a response to the pressures of political competition in the UK and in Galicia respectively, as both parties sought to boost their electoral appeal and attract a broader support base. For Plaid Cymru, a moderation of the party's socialist values was one factor that prompted a reassessment of the opportunities for Wales within a European free market; abandoning its opposition to supranational capitalism enabled the party to argue the case for regional economic growth and competitiveness within the EU. The BNG moderated its radical Marxist–Leninist values as it sought to compete for the political centre ground from the late 1980s onwards, although a formal change in rhetoric did not alter the basic ideological antipathy of the party's membership towards supranational economic integration. Corsica Nazione also abandoned its early radical socialist ideals, although this must be understood as an adjustment to de-ideologicalised Corsican politics, as well as to the pressures of party competition.

These two ideological dimensions together – centre–periphery and left–right – thus define the starting point of a minority nationalist party's stance on Europe, but also constrain its end point. None of the parties studied have made the complete transformation from a Euro-rejectionist party to a Euro-enthusiastic party (Figure 6.1). Basic ideology thus serves to distinguish between those parties that are instinctively predisposed to the idea of Europe (Plaid Cymru and the UPC/PNC) and those inherently suspicious of this same Europe (the BNG and the FLNC/Corsica Nazione). For the BNG and radical Corsican nationalist parties, a tradition of anti-Europeanism continued to inform an enduring scepticism towards the European project in spite of formal declarations in support of Europe in principle, as a framework for securing national self-determination. These values also contributed to these parties' relative disinterest in, and superficial engagement with, the realities of European integration.

Within the basic attitudinal parameters defined by ideological values, however, there is clearly scope to fine-tune a minority nationalist party's position on Europe. A number of other influences often come into play that can push and pull a party in different directions over Europe. Before considering what these factors are, however, and how they have modified minority nationalist party attitudes towards European integration, it is necessary to evaluate to what extent differing pressures to adopt different stances on Europe have led to factional strife within minority nationalist parties.

Internal factions on the issue of Europe

The case studies have found no evidence that the issue of Europe has created deep internal divisions within parties. On the contrary, one of the most striking things about the ways in which minority nationalist parties have adapted and changed their positions on Europe over time is that such changes have been relatively unproblematic. Minority nationalist parties have thus far been exempt from the serious factionalism that the issue of Europe has provoked within many other party families. It is not that such intra-party dissent has never existed, although 'issue groups' (as suggested by Johanssen and Raunio, 2001, see Chapter 2) or tensions is a more accurate description of these divisions than well-organised, well-resourced and durable factions. On the one hand, these differences have been ideological. The BNG is the best example in this respect. At the end of the 1980s, the party began to incorporate several ideologically heterogeneous groups into its organisation, groups that espoused very different opinions about the European project. Differences over Europe were inevitable, although they did not evolve into a serious confrontation within the BNG. On the other hand, tensions to do with Europe have been related to party strategy. Within Plaid Cymru during the late 1970s, party members against the EEC campaigned for the withdrawal of the UK from the European club, whilst others defended a more moderate approach which placed the emphasis on reforming the EEC from within. More recently, the BNG and Corsica Nazione faced intra-party divisions on the best strategy to adopt in the referendum on the European Constitution.

And yet, at no point have these tensions escalated to such a degree as to seriously threaten party unity or damage the party's political credibility and, therefore, vote-maximisation potential. There are two main reasons as to why this has not been the case. Firstly, specific factors exclusive to individual cases have mitigated the potentially damaging effects of intra-party dissent on Europe. The BNG's deliberative organisational structure, for example, facilitated the reconciliation of different ideas within the party on Europe; this factor was also crucial in reconciling different opinions when it came to deciding the party's position in the referendum campaign on the European Constitution. In the case of Corsica Nazione, the relative unimportance of the European dimension for the party's political programme in general, combined with the specific decision of the party leadership to allow a free vote in the referendum on the European Constitution, limited the potential of the European issue to divide the party.

Secondly, all three case studies have demonstrated that there is a further factor that has exerted an important pressure on these parties to subjugate internal tensions for the sake of party unity: the quest for electoral success in the domestic political arena. As parties which, during the late 1970s, were politically and electorally marginalised in their respective political systems, aspirations for electoral growth and public office exerted a strong pressure for maintaining party unity at all costs. It was the centripetal pressures of party competition, and the success of these parties in meeting their electoral goals, that kept minority nationalist parties united on the issue of Europe, at least until the late 1990s.

The reversal in the electoral fortunes of the BNG and Plaid Cymru from the early 2000s onwards, in contrast, led to the re-emergence of intra-party tensions on the European issue. In both cases, these tensions did not result in serious intra-party dissent because the success of both parties in entering regional government meant party energies were directed onto the new challenges of government incumbency. Nevertheless, the fact that electoral defeat fuelled the emergence anew of tensions vis-à-vis Europe provided further testimony of the powerful impact of party performance on the ability of minority nationalist parties to manage and limit intra-party dissent. In this respect, minority nationalist parties are subject to the same pressures as any other political party (Taggart, 1998; Sitter, 2002). It was argued in Chapter 2 that factions on the issue of Europe tended to be confined to those parties that are central to the political system, for example major political parties that are either in government or are main opposition parties. The fact that minority nationalist parties in Wales, Galicia and Corsica have established themselves as central actors in their respective regional political systems – either as parties of government or as major opposition parties – is thus likely to increase their susceptibility to intra-party divisions in the future.

Factors within the domestic political context

The fact that each minority nationalist party is embedded in a particular domestic political context exerts a major influence on what these parties have to say about Europe. Party ideology may determine basic party attitudes on this issue, but other factors within the domestic political context have been more important in informing what parties choose to communicate to their voters on this issue. The findings of this study thus concur with those of Featherstone's (1988) study of socialist party positions on Europe, which identified domestic political factors as the primary determinants of party attitudes towards Europe.

Some domestic influences are unique to each case and are not comparable. In Corsica, a strong clanist political culture and the chronic instability of the minority nationalist movement limited the engagement of minority nationalist parties with European affairs. In Galicia, the experience of Francoism and Spain's late transition to democracy during the 1970s provided a specific context within which the Galician nationalist movement emerged and evolved. Without wishing these specificities away, however, the evidence gathered in the preceding chapters confirms that a number of other factors within the domestic political context have exerted a common pressure on minority nationalist parties to adapt their attitudes towards European integration in specific ways. These factors include the structure of the domestic political system (which in turn has shaped party strategy and goals), the political space available on the European issue and public opinion towards Europe. In addition, the ability of minority nationalist parties to cross the threshold of representation for the European Parliament has been important in determining the salience of the European dimension in different party programmes and strategies. The exact form or strength of a factor has varied from context to context and from party to party, and the timing and extent of programmatic adaptation may thus differ. Nevertheless, the common patterns of influence enable several generalisations to be made about how the domestic political context has shaped minority nationalist party attitudes towards European integration.

The changing dynamics of party competition

The case studies in the preceding three chapters demonstrated clearly that the changing political status of minority nationalist parties within their respective political systems has had a dramatic impact on party attitudes towards European integration. During the time period covered by this study, Plaid Cymru, the BNG and the main radical Corsican nationalist parties evolved from being marginal actors in state/regional politics to being major players on the regional level, either as main opposition parties or as parties of government. In these cases, the changing political and electoral status of the parties prompted a re-evaluation, moderation and re-prioritisation of what could be said about Europe. Other minority nationalist parties who were not subject to such a change in their political status were not exposed to these pressures. The UPC/PNC, for instance, has remained a marginal electoral force within Corsican politics, and has not altered the basic tenets of its position on Europe since it was first defined in the 1970s. Other smaller radical nationalist parties in Corsica (such as the ANC) also continue to be politically and electorally insignificant, and still espouse the same Euro-rejectionist positions articulated by the FLNC during the 1980s.

The source of this adaptive pressure on party attitudes towards European integration derived, in large part, from the strategy pursued by a minority nationalist party within the domestic political sphere. The impact of changing party strategies on attitudes towards Europe was clearest to see in the case of the BNG and the FLNC/Corsica Nazione. As proposed in Chapter 2, the anti-system strategies adopted by the BNG and FLNC in the early 1980s saw opposition to the domestic political system being translated into opposition to the European polity, the latter merely an extension of the ills of the state's values and institutions. However, once these parties took the decision to abandon outright opposition to the extant political system and to compete in elections, they were exposed to a very different kind of pressure to modify their political message in specific ways. The prioritisation of vote maximisation required both the BNG and the different fronts of the FLNC to cultivate a broader support base based on a more moderate and pragmatic political agenda. As part of this adaptation, these parties replaced their opposition to Europe in principle with a commitment to securing national self-determination within a European framework. The imperatives of electoral competition thus trumped basic ideology in determining the party's position vis-à-vis the general idea of Europe. However, this discursive moderation was less far reaching than was anticipated in Chapter 2. Firstly, discursive moderation was limited to symbolic declarations that linked national self-determination to a future regional Europe; a revision of the party's formal position on Europe did not, however, filter down to the attitudes of party members and some leaders, who remained deeply suspicious of supranational co-operation. Secondly, and as a consequence of the resilience of anti-European sentiments within these parties, discursive moderation did not prompt either the BNG or Corsica Nazione to engage with European affairs in any serious or thorough way. These parties remained uninterested in working out the details of their newly adopted constitutional policies, as well as in the specifics of how European legislation impacted upon the minority nation. Whilst formally committing to the fundamental idea of national self-determination within a European framework in response to strong political and electoral pressures, Europe failed to sway the hearts and minds of the vast majority of Galician and Corsican nationalists.

Plaid Cymru's adaptation of its position on Europe to changes in its political and electoral circumstances responded more closely to the expectations set out in Chapter 2. In the early 1980s, Plaid Cymru was a Euro-sceptic party confined to the margins of British politics. The party's moderation of its brand of 'democratic socialism' and abandonment of opposition to the EEC were motivated by the desire to relaunch Welsh nationalism as a progressive political force that would appeal to Welsh voters increasingly disillusioned with the Conservative Party in government in Westminster. The reformulation of the party's long-term constitutional goals was thus motivated by a desire to carve out a new nationalist political space within Welsh politics. This formal change in party attitude towards Europe was accompanied by an effort to work out the details of how to achieve the goal of 'full national status' for Wales in Europe, as well as the concrete implications of European policy making for Wales. Paradoxically, one consequence of this greater engagement with Europe was that Plaid Cymru was much quicker to appreciate the limitations of European integration in meeting its nationalist demands. By the late 1990s, growing frustration within the party at the stalling of the Europe of the Regions dynamic, as well as disillusionment with concrete policy developments on the supranational level, contributed to a new wave of scepticism towards the EU as it then existed. The creation of a new Welsh political space in 1999 had two contradictory effects on Plaid Cymru's position on Europe. On the one hand, the new political visibility, brought as a result of being the main party of opposition within the NAW forced a clarification of the party's long-term constitutional goals for Wales within Europe. On the other hand, devolution provided new incentives for Plaid Cymru to focus on the opportunities for influencing policy making within Wales. The prioritisation of politics at home, combined with the increasingly problematic direction of European integration, contributed to a decline in the references to Europe in Plaid Cymru's political declarations and activities.

The entry of the BNG and Plaid Cymru into regional government in 2005 and 2007 respectively has created new pressures on each party to adapt their positions on Europe. Two trends have thus far been evident. Firstly, these parties have changed their strategies for securing greater autonomy for their respective nations. As parties of government, the BNG and Plaid Cymru have been able to push for new negotiations between regional and state authorities for a revised constitutional settlement that would bolster national self-determination. No agreement has yet been reached in either place as to how regional competencies can or should be enhanced. But the prospect of such reforms has led both parties to focus on the state, rather than Europe, as the actor that can realistically deliver on the goal of territorial autonomy. The rhetoric of a regional Europe that defines the long-term ambitions of the BNG and Plaid Cymru is increasingly confined to summary statements of these parties' long-term visions for Wales and Galicia respectively. Such symbolic statements aside, however, short-term pragmatism has led to the prioritisation of other channels in the pursuit of the territorial goal that constitutes the *raison d'être* of these minority nationalist parties. Europe no longer constitutes the most attractive or promising arena for resolving key minority nationalist demands.

Secondly, there is evidence of a new engagement with the realities of how European integration impacts upon policy making within the minority nation. The fact that both parties hold portfolios with a significant European legislative dimension requires party representatives in government to become familiar with the technical and financial parameters that constrain policy innovation. The formal Europeanist rhetoric adopted by these parties when in opposition has, as expected, been replaced by a focus on the pragmatic ways in which European integration comes to bear on regional policy making. This new form of engagement with Europe is particularly novel for the BNG, given the party's general lack of interest in European affairs beyond the stock critique of European policies that are deemed to have had a disastrous impact on the Galician economy. It is easy to imagine how the constraints imposed by European legislation on regional policy innovation could generate tensions between the party in office and party members anxious to maximise policy influence. This danger was greatest for the BNG, given the party's deep-rooted antipathy towards the concrete realities of European politics. At the time of writing, however, such tensions had not emerged. The party's strategy of decrying the constraints imposed upon it by statewide and European policy makers has thus far been effective in maintaining the party's image as the defender of Galician interests vis-à-vis the damaging effects of economic integration.

Whether such tensions will emerge within Plaid Cymru or the BNG in future will likely depend on two things: firstly, the degree to which these parties are able to exploit channels of access to EU policy making via the state to defend nationalist interests; and secondly, the more general success of these parties in meeting their policy goals within regional government. In neither case has the nationalists' first experience of regional government been put to the electoral test. When it is, a negative evaluation from voters is likely to constitute an external shock which could bring tensions on the issue of Europe to the fore once more, as part of a more profound questioning of the goals and strategies of these two parties within Welsh and Galician politics respectively. On the contrary, a positive evaluation is likely to reinforce the pragmatic approach of these parties towards Europe, at the expense of symbolic declarations in favour of a future regionalised European polity.

Political space on the issue of Europe

A further aspect of political competition relates to the degree of political space a party has to exploit the European issue for political and electoral gain. Being

156 *Conclusions*

able to do so has in large part depended on the positions adopted by other (usually statewide) political parties on Europe. The case studies provided several examples of parties exploiting differences in party positions on European integration to score easy political points against their partisan rivals, by drawing attention to the differences that exist in partisan approaches to Europe. This included highlighting the internal divisions of other parties over Europe (Plaid Cymru vis-à-vis Labour in 1975), contrasting opposing visions of Europe (Plaid Cymru versus the Conservatives during the 1980s, the BNG versus the Spanish political class at the time of Spain's accession to the EEC, and the UPC and FLNC versus a centralised French government during the 1980s) and drawing attention to the incompetence of others in managing European affairs (Corsica Nazione versus the French authorities in the late 1990s).

However, maintaining such a European political space over time has proved difficult. Minority nationalist parties were not the only ones to adapt their political programmes to developments in European integration and in response to party competitive pressures at home. Statewide parties in Wales, Galicia and Corsica were just as adept at modifying their European discourses in response to ever-changing supranational and domestic political realities. This has usually had the effect of constraining the ability of minority nationalist parties to play the European card to their own political advantage. For Plaid Cymru, the Labour Party has largely overcome its previous divisions over Europe whilst the Conservative Party has managed to downplay intra-party divisions on this issue and is now more in tune with British public opinion towards Europe (see below). Corsican nationalist parties have increasingly faced competition from the traditional clans who have also adopted a regional Europeanist discourse. The BNG can still claim to be the only party that is critical of European integration and its negative effects on the Galician economy. However, it has become less easy to articulate such Euro-scepticism as a party of regional government, whilst other smaller, more radical nationalist parties have taken on the Euro-rejectionist arguments once defended by the BNG.

The problem of defending a political space on the European issue has been symptomatic of a much bigger challenge faced by minority nationalist parties in fending off partisan competition on core nationalist issues. The creation of new regional political spaces in Wales, Galicia and Corsica, and the growing political and electoral salience of minority nationalist parties within these arenas, has forced other statewide political parties to take on the nationalist challenge directly by adopting themes from their political programmes. This direct competition for votes brought an end to the electoral rise of Plaid Cymru and the BNG by the early 2000s, and has halted the further electoral expansion of Corsica Nazione. Electoral decline/stagnation has prompted new debates within these parties with regard to party identity and strategy. Attempts at defining a new nationalist political space have often pitted modernists against traditionalists on questions of ideology and strategy. The programmatic moderation and electoral strategies adopted as a means of moving towards the political centre have been challenged by defenders of a return to ideological purity and oppositional politics. Such tensions are not exclusive to the minority nationalist parties studied here. Rather, they are symptomatic of the trade-off faced by many political parties between adopting a 'catch-all' strategy as a means of influencing policy and securing public office, and faithfulness to original ideals and values (Strøm and Müller, 1999; Elias and Tronconi, 2006).

Nevertheless, the case studies did not provide any evidence that such internal debates have led to a further revision of party attitudes towards Europe. As noted earlier in this chapter, none of the parties studied have abandoned their support in principle for a European framework for national self-determination. Instead, minority nationalist parties have sought to switch attention away from European integration and onto other less contentious policy issues where they have a greater political advantage vis-à-vis other political parties. This has been relatively easy for Corsica Nazione, given the party's general lack of interest in, or engagement with, European affairs. Plaid Cymru and the BNG, in contrast, have focused instead on concrete policy goals that can be realistically achieved within the domestic political arena. As noted above, the entry of these parties into regional government has reinforced the pragmatism with which European affairs have increasingly been approached.

The structure of the domestic political system

The changing patterns of party competition summarised above cannot be fully explained without taking into account important changes in the structure of the political system within which different minority nationalist parties have mobilised since the 1970s. In each of the three case studies, the creation of new regional institutions provided a new political opportunity structure for minority nationalist parties to articulate and pursue their nationalist demands. Institutional reform has taken different forms in different places. Spain's transition from dictatorship to democracy in the late 1970s was the context for the design of a new constitutional architecture that established a new regional political space for minority nationalist parties. Decentralisation in Corsica has been more gradual, with several waves of reform since 1982, but also less far-reaching in terms of the scope of regional government. In Wales, devolution occurred only very recently, in 1999, before which Plaid Cymru's main goal was to secure representation and to influence policy at the state level.

The timing of reform aside, however, the restructuring of the domestic political system enabled parties that were previously excluded from, or marginal within, statewide politics to articulate their grievances through electoral competition at the regional level. These new opportunity structures below the state constituted a major incentive for minority nationalist parties to moderate their political programmes in ways outlined above, and to compete for votes with other (usually statewide) political parties within the regional political arena. Having established themselves as major political players in their respective regional political arenas, some parties (Plaid Cymru and the BNG) have also had their first experience of government office at the regional level. The impact this has had on party attitudes towards Europe has already been considered above.

158 *Conclusions*

As argued in Chapter 2, the primacy given by minority nationalist parties to political competition at the regional level is understandable, given that the *raison d'être* of the party is to exercise political authority within an autonomous 'national' territory. Nevertheless, and as expected, other territorial levels remain important for minority nationalist parties in addition to being present and influencing policy within the minority nation itself. With regard to the state level, for example, for most of Plaid Cymru's existence, the absence of a regional tier of government meant that elections to Westminster were the only game in town (Wyn Jones and Scully, 2006). The nature of political competition within British politics was thus the main factor shaping Plaid Cymru's attitude towards Europe until 1999. Even after devolution, however, having MPs sitting in the House of Commons remained a priority in order to give expression to Welsh interests in debates on non-devolved policy areas, and to push for further devolution via new state legislation. The reverse is true of the BNG. The party was uninterested in state-level politics until the mid-1990s, with the dynamics of Galician politics being the primary determinant of the party's stance on Europe. The party's changing electoral ambitions within the Galician Parliament, however, led the party to recognise the importance of being present on the state level, for symbolic purposes as well as in order to influence policy. On the one hand, representation within the Spanish Congress of Deputies reinforced the BNG's newly adopted symbolic Europeanism. On the other hand, however, the party also experienced how multilevel politics can constrain a party's position on Europe. The BNG's pursuit of alliances with minority nationalist parties with a strong Euro-enthusiast profile at the state level did not play favourably with the party's electorate at home, and the party was punished by its supporters for having compromised on the party's long-standing scepticism towards the EU. In the Corsican case, minority nationalist parties have always been, and remain, excluded from the statewide political arena, given the nature of the electoral system and the delimitation of parliamentary constituencies. This fact of exclusion has been crucial in shaping the attitudes of different parties towards Europe.

Finally, the case studies also revealed the importance of securing representation at the European level for minority nationalist parties. The impact of having an MEP in the European Parliament on minority nationalist party discourses on Europe is considered in detail below. However, securing a representative within the European Parliament also had indirect political advantages for minority nationalist parties. For example, getting an MEP elected served to boost a minority nationalist party's credibility in the eyes of its electorate; the ability to be elected at several different territorial levels reaffirmed the political appeal of Plaid Cymru, the BNG and the UPC. Moreover, the linking of Welsh, Galician or Corsican interests to those of a broader nationalist constituency across western Europe was a highly effective strategy for conveying the legitimacy of nationalist demands. The rhetoric of being able to go directly to Brussels (or Strasbourg) to defend the interests of the nation also brought valuable political capital to parties anxious to portray themselves as key political actors in European decision making. Securing a presence within the European Parliament has thus been important not only as a prerequisite for defending minority nationalist interests at the supranational level, but also because of the positive knock-on effects on party image and credibility in other arenas of political competition.

The role of public opinion

Public opinion towards Europe has also influenced the degree to which minority nationalist parties have a free hand in articulating a position on this issue. As proposed in Chapter 2, when party positions on Europe have resonated with broader popular sentiment, minority nationalist parties have reaped considerable political and electoral benefits. The clearest example of this was provided by the BNG during the 1980s. The party's dogged opposition to the economic reforms implemented in Galicia as part of a programme of restructuring ahead of Spanish accession to the EEC rang home with Galician voters who were suffering directly as a result of these reforms.

More often than not, however, public opinion has constrained the ability of minority nationalist parties to emphasise their European attitudes. The nature of this constraint has been different in each of the three cases. Plaid Cymru's slogan 'independence in Europe' remains out of sync with an increasingly Euro-sceptic Welsh electorate that does not favour far-reaching constitutional reform. A similarly Euro-sceptic electorate in Corsica contrasts with the Europe of the Peoples rhetoric of moderate nationalist parties, and there is just as little appetite for independence along the lines advocated by Corsica Nazione. In contrast, it is the growing pro-Europeanism of the Galician electorate that is problematic for the BNG, in contrast to the resilient scepticism of its core nationalist support base. The growing discrepancy between the attitudes of minority nationalist parties and their electorates on Europe has been a further factor that has contributed to the playing down of the European dimension in nationalist party programmes in Wales, Galicia and Corsica in recent years.

The role of European Parliament elections

Finally, European Parliament elections have had a divergent impact on the European attitudes of minority nationalist parties. Only in the case of Plaid Cymru was the second-order effect usually associated with these elections identifiable. The party's better than average performance in these elections from 1979 onwards was crucial in prompting, and later reinforcing, a revised assessment of the opportunities for Wales within Europe. For other minority nationalist parties, structural and political factors – the rules governing the electoral process, the definition and number of electoral constituencies and the role of the media – mitigated against the second-order electoral benefit enjoyed by Plaid Cymru. The disadvantages faced by the BNG and the Corsican nationalist parties, and the resultant difficulties of getting a representative elected to the European Parliament, meant that these elections were given very little priority by these parties for much of the time period covered by this study. For the BNG and the FLNC/Corsica Nazione, the closure of the European parliamentary arena was a further factor that encouraged these parties' disengagement with Europe.

And yet, when the political circumstances were right and when minority nationalist parties did succeed in crossing this threshold of representation on the supranational level, direct representation within the European Parliament had a major impact on these parties' attitudes towards Europe. The effects of supranational co-operation and representation are considered in detail in the next section.

Factors at the supranational level

Developments in European integration

Existing academic accounts of minority nationalist party attitudes towards Europe have often argued that developments in European integration – especially during the late 1980s and 1990s – encouraged the supportive attitudes associated with this party family. This literature was summarised in Chapter 1. As noted above, the findings of this study confirms the general trend for minority nationalist parties to become more favourable towards European integration over time.

At the same time, however, the case studies demonstrate that it is certainly not the case that minority nationalist parties have responded to developments in European integration in a uniform way. In the first place, different parties came to make the linkage between national self-determination and European integration at very different points in time. In Corsica, the UPC was already calling for a Europe of the Peoples in 1979, but it would take another decade for Plaid Cymru to be converted into a zealous Euro-enthusiastic party. Yet another ten years would go by before the BNG would formally adopt a commitment to a Europe of the Peoples; Corsica Nazione settled for the slogan 'independence in Europe' at around about the same time. To some extent, the fact that individual parties discovered the transformational potential of Europe at different times can be linked to the different timing of European membership in each case. Thus, for example, the fact that France was a founding member of the EEC meant that Europe had long constituted a backdrop for minority nationalist mobilisation in Corsica (even if, for ideological reasons, radical nationalist parties chose to reject this supranational reality). In contrast, the later accession of the UK and Spain to the European club saw the European dimension catapulted onto the nationalist agenda at different times. The importance of this variable should not be overstated, however. Far more important in conditioning minority nationalist party attitudes towards Europe were ideological and contextual factors, as set out in the preceding section.

Secondly, and once more contrary to standard explanations of minority nationalist party support for European integration, not all minority nationalist parties have responded to developments in European integration positively. It is true that innovations such as the reform of European regional policies, the Committee of the Regions and the principle of subsidiarity encouraged the enthusiasm of some parties – Plaid Cymru and the UPC – towards Europe. But other ideological and

Conclusions 161

domestic-related factors had also already pushed these parties towards the realisation that the European polity seemed to offer the best prospect for meeting their territorial demands. For others – the BNG and radical Corsican nationalists – these developments did little to appease the ideologically driven critique of European integration in all its damaging forms. As has been outlined above, the European turn of these Euro-rejectionist parties was due to other political and electoral factors, rather than because of specific developments in European integration.

These observations demonstrate that the oft-asserted argument that minority nationalist parties support European integration because they have more to win than to lose, must be qualified in two important ways. Firstly, minority nationalist support in principle for European integration cannot be taken as a proxy for the attitude of these parties towards the European polity that actually exists at any given point in time. Whilst scholars have frequently assumed the former to be a reliable indicator of the position of minority nationalist parties on Europe, this study has demonstrated the importance of examining party attitudes towards the realities of actually-existing Europe, since it is not necessarily the case that these different facets of European integration will be evaluated in the same way. Secondly, the support of minority nationalist parties in principle for European integration in some cases has very little to do with a cost–benefit analysis of what is on offer for the nation within Europe. As the examples of the BNG and Corscia Nazione have demonstrated, such support is rather the product of other intra-party or domestic factors.

These two observations are important for understanding why some minority nationalist parties have become increasingly sceptical towards the EU in recent years, and the significance of this for the way in which these actors position themselves on Europe. Parties like Plaid Cymru have been increasingly frustrated with European integration because of the repeated failures to put in place an institutional and policy framework conducive to meeting key nationalist goals. The lack of progress towards a more regionalised Europe has also reinforced the long-standing hostility of the BNG towards the European polity as it has developed thus far. However, this tendency towards Euro-scepticism must be qualified in two ways. Firstly, in both cases, dissatisfaction with the EU has been accompanied by a playing down of the European dimension to nationalist politics, as parties have focused on other opportunities for advancing nationalist goals within the regional/ state context. Secondly, scepticism towards the realities of European integration has not yet translated into a more fundamental revision of these parties' support for the basic idea of a European framework for achieving self-determination. There are two important reasons why minority nationalist parties are unlikely to abandon their support for Europe in principle in the near future.

In the first place, the EU remains the only realistic option for parties whose basic aim is to loosen the binds that tie them to the sovereign state. The fact that debates about the nature and scope of the European polity are still ongoing means that there is still scope for minority nationalist parties to shape the future direction of European integration by articulating their own vision of what such a polity should look like. Symbolic politics thus remains important since it enables

162 *Conclusions*

minority nationalist parties to stake a claim in negotiations over how best to organise political authority within the European polity (Keating and Bray, 2006).

Secondly, the EU continues to provide important resources that minority nationalist parties can draw upon in their attempts at articulating a credible discourse in favour of greater national autonomy. Access to European and global markets makes arguments about economic sustainability easier for more prosperous minority nationalist parties to make, whilst for others the receipt of European monies is a key tenet of arguments about achieving economic regeneration and growth. Representation within supranational institutions remains an important mechanism for ensuring that nationalist interests are heard within the European policy-making process. Presence within the European Parliament and, for some parties, within the Council of Ministers, has allowed minority nationalist party politicians to project themselves as important participants in the policy-making process. The supranational arena has enabled minority nationalist parties to pursue new transnational and cross-border alliances that reinforce the presence of a nationalist/regionalist agenda at the supranational level. The significance of such networks for the ways in which minority nationalist parties position themselves on Europe is considered in the next section.

Co-operation and representation at the supranational level

If developments in European integration have not exerted a uniform influence on party attitudes over time, the case studies demonstrated that representation and co-operation on the supranational level played a more uniform role in reinforcing minority nationalist party attitudes towards Europe. This effect was highly significant in the three parties who were members of the EFA and who sat with the EFA group within the European Parliament. Only Corsica Nazione was exempt from this influence due to its infrequent transnational contacts and its failure to secure a presence within the European Parliament.

The effects of co-operation and representation at the supranational level can be summarised as follows. Firstly, membership of the EFA brought a number of practical benefits. The EFA has provided financial and campaigning resources for European election campaigns in different minority nations. In the case of the UPC, the Green/EFA alliance within the European Parliament facilitated the formation of a joint Green–EFA list in the French European Parliament elections in 1989. For parties not represented in the parliament, the EFA provided the mouthpiece for their interests; once elected, the EFA provides a ready-made organisational framework within which new representatives can take up their seat, and provides access to the parliament's deliberative and policy-making forums.

Secondly, the case studies demonstrated the strong socialisation effect to which Plaid Cymru, the BNG and the UPC were exposed within the EFA. This effect was particularly salient when these parties were directly represented within the European Parliament. The regionalist arguments developed by the EFA provided a new vocabulary and rhetoric to minority nationalist party articulations of their individual nationalist projects. The diffusion of a shared set of themes within the alliance brought added substance to previously abstract aspirations for some kind of a regional Europe. The framework provided by the EFA also facilitated the exchange of information and ideas about a whole range of European issues that had hitherto not been explored in detail by individual parties.

However, the degree to which this socialisation effect trickled down to, and was incorporated into, more general party thinking was not uniform. For Plaid Cymru, it was very easy to reconcile the European regionalist ideas propounded by the EFA with the party's ideological commitment to the idea of Wales as a European nation. This was much more difficult for the BNG since a strongly Europeanist symbolic discourse was at odds with the instinctive anti-Europeanism of the party's membership. The result was a clear disjuncture between different dimensions of the party's attitude towards European integration, as outlined above. The top-down effects of socialisation as a result of transnational co-operation are not, therefore, automatic. Rather, for such an effect to take place, certain conditions must be present in order to make the party receptive to these ideas. These conditions once again point to the role of other context and actor specific factors in influencing a party's attitude towards Europe.

So what? The implications for minority nations, minority nationalist parties and the EU

This study has examined the European attitudes of minority nationalist parties in three specific contexts. Its findings have challenged the prevailing scholarly portrayal of minority nationalist parties as the enthusiastic champions of European integration. Instead, minority nationalist party attitudes towards Europe have been demonstrated to be highly complex and contingent, as a result of a number of competing factors that shape the way European integration is perceived and understood by these actors. This chapter concludes by considering some of the broader implications of these findings. In particular, what can the findings of this study tell us more generally about the nature of politics in Wales, Galicia and Corsica as a result of minority nationalist mobilisation, minority nationalist parties as an object of study and the role of nationalism within EU studies?

The implications for politics in Wales, Corsica and Galicia

This study has argued that the linking of core nationalist demands with the transformative potential of European integration was key to the success of minority nationalist parties in Wales, Galicia and Corsica in creating a new nationalist political space within these territories. The fact that Plaid Cymru, the BNG and Corsica Nazione have become important political and electoral forces has had major implications for the structure of the political system in these different places, as well as for political dynamics within these systems.

Firstly, minority nationalist party mobilisation has constituted an important challenge to the internal structure of the state. The demands made by these parties have contributed towards pushing state authorities to undertake important

164 *Conclusions*

institutional reforms that have either created from scratch, or strengthened, a regional tier of government in these three places. Such decentralising reforms were not exclusively a response to the electoral growth of the three political forces examined in this study. In the UK and Spain, institutional reform was also in large part the result of pressure from other, more successful, minority nationalist actors elsewhere within the state's territory (Mitchell, 1998; Pérez-Nievas, 2006; Barberà and Barrio, 2006). In France, the process of regionalisation was also informed by the ideological preferences of different socialist governments, rather than being a direct response to the political demands and terrorist activism of different nationalist groups from the Corsican periphery (Loughlin and Seiler, 2001: 189). Nevertheless, the growing prominence of nationalist demands for self-determination in Wales, Galicia and Corsica throughout the 1980s and 1990s were important considerations that informed the decision taken by different state authorities at different times to create or enhance the regional tier of government in these three places.

Secondly, minority nationalist parties have had a major impact on the party systems within which they operate, both in terms of their core structures – such as the number and relative strength of parties – and the nature of the interaction between parties. Within the Welsh, Galician and Corsican political arenas, the presence of one or more minority nationalist parties competing within the regional party system has led to changes in the direction of party competition (with minority nationalist parties having chosen to moderate their programmes in order to compete with other, usually statewide, political parties for the median voter), the degree of competitiveness within the party system and the formulation of party strategies, including the patterns of coalitions between parties. As a result, regional political systems have become more differentiated from the statewide arena. At the same time, however, and in a more indirect manner, minority nationalist parties have contributed to the increasing interlinking of state and substate systems of party competition (Thorlakson, 2006: 39). This can be seen in at least two ways. Statewide parties have been forced to respond to the nationalist challenge by giving their programmes and organisations a more 'regional' face. The need to appeal to different electorates at different territorial levels has generated new tensions within some previously unified statewide political parties. At the same time, the entry of Plaid Cymru and the BNG into regional government in Wales and Galicia respectively has posed a new challenge for some statewide parties that can govern alone at the state level, but are constrained by coalition obligations at the regional level. In short, minority nationalist parties have contributed to making politics considerably more complex, as all political actors strive to adapt to the requirements of multilevel electoral politics.

Implications for the study of minority nationalist parties

This study also has important implications for the way in which minority nationalist parties are understood and studied. To date, scholars of minority nationalist parties have been mainly concerned with understanding what makes this party family different from other major party families. Significant effort has, accordingly, been dedicated to examining the conditions that gave rise to minority nationalist contestation, the electoral fortunes of minority nationalist parties, their organisations and support bases and, most importantly, the nature of their territorial demands. As a result of these efforts, there is now a substantial literature on the origins and distinctive features of minority nationalist parties and the key demands that they articulate.

This focus has been at the expense, however, of examining other important aspects of minority nationalist party politics that are not specific to this party family. This study has pointed to two ways in which minority nationalist parties can be said to be less distinctive, and more conventional, political actors than is usually acknowledged in the extant literature. Firstly, minority nationalist parties are not exclusively concerned with the core business of territorial politics. These parties also espouse other more conventional ideological values that complete these actors' projects for society, such as left–right values. This is important because this repertoire of values constitutes the prism through which minority nationalist parties perceive and respond to new issues that arise. To date, however, there is very little research on how these additional ideological values inform the nation-building projects that minority nationalist parties are engaged in. Particularly in light of the fact that an increasing number of minority nationalist parties are now in government in different places, and have to engage in policy making on a range of issues that go beyond the core business of territorial autonomy, a systematic examination of minority nationalist parties as more sophisticated ideological animals is long overdue.

Secondly, this study has demonstrated how minority nationalist party attitudes on a given issue are affected by party competitive pressures emanating from the political context in which they are active. Minority nationalist parties that move from the margins of a political system towards the centre ground, and those that alternate between government and opposition, will face different constraints on what they can say on a given issue. Such pressures are certainly not exclusive to minority nationalist parties. Research on other political party families has demonstrated that these are constraints that face any political party whose political and electoral status changes significantly within a political system (Deschouwer, 2008; Harmel, 1985; Heinisch, 2003; Müller-Rommel, 2002; Müller-Rommel and Pridham, 1991; Poguntke, 2002; Rihoux and Rüdig 2006).

As yet, however, scholars have paid very little attention to how such pressures of party competition impact upon the way in which minority nationalist parties articulate their goals, and the strategies that they formulate to meet these goals. Neither have scholars seriously attempted to answer questions about the degree to which, and in what ways, minority nationalists 'matter' in their respective political systems (for example, in terms of their impact on the territorial structure of the state and on political dynamics at different levels within the state). The Welsh, Galician and Corsican case studies presented in this study demonstrate that minority nationalist parties clearly do matter, in ways that have been outlined above. Scholars of minority nationalism would do well to draw on the theoretical and

166 *Conclusions*

empirical insights of a burgeoning literature on political parties and party systems in order to provide further systematic comparative analyses of the ways in which minority nationalist parties have been impacted by, and have themselves impacted upon, established political systems and dynamics.

Implications for the study of the EU

Finally, the findings of this study have important implications for the way in which the EU is understood and studied. In particular, they point to the importance of nationalism as a prominent force within European politics, even though to date scholars have not given sufficient attention to the precise ways in which this phenomenon shapes the identities and discourses of different actors within the EU.

The European project was originally conceived as a response to the horrors of war in Europe, and as a means of taming, or at least moderating, destructive nationalism (Rich, 1996: 21–22; Marks, 1999: 69). Many of the earliest theorists of European unity advocated supranational co-operation as a means of overcoming national rivalries and hostilities, and of fostering new shared understandings and loyalties (Scully, 2005: 46–48). The occasion of the fiftieth anniversary of the signing of the Treaty of Rome, celebrated on 25 March 2007, was an occasion to rejoice in the success of the EU in achieving the first of these goals, namely to bring peace to western Europe. However, the EU has failed to rid Europe of the emotive power of nationalism. At the beginning of the twenty-first century, there are no signs that nationalist ideology has lost its remarkable capacity to mobilise in defence of the nation's historical, political and cultural rights.

The EU's founding fathers not only underestimated the resilience of existing national identities, but also failed to anticipate the role of European integration in creating new spaces for the (re)discovery of alternative conceptualisations of nationhood. As European integration has put pressure on established systems of political, functional and identity structuring, new spaces have been created beyond the state for the reassertion of alternative claims to collective solidarity (Laffan, 1996; Bartolini, 2005). This study has examined one manifestation of this national assertiveness, namely by nationalist actors below the state. But there are also myriad other ways in which the EU has facilitated the articulation of competing narratives of nationhood. Those fearful of the decline of the nation-state have mobilised in opposition to Europe, whilst more extreme versions of nationalism have blamed European integration for facilitating immigration and undermining national solidarity. Other political actors and commentators have debated the prospects and/or desirability of the emergence of a European identity, either as a complement to or a replacement for pre-existing national identities.

From these observations, apart from the obvious conclusion that territorial politics remains highly prominent within the EU, there are two implications for the way in which the EU is studied. Firstly, scholars should take nationalism seriously as a phenomenon that continues to exert a strong and pervasive influence on how different actors perceive and understand the EU. This requires overcoming the prevalent view in many journalistic and political circles that 'nationalism only comes in small sizes and bright colours' (Billig, 1995: 6); it also requires a recognition that nationalism can assume myriad forms, and may not be immediately recognisable when hidden behind the language of patriotism or citizenship. Doing so paves the way for examining the explicit and implicit ways in which ideas about nationhood and national belonging frame the actions of various individuals and groups within the EU. The challenge for the researcher is thus to take these competing discourses of the nation in their own terms, and to understand how these different narratives of identity compete to shape the parameters of debates on 'What Europe?', 'How much Europe?' and 'Whose Europe?'.

Secondly, however, whilst European integration has provided a new arena within which different groups have been able to reassert and defend their collective identities as a basis for a new political order, it is far from clear how competing claims for territorial authority can be reconciled within the emerging European order. European integration has the process of fundamentally restructuring the relationship between territory, identity and political authority established within the framework of the sovereign state system. But it remains unclear where this process will end, and what new configuration will be proposed between these fundamental components of any legitimate political order.

As the EU continues to debate the answers to difficult questions about democracy, legitimacy, accountability and transparency, however, everyday politics carries on. Political actors must balance their normative demands with pragmatic strategies for advancing their goals within a complex multilevel political system. As this study has argued, minority nationalist parties will always have a vested interest in shaping the evolution of a future EU in order to make sure that there is a better fit between the 'national' and the 'political' in Europe. At the same time, however, minority nationalist parties must engage in the day-to-day task of building the nation within the territory itself, if claims to national self-determination are ever going to be taken seriously within the supranational arena. And this means taking the practical opportunities for, and constraints on, decision making within the national territory seriously. Scholars of EU politics would do well to do likewise, in order to better understand the challenges of making and shaping policy within an increasingly complex multilevel European polity.

Appendix
List of interviews

The interviews conducted for this study are listed below, according to party and in alphabetical order by surname. The dates on which interviews were conducted have been noted in the main text, and are not noted here in order to preserve the anonymity of interviewees.

Plaid Cymru

Cynog Dafis, Plaid Cymru MP (1992–2000) and Assembly Member (AM) (1999–2003).
Jonathan Edwards, assistant to Rhodri Glyn Thomas AM.
Jill Evans, spokesperson for international affairs and MEP (1999–present).
Lowri Gwilym, ex-policy development officer with responsibility for European affairs.
Dafydd Elis Thomas, President of Plaid Cymru (1984–1991), Presiding Officer of the National Assembly for Wales.
Rhodri Glyn Thomas, AM and Minister for Culture (2007–present).
Simon Thomas, Plaid Cymru MP (2001–2005), Plaid Cymru special advisor in the National Assembly for Wales.
Dafydd Trystan, Chief Executive of Plaid Cymru (2002–2007).
Eurig Wyn, Plaid Cymru MEP (1999–2004).
Ieuan Wyn Jones, Plaid Cymru leader in the National Assembly for Wales, Deputy First Minister (2007–present).

Bloque Nacionalista Galego

Carlos Aymerich, BNG deputy in the Spanish Congress (1996–2000), BNG spokesperson in the Galician Parliament (2005–present).
Francisco Jorquera, executive co-ordinator, BNG representative in the Spanish Senate (2004–2008).
Domingos Merino, ex-Secretary General of Unidade Galega, BNG representative in the Galician Parliament (until 2005).
Ana Miranda, assistant in the European Parliament (1999–2004), member of BNG National Council.

Camilo Nogueira, ex-leader of Esquerga Galega and Unidade Galega, MEP (1999–2004)
Encarna Otero, BNG spokesperson for international affairs.
Alberte Rodríguez Feixóo, Secretary General of Esquerda Nacionalista, BNG representative in the Galician Parliament (until 2005).
Enrique Rodriquez Peña, Secretary General of PNG-PG, BNG representative in the Galician Parliament (until 2005).
Alfredo Suárez Canal, BNG parliamentary spokesperson (until 2005).
Xesus Veiga Buxán, Secretary General of Iznar, BNG representative in the Galician Parliament (until 2005).

Corsican nationalist movement

Francois Alfonsi, ex-Secretary General UPC, senior member of PNC.
Jean Christophe Angelini, leader of PNC, representative in the Corsican Assembly.
Leo Battesti, ex-FLNC leader, founder of MPA.
Jean Biancucci, ex-aNC leader, member of A Chjama, representative in the Corsican Assembly.
Christine Colonna, member of Corsica Nazione, representative in the Corsican Assembly.
Pierre Poggioli, ex-FLNC leader, founder of ANC.
Max Simeoni, leader of UPC, MEP (1989–1994).
Jean-Guy Talamoni, leader of Corsica Nazione, representative in the Corsican Assembly.

Notes

1 Introduction: minority nationalist parties and European integration

1 Referred to as regionalist parties in their study.
2 See, for example, the case studies in the edited volume by De Winter *et al.* (2006a).
3 Despite the formal demand for 'independence', however, the party has been quick to argue that such a goal does not envisage Wales first becoming a fully sovereign state as a precondition to its entry into the EU, since sovereignty in the classical sense is no longer meaningful in the twenty-first century (Elias, 2006). The implications of Plaid Cymru's constitutional ambitions are examined in more detail in Chapter 3.
4 One exception is the analysis by Chari *et al.* (2004) of the changes in the Lega Nord's position on the European issue. The authors develop and evaluate different hypotheses to explain the Lega Nord's Euro-scepticism, and find that domestic-level politics provide the most powerful explanation of this change in attitude towards Europe since the late 1990s.
5 After the 1979 European elections, the members of the EFA formed a technical group with some extreme left parties. In the following legislature (1984–1989), the Rainbow Group was formed jointly with the Greens. After the 1989 elections, the Green parties formed their own political group, leaving the EFA members as the dominant force within a reconstructed Rainbow Group (Lynch, 1998: 200). Disastrous results in the 1994 European elections and the loss of all but three of its MEPs led the EFA to join the French and Italian radicals to form the European Radical Alliance Group. The EFA resumed its alliance with the Greens in the 1999–2004 legislature, and this alliance has been reconstituted in the current legislature.
6 For example, France and the UK abstained from voting in favour of the Charter on Regional or Minority Languages in 1992, with their abstentions counting as negative votes that contributed to the rejection of the proposal. They also delayed signing up to the charter, with France doing so in May 1999 and the UK in March 2000. While the UK and Spain eventually ratified the charter in March and April 2001 respectively, France has yet to do so since its constitutional court declared the document to be contrary to the French constitution in 1999.
7 See, for example, the collection of case studies in De Winter *et al.* (2006a).
8 One exception is the study by Lynch (1996), which examines how minority nationalist parties in Scotland, Wales, Brittany and Flanders developed linkages between their own nationalist political projects and European integration from the 1920s to 1995. However, the study is largely descriptive, and does not develop a systematic comparative framework for analysing minority nationalist party attitudes towards European integration. Moreover, the study is over ten years old, and thus can tell us nothing about changes in minority nationalist party attitudes towards developments in European integration over the last decade.

2 Theorising the European attitudes of minority nationalist parties

1 For a summary of this literature, see Hix *et al.*, (2003).
2 According to Mair (2000), European integration might be said to have a direct impact on national party systems if (i) new parties have been established that either add to, or substitute, the number already in contention; and (ii) if the way in which the parties interact with each other changes, either by modifying the ideological distance separating the relevant parties, or by encouraging the emergence of wholly new European-centred dimensions of competition. Mair concludes that there is very little evidence of any direct impact on these features of party systems, as it is difficult to attribute evidence of party-system change exclusively to the impact of Europeanisation as such.
3 These referendums revealed a gulf between elite and popular sentiments towards Europe. The French electorate voted to reject the European Constitution by 54.8%, followed a few days later by a more emphatic rejection by the Dutch electorate with 61.5% voting 'no'.
4 The participation of government leaders in EU forums may strain relations with the party on particular policies, and may lead to changes in the nature of party–government relations over time. Ladrech explains the logic of such a change as follows: 'Party–government relations on EU matters may become "push–pull" in nature. Government is "pushed" by the party to maximise positions on matters close to the party programme . . . [whereas] Government is "pulled" by the party to minimalist positions on institutional change . . . that run counter to notions of state sovereignty' (p. 398).
5 For further categorisations of usages of the term see Olsen (2002) and Featherstone (2003). Radaelli and Pasquier (2006) provide a useful overview of the state of the art in terms of the conceptualisation of Europeanisation.
6 One exception is the analysis by De Winter and Gómez-Reino (2002) of the Europeanisation of the goals and strategies of nationalist and regionalist parties, which focuses on the evolution and consolidation of the EFA as a new European party family.
7 As opposed to political parties whose ambitions and political project are statewide, but for various reasons they have been unable to realise this breadth of appeal and are therefore geographically limited in their support base.
8 This distinction by Kopecký and Mudde (2002) is inspired, in turn, by Easton's (1965) work on different forms of support for political regimes. Conti (2003) has argued that the application of Kopecký and Mudde's distinction (diffuse versus specific support for European integration) is not appropriate for political parties in western Europe, since it is difficult to find parties that do not have a vision of Europe of some kind, and therefore the idea of diffuse support for European integration – or support for European integration in principle – becomes redundant. The reasoning put forward for this rejection is that most political parties in western Europe have been around for a sufficiently long time to take European integration as a given, therefore rejecting Europe completely is no longer a policy that makes sense (p. 22). Only the specific nature of European integration is subject to differing partisan evaluations. This may be true of long-established mainstream political parties in western Europe. However, Kopecký and Mudde's analysis demonstrates that for political parties of more recent creation (such as radical extremist parties), opposition to the very idea of Europe is a policy often espoused. Such parties reject both the idea of Europe and the specific project of European integration (2002: 316–17). Since many minority nationalist parties are also young (having been established in the 1970s and 1980s) and are often established as protest parties vis-à-vis the state-dominated status quo, it is necessary to allow for the possibility that such parties may also assume Euro-rejectionist positions. For this reason, the distinction between diffuse and specific support for European integration is an appropriate one for the conceptualisation of minority nationalist party attitudes towards European integration.

9 The major party families that these studies refer to are the Conservative, Liberal, Christian Democratic and Socialist party families.
10 As Capoccia (2002) notes, the term 'anti-system' has been subject to substantial conceptual stretching since being first employed by Sartori in his analysis of party systems in the 1960s and 1970s (Sartori, 1976/2005). The idea of an anti-system party is used here to refer to a party that 'does not share the basic values of the political order within which it operates' (Sartori, 1976/2005: 133), values which other political parties within the political system embrace. This does not necessarily mean opposition to democracy *per se*, but rather to the nature of the extant political system (Capoccia, 2002).
11 These are: the European People's Party and European Democrats (EPP-ED), the Party of European Socialists (PES), the European Liberal and Democrat Reform Party (ELDR), the Greens/European Free Alliance (Greens/EFA), the Union for European Nations (UEN), the European United Left/Nordic Green Left (GUE), the Independence/Democracy group (ID), and the Identity, Tradition and Sovereignty group (ITS).

3 Wales: Plaid Cymru

1 Traditionally, Plaid Cymru's leaders had always rejected defining the party in classic left–right terms. The party's nationalism was conceptualised as an ideology that did not fit neatly into this conventional ideological dichotomy. The political ideas usually associated with left or right political agendas were also considered to be inadequate for Wales's socio-economic and political situation. For a more detailed discussion of Plaid Cymru's ambivalent relationship with socialism, see Wyn Jones (2007, ch. 6).
2 For more on the changing attitudes of the Labour Party towards European integration, see George and Haythorne (1996) and Daniels (1998).
3 The issue of devolution for Scotland and Wales was first mooted in the late 1960s, when the unexpected success of Welsh and Scottish nationalists in a series of Westminster by-elections pushed Harold Wilson's Labour government to set up a commission of inquiry into the relationship between Westminster and the nations and regions of the UK (Lynch, 2002; Wigley, 1992: 73–83). After the October 1974 general election, the narrow majority of the Labour Party in the House of Commons allowed the SNP and Plaid Cymru to exchange parliamentary support for the government for an agreement to hold a referendum on devolution to Scotland and Wales.
4 Such was the conclusion of Plaid Cymru's own analysis of its political situation at the end of the 1970s; see, for example, the discussion in Jones (1985).
5 The negative effects of European integration on the Welsh economy are discussed repeatedly in the party's monthly publication *Welsh Nation* during the years 1980–1983 (*Welsh Nation*, 1980a, b; 1982a, b; 1983a, b).
6 This argument was set out by, among others, the party's leader at the time, Dafydd Elis Thomas. See Elis Thomas (1987).
7 Dafydd Wigley, the president of Plaid Cymru by 1994, also stood as a candidate in the 1994 European Parliament elections.
8 In fact, the party did not perform badly at all; Plaid Cymru's 12.9% share of the Welsh vote was an improvement on the 1984 European Parliament elections, and was significantly better than the 7.3% of the Welsh vote polled by the party in the general election two years previously.
9 Interestingly, this phrase is used in the party's propaganda for the 1989 European Parliament elections as the basis for 'self-government within the European Community to safeguard the social and economic life of each community, to defend the values that they represent and to preserve the Welsh language that has expressed those values for nearly two thousand years'. See Plaid Cymru (1989: 2).
10 These policy areas included education, the environment, leisure, culture, the Welsh language, health, transport and tourism, agriculture, town planning, economic development,

industry, local government, housing and social services. For fuller details, see Osmond (1998).
11 Of the assembly's sixty seats, forty represented individual constituencies and were elected using the same first-past-the-post system as used for Westminster elections. The remaining twenty were selected from party lists using a proportional 'alternative member system', and represented five larger regional constituencies within Wales.
12 The party still uses this argument as a justification for Welsh membership of the EU. For example, 'many nations smaller than Wales are already fully independent members of the international community. We want our nation to be treated equally' (Plaid Cymru, 2006: 14).
13 In its evidence submitted to the convention, Plaid Cymru called for the recognition of the role of nations and historic regions in the EU, the incorporation of the Charter of Human Rights, a definition of the subsidiarity principle to encompass regional and local levels of government, more involvement for regional governments in European policy making, the recognition of the principle of 'internal enlargement' to allow nations and regions to become full members of the EU in their own right, and direct access to the European Court of Justice. See Plaid Cymru (2003).
14 See, for example, Melding (2003). A more detailed account of the adaptation of political parties in Wales to post-devolution politics can be found in Osmond (2003).
15 This is the suggestion of the document by Thomas (2003).
16 For an account of public attitudes towards European integration in Britain as a whole, see Spiering (2004).
17 Since 1933, Plaid Cymru's logo was three green peaks, representing Plaid Cymru's key values of self-government, cultural prosperity and economic prosperity. More recently, a red dragon was added onto the three peaks. The new logo is based on a yellow poppy, and the party will no longer use the word 'Cymru', Welsh for Wales, referring to itself simply as 'Plaid' (although its full name remains 'Plaid Cymru – The Party of Wales').

4 Galicia: the Bloque Nacionalista Galego

1 'Galeguismo' is defined by Beramendi and Núñez Seixas (1996: 17) as the emergence of a political agenda that conceived of Galicia as a distinct territorial identity. Within this general definition of galeguismo, one can further distinguish between cultural, political and, eventually, nationalist conceptualisations of Galicia as a distinct territorial, cultural, ethnic or political entity (Fernández Baz, 2003: 29–30).
2 For a more detailed account of the historical origins of Galician nationalism, see Beramendi and Núñez-Seixas (1996), Beramendi (1997) and Máiz (1996).
3 Other parties active during the 1970s originated from ideological and strategic dissent within the UPG. These included the Partido Obrero Galego (POG), created in October 1977 in opposition to the UPG's uncompromising attitude towards the proposed constitutional model for Spain; the POG would change its name to Esquerda Galega (EG) in May 1981 under the leadership of Camilo Nogueira. The more explicitly independentist Partido Galego do Proletariado (PGP) shared the UPG's Marxist–Leninist ideology but also advocated the creation of an armed branch.
4 These were Galicia Ceibe, Asamblea Nacional-Popular Galega (AN-PG) and Arco de Vella. Parties that did not participate in the formation of the BNG included, among others, EG and the PG.
5 Other parties who began negotiations withdrew at various stages in the deliberations in disagreement with the model proposed for the BNG. While the PSG also withdrew from the BNG, a small core of its members who preferred to stay within the BNG formed their own group, Coalición Socialista, which remains one of the component parties of the BNG.

6 The PSG and the EG joined forces in 1984 to form the Partido Socialista Galega-Esquerda Galega (PSG-EG).
7 In the wake of the definitive decline of the statewide Unión de Centro Democrático (UCD) during the 1980s, a certain number of ex-UCD adherents joined forces with the right-wing nationalist party, the PG, rebranding itself as Coalición Galega (CG). However, internal tensions led to the PG's withdrawal from the right-wing coalition in 1987. The PG subsequently fused with a further group from within the CG, Partido Galego Nacionalista, to create the Partido Galego Nacionalista-Partido Galeguista (PNG-PG) in December 1988.
8 PSG-EG renamed itself Unidade Galega (UG) in March 1993.
9 Composed of previously independent members of the BNG, the EN was first established as a 'current of thought' inside the BNG in 1992, and was established as a political party in 1995.
10 It should be noted that, in spite of this consolidation process, a number of smaller nationalist groups and associations remained outside the BNG, such as the Frente Popular Galega and Nós-Unidade Popular (Nós-UP). However, as these parties have been, and remain, marginal within the Galician political system, they have been excluded from this study.
11 See, for example, the special edition of *A Nosa Terra* (2003).
12 For an analysis of the origins and development of the Celtic roots of Galician nationalism, see Máiz (1984).
13 In Galicia, support for the Spanish Constitution in the referendum was 90.1% in favour, with a mere 5.9% against (turnout 50.2%). In the referendum on the ratification of the Galician Statute of Autonomy in 1981, 73.1% of those who voted did so in favour, with 26.9% against (turnout 29%).
14 The newspaper *Faro de Vigo*, for example, described 13 June 1985, the day of the signing of Spain's accession treaty to the EEC, as 'a day on which our country lives a historic event, a positive event that creates hope that the frontier of difference that has separated one part of Europe and another will be brought down' (*Faro de Vigo*, 1985).
15 In June 1987, European Parliament elections were held in Spain and Portugal to provide these two new members of the EEC with representatives in the European Parliament following their accession in the previous year, after which date elections followed the normal five-yearly cycle as elsewhere in western Europe.
16 The stabilisation and simplification of the Galician political system, in comparison to the volatility of the earliest years of Galician autonomy, also contributed to the BNG's electoral growth (Vilas Nogueira *et al.*, 1994).
17 Manuel Fraga Iribarne, originally from Vilalba in Galicia, held several posts in Franco's government. At the beginning of the process of transition to democracy, Fraga joined other former Francoist ministers to form the right-wing party Alianza Popular (AP). The party's disastrous results in the 1986 Spanish general elections led to its refoundation as the Partido Popular (PP) under the presidency of José María Aznar. Fraga returned to Galicia as president of the PPdeG; he provided the strong personality necessary to unify the hitherto heterogeneous preferences and strategies of the Galician branch of the AP (Lagares Díez, 2003: 70).
18 The name 'Galeusca' was first used to mark the alliance between the three nationalist tendencies formalised by the Triple Alliance of 1923, leading to the Galeuzca Pact of 1933. It was motivated by the shared desire to articulate demands for a confederal state during the Spanish Second Republic. During the early years of the Franco regime, a political review bearing the same name, *Galeuzca*, was published by Galician, Catalan and Basque nationalists in exile in Latin America and continental Europe. See *A Nosa Terra* (1980b).
19 Alone or in coalition, the PNV has been in government in the Basque Country since 1980 and the CiU in Catalonia from 1980 to 2003. Both parties have been represented in the Spanish Congress of Deputies since 1977.

Notes   175

20 Up until 1994, Spain had sixty seats in the European Parliament. Before the 1994 elections, this number was increased to sixty-four. The number of Spanish seats was reduced again in the run-up to the 2004 elections to fifty-four seats.
21 In 1987, the BNG was the only nationalist party to present a Galician-only list; the PSG-EG participated in the coalition Esquerda dos Pobos alongside Unión del Poble Valenciá, Entesa dels Nacionalistes d'Esquerra de Catalunya, Partido Socialista de Mallorca and Partido Socialista de Menorca. The PNG, on the other hand, participated in a list called Por la Europa de los Pueblos jointly with EA, Esquerda Republicana and the PNV. A similar pattern of alliances was repeated in the 1989 European Parliament elections.
22 Relations with HB were formally broken off in 1987 due to its unacceptable links to the Basque terrorist group Euskadi 'Ta Askatasuna (ETA).
23 An initial text proposed by the executive committee proposing a negative vote in the forthcoming referendum, and a second text produced by Esquerda Nacionalista in favour of a 'critical yes' position, were circulated to all the BNG's local branches. Once these branches had voted in favour of one or other position, the BNG's national council then adopted a final official voting intention in the referendum.
24 On a turnout of 42.3%, 81.3% of those who voted did so in favour of the constitution, with only 12.2% voting against (abstention 6.5%).
25 Camilo Nogueira's party, Unidade Galega, was disbanded in September 2003, with its members remaining as a 'current of thought' within the BNG.
26 Within the Galician government, the BNG has responsibility for the following policy portfolios: rural affairs, culture and sport, housing, equality and well-being, and innovation and industry.
27 Such is the argument put forward, for instance, in an interview with Francisco Jorquera, the co-ordinator of the BNG's executive, in *BeNeGa* (2006b).

5 Corsica: a comparison of moderate and radical Corsican nationalist parties

1 In the 1920s, a group of journalists and intellectuals sought to create a 'corsiste' movement which led to the creation of the Partitu Corsu d'Azione in 1923, which became the Partitu Corsu Autonomistu in 1927.
2 Corsica was under Genoese rule until 1659, when control, and eventual sovereignty, was handed over to France (Caratini, 2003).
3 This was especially the case in the agricultural sector, where repatriated French Algerians were given preference in the sale of newly reclaimed and very fruitful agricultural land. In these zones of new economic development, Algerians soon outnumbered native Corsicans in terms of ownership of large and profit-making farms and vineyards (Crettiez, 1999: 27).
4 The Hudson Institute, based in New York, had been commissioned by the French government to produce a study of economic and social development in Corsica, as a basis for the development of a management plan for the island. A leaked copy of the study set out the different options for the future of the island in the following unambiguous terms: 'Accelerate the disappearance of the Corsican cultural identity by encouraging a new wave of massive immigration . . . [or] conserve and restore the Corsican cultural identity and traditions through the development of its own endogenous potential' (quoted in Crettiez, 1999: 24).
5 The public front of the FLNC underwent several name changes during the 1980s. The CCN was dissolved by the French authorities on 21 September 1983 due to its close links to the FLNC. It was replaced by the Muvimentu Corsu per l'Autodeterminazione (MCA), which was also declared illegal in January 1987. A third political front was created in June 1987, A Cuncolta Naziunalista (aCN).
6 Other groups to have emerged in the late 1990s and early 2000, such as Rinnovu Naziunale, A Chjama, A Manca Naziunale and A Presenza Naziunale, can be grouped within

the moderate tendency, the majority of which have either emerged from the UPC or have abandoned radical nationalist politics in favour of a more moderate interpretation of the nationalist struggle.
7 In March 1996, the MPA declared itself in favour of autonomy and the end of violence, and dissolved the FLNC 'canal habituel'. The legal party was itself disbanded in 1999, with its members largely joining the newly created Rinnovu Naziunale (RN), a party set up by dissidents from Corsica Nazione, ANC and UPC. Opponents to the disappearance of the MPA opted to created yet another group, Corsica Viva, who established its own clandestine group called FLNC du 5 Mai.
8 These parties included the ANC, Chjama per l'Indipendenza, Corsica Viva, Corsica Nazione, Cuncolta Indipendentista, Associu per a Suvranita, Partitu per i Indipendenza, and I Verdi Corsi. Notably absent from this alliance was the UPC.
9 Among the groups making up the FLNC 'Union des combatants' were FLNC Historique, FLNC du 5 Mai, Resistenza, Clandestinu and Fronte Ribellu.
10 The participants in Unione Naziunale included Indipendenza-Corsica Nazione, PNC, A Chjama, ANC and Partitu Sucialistu per l'Indipendenza (PSI). The latter two parties left the alliance in March 2005 in disagreement with the institutional strategy adopted by the group.
11 Many references are made to the United Nations and UNESCO as possible forums that might be sympathetic to the demands of moderate Corsican nationalism. See *Arritti* (1986).
12 In 2002, it was proposed that these two insular constituencies should be merged to form a single Corsican constituency, a move widely interpreted as an attempt to undermine the stranglehold of the clans on representation at the statewide level. However, these proposals were rejected by the Corsican electorate in a referendum on 6 July 2003.
13 The original electoral rules specified an electoral threshold of 1.6% to enter the Corsican Assembly. However, extreme political instability within the Assembly after the first round of elections led to new elections being held in 1984, with the electoral threshold being raised to 5%.
14 More specifically, the Statut Joxe created an executive of seven members with new responsibilities for economic and social development, spatial management, the promotion of culture, and improved educational and linguistic provision. On 9 May 1991, the French Constitutional Court declared Article 1 of the legislation – which referred to the existence of a 'Corsican people' – unconstitutional, although all other provisions were approved.
15 Although Poggioli (1996: 26) also claims that the relative youth of the party, its lack of organisational structures and a weak support base meant the party simply was not ready to undertake such a task.
16 Although it is not clear at which date the UPC officially joined the organisation. Interviews suggested that the UPC retained observer status until around 1984, at which point it became a full member. However, no official data is available to confirm this. The PNC took over the UPC's membership of the EFA upon the latter's dissolution in 2002 (Dominici, 2004).
17 This list has been presented at all European Parliament elections since 1994.
18 One interviewee attributed this lack of co-operation to the fact that minority nationalism in, for example, the French Basque Country, Alsace and Brittany, had very little in common with the historical experiences and evolution of Corsican nationalism. This lack of common ground made defining a common nationalist agenda a very difficult task (interview, 16 March 2004).
19 For example, language schools to teach Corsican and a co-operative bank to finance economic activities.
20 Crettiez (1999: 159–63) argues that the FLNC's moderation in practice was also evident in the limits of the revolutionary model that inspired the movement's strategy of

violence. The notion of a 'logique de guerre' associated with Third World liberation struggles and which envisaged a full military confrontation with the state, was rejected by the FLNC in favour of a much narrower 'political' definition of the Corsican problem, which justified the use of violence as a political resource for political ends – the legal and political recognition of the Corsican people – rather than as an end in itself. This translated into the prioritised targeting of highly symbolic representations of the French state's insular presence – police stations, court houses and civil service buildings – and property owned by foreign citizens, as opposed to the blind violence that risked civilian casualties adopted by other national liberation movements, such as the IRA (Northern Ireland) and ETA (Basque Country).

21 See, for example, Poggioli (1996: 96) and ANC (1990).
22 Article 74 of the French Constitution allows the creation of special legislative statutes, institutions and competencies for France's overseas territories. Designation as a Territoire d'Outre Mer (renamed Collectivité d'Outre Mer after constitutional revision in 2003) would give Corsica the same status as the islands of French Polynesia, Mayotte, Saint Pierre et Miquelon and Wallis et Fauna.
23 Thus, for example, the two dominant clans in Corsican politics and society in the latter half of the twentieth century, headed by François Giacobbi and Jean-Paul Rocca Serra, aligned themselves with the French statewide parties on the left and right of the political spectrum, namely the Movement des Radicaux de Gauche (MRG) and Rassemblement pour la République (RPR) – later to be called L'Union pour un Mouvement Populaire (UMP) – respectively. See Briquet (1997: 160–62).
24 See, for example, the so-called 'Rapport Glavany' produced at the behest of the French Parliament in 1998 (Assemblée Nationale, 1998); also Follorou and Nouzille (2004).
25 Corsica was classified as an Objective 1 region under the first programme of the reformed structural funds (1989–1993), and received 138 million ecus. In the subsequent budgetary programme (1994–1999), the island saw its allocation of Objective 1 funds nearly doubled to 250 million ecus. See Le Monde (1999).
26 These included the proposal to teach the Corsica language as part of the primary school curriculum.
27 Whilst 50.8% of French voters voted 'yes' to the ratification of the TEU, only 42.4% of Corsican voters did the same.
28 The survey was conducted by the company BVA on behalf of the French newspaper, *Paris Match*. A random sample of 505 Corsicans were interviewed. The full results of the survey can be found in *Paris Match* (1991).
29 As for the 1991 survey, a random sample of 505 Corsicans was interviewed. For the full results, see *Paris Match* (1998).
30 The programme includes Corsica, Sardinia and the Balearics, and was originally established as a 'durable space of co-operation for the exchange of experiences and the promotion of common interests within the European Union' (quoted in Lefevre, 2000: 304).
31 For the budgetary period 2007–2013, Corsica continues to receive funding under the objective 'competitiveness and employment' of the European Regional Development Fund. The sum earmarked for Corsica equates to €148,88 million (Ministry of the Economy, Finance and Employment, 2006).

Bibliography

Primary sources

ANC (1990) *Pruposti Pulitichi*. Ajaccio: ANC.
A Nosa Terra (1980a) '¿Por qué xurdeu e a quen serve a CEE?', 15 January 1980, p. 9.
—— (1980b) 'Galeuzca: as súas bases', 29 May 1980, p. 6.
—— (1980c) 'A política agraria no mercado común', 19 September 1980, p. 9.
—— (1980d) 'Crónica política', 14 November 1980, p. 5.
—— (1981) 'A pesca galega e as licencias para o gran sol', 18 February 1981, p. 9.
—— (1982) 'Galiza e a CEE (I)', 5 November 1982, p. 9.
—— (1984) 'Por qué os labregos nos opomos á entrada na CEE e á política do PSOE', 6 December 1984, p. 7.
—— (1985a) 'A mercado comun, negócio ruinoso para Galiza', 13 April 1985, p. 5.
—— (1985b), 'A ruralización, economia sumergida e o paro', 18 July 1985, p. 14.
—— (1985c) 'Galiza en órbita ascendente: do mercado comun español ao mercado comun europeu', 18 July 1985, p. 9.
—— (1987a) 'Acta Única Europea', 10 September 1987, p. 8.
—— (1987b) 'Pésie á falla de discrepancias visíbeis non foi posible o acordo PNG, PSG-EG, BNG', 23 April 1987, p. 5.
—— (1988) 'Entrevista: Camilo Nogueira', 17 November 1988, p. 11.
—— (1989) 'Nengunha política regional poderá menguar os desequilíbrios causados pola liberación de capitais', 8 June 1989, p. 2.
—— (1992) 'Maastricht (a CEE) inviabel. O BNG (non embargantes) impotente', 26 November 1992, p. 14.
—— (1994) 'Domingos Merino: "A entrada de UG no BNG non convén á estratéxia do centralismo"', 21 July 1994, p. 8.
—— (1995a) 'PP, PSOE e IU pensan o mesmo da UE, todos dan por boa a integración', 6 April 1995, p. 3.
—— (1995b), 'Europa', 15 June 1995, p. 8.
—— (2001a) 'Encrucillada na Unión Europea', 24 May 2001, p. 12.
—— (2001b) 'O Euro será moeda de referencia internacional, xunto co Dólar', 13 December 2001, p. 2.
—— (2001c) ' Buscan alternativas para consultar os fondos da UE', 13 December 2001, p. 6.
—— (2003) '25 de xullo: Galiza nación Europea', 24 July 2003, pp. 1–16.
—— (2004) 'Galiza e a UE', 20 May 2004, p. 10.
Arritti (1972) 'Corse – France – Europe', 6 July 1972, p. 3.
—— (1977a) 'Les grandes lignes da la lutte future', 27 August 1977, p. 4.

—— (1977b) 'Contacts internationaux du UPC', 11 November 1977, p. 5.
—— (1978) 'L'UPC à Bruxelles', 27 December 1978, p. 5.
—— (1984a) 'L'UPC et les élections Européennes', 24 May 1979.
—— (1984b) 'L'intervention de L. Alfonsi au Congres de l'Union Valdotaine', 29 November 1984, p. 7.
—— (1986) 'Propositions sur le terrain international', 21 August 1986, p. 7.
—— (1987a), 'La Corse et l'enjeu europeen', 26 February 1987, p. 5.
—— (1987b) 'Après bientôt deux années', 16 April 1987, p. 3.
—— (1990) 'Positions nationalistes', 14 September 1990, p. 3.
—— (1991a) 'Qu'est-ce que l'Europe? Que peut-elle être ?' 9 March 1991, p. 3.
—— (1991b) 'Editorial de Max Simeoni', 24 May 1991, p. 2.
—— (1994) 'La liste Régions et Peuples Solidaires', 5 May 1994, p. 3.
—— (1996a) 'UPC/LLN: Rapports démocratiques contre rapports de force', 21 March 1996, p. 6.
—— (1996b) 'Editorial de Max Simeoni', 27 June 1996, p. 2.
—— (2005) 'Auropa: Avvene', 7 March 2005, p. 1.
Assemblée Nationale (1998) *Rapport Fait au Nom de la Commission d'Enquête sur l'Utilisation des Fonds Publics et la Gestion des Services Publics en Corse*. Online. Available at www.assembleenationale.fr/11/dossiers/corse.asp (accessed 15 June 2004).
BeNeGa (2006a) 'O nacionalismo transforma xa o campo galego', No. 14, May 2006, p. 4.
—— (2006b) 'Avanzamos no primeiro ano de Goberno, pero Galiza necesita máis poder político', No. 15, June 2006, p. 6.
BNG (1982) *Programa Político e Organizativo. I Asamblea, 26–27 September 1982.* Santiago de Compostela: BN-PG.
—— (1985) *Programa Electoral do BNG. Balance da Situación de Galicia: Análise e Alternativas.* Santiago de Compostela: BNG.
—— (1989) *Ponencias e Discursos. IV Asamblea, 11–12 March 1989.* Santiago de Compostela: BNG.
—— (1991) *Enerxia Alternativa. Ponéncias V Asamblea Nacional, 25–27 January 1991.* Santiago de Compostela: BNG.
—— (1992) *O Tratado da Union Europea (TUE) Asinado en Maästricht. Análise e Posición Política do Bloque Nacionalista Galego.* Santiago de Compostela: BNG.
—— (1994) *Programma. Eleccións Europeas 1994.* Santiago de Compostela: BNG.
—— (1997) *Ponencia Política. VII Asamblea, 14–15 December 1991.* Santiago de Compostela: BNG.
—— (1998) *Galiza Sairá Gañando con Intelixéncia e Ilusión. VIII Asamblea Nacional, 27–8 June 1998.* Santiago de Compostela: BNG.
—— (1999) *Galiza con Voz Própria en Europa. Programa Eleitoral.* Santiago de Compostela: BNG.
—— (2003) *XI Asemblea Nacional do BNG, 22–23 November 2003.* Santiago de Compostela: BNG.
—— (2004a) *Galiza: Unha Nación Europea.* Electoral Manifesto for the European Parliamentary Elections, 23 June 2004. Santiago de Compostela: BNG.
—— (2004b) 'O BNG recomenda o non ao Tratado Europeo dende o seu inequívoco si a Europe', press release, 18 December 2004.
—— (2005) *Estatuto de Galiza.* Santiago de Compostela: BNG.
—— (2007) 'Anxo Quintana asegura que as forzas políticas que compoñen Galeuscat serán decisivas para decidir quen vai sentar na Moncloa', press release, 15 September 2007. Available at www.bng-galiza.org/galeuscat (accessed 23 October 2007).

BN-PG (1977) *Bases Constitucionais pra a Participación da Nación Galega nun Pacto Federal, e de Goberno Provisorio Galego.* Santiago de Compostela: BN-PG.

Corscia (2005) 'La division nationaliste', May 2005, p. 34.

—— (2007a) 'L'unité des nationalistes est soluble dans les urnes', No. 95, August 2007, no page number.

—— (2007b) 'On prend les mêmes, ils se divisent', No. 96, September 2007, no page number.

Corsica Nazione Independente (2006) 'Sarkozy: une visite pour rien', press release, 27 April 2006. Online. Avaliable at www.unita-naziunale.org/portail/sarkozy-corse-flnc.htm (accessed 26 November 2006).

Dafis, C. (2001) 'Wales in an expanding Europe', Speech given at unknown location, 16 November 2001.

—— (2003) 'Dyfodol Plaid Cymru: Datganiadau i'w Trafod', document presented to the Plaid Cymru National Council, November 2003.

—— (2005) *Mab y Pregethwr,* Talybont: Y Lolfa.

Davies, D.J. (1931/1958) *Towards Welsh Freedom*, Cardiff: Plaid Cymru.

Elis Thomas, D. (1979), 'Foreword', in G. Miles and R. Griffiths, *Socialism for the Welsh People,* Cardiff: Cleglen Publications, p. 3–4.

—— (1987) 'Strategy paper for the European Elections', paper presented to the Plaid Cymru National Council, 28 November 1987.

—— (1989) 'Strategy Paper for 1989 European Elections', paper prepared for unknown meeting.

Evans, G. (1967) *Gwynfor yn y Senedd*, Cardiff: Plaid Cymru.

Evans, J. (1997) 'Wales and Maastricht', discussion paper presented at the Plaid Cymru National Council, 26 September 1997.

Faro de Vigo (1985) Title unknown, 13 June 1985, p. 2.

Fernán-Vello, M.A. and Pillado Mayor, F. (1989) *A Nación Incesante. Conversas con Beiras,* Barcelona: Sotelo Blanco.

—— (2004) *A Estrela na Palabra. Novas Conversas con Xosé Manuel Beiras,* A Coruña: Edicións Laiovento.

FLNC (1977) *Livre Vert du FLNC,* Publisher unknown.

Golwg (1989) 'Rhoshirwaun, Rossett a Strasbourg', June 1989, p. 13.

Jones, T. (1985) *Plaid Cymru and Welsh Politics: 1979–85,* Cardiff: Plaid Cymru.

Keelan, P. (1989) *Beyond Thatcher – Wales 2000 in a Green Europe*, Cardiff: Plaid Cymru.

La Voz de Galicia (2004) 'El Supremo declara que el BNG no tendrá voz en el Parlamento Europeo', 23rd July 2004. Online. Available at www.lavozdegalicia.es/buscavoz/ver_resultado.jsp?TEXTO=2877321 & lnk=GALEUSCA (accessed 25 July 2004).

Labour/Plaid Cymru (2007) *One Wales. A Progressive Agenda for the Government of Wales.* Coalition agreement between the Labour Party and Plaid Cymru, 27 June 2007. Online. Available at http://news.bbc.co.uk/2/shared/bsp/hi/pdfs/27_06_07_onewales.pdf (accessed 28 June 2007).

Le Monde (1999) 'La Corse et l'aide européenne', 31 August 1999, no page number.

Lewis, S. (1926) *Egwyddorion Cenedlaetholdeb*, Machynlleth: Plaid Genedlaethol Cymru.

Mathews, G.E. (1971) *Wales and the Common Market*, Cardiff: Plaid Cymru.

Melding, D. (2003) *New Dawn or Sunset Boulevard – What Role for the Welsh Conservative Party?* speech to the Institute of Welsh Politics, University of Aberystwyth, 27 October 2003.

Ministère de l'Intérieur (2004) 'Scrutin du 28 mars 2004: Corse'. Online. Available at http://www.interieur.gouv.fr/sections/a-votre-service/resultats-elections/reg2004/094/index.html (accessed 12 November 2007).

Ministry of the Economy, Finance and Employment (2006) *Les Fonds Structurels 2007–2013*. 29 May 2006. Online. Available at www.industrie.gouv.fr/infopresse/fonds2007-13.pdf (accessed 15 December 2006).
Morgan, S. (1987) *Statement to the Plaid Cymru Executive Committee on the European campaign strategy*, 30 December 1987.
Nogueira, C. (2006) *A Terra Cantada*, Vigo: Edicións Xerais.
Parlamento de Galicia (2005) 'Eleccións 19 de Xuño de 2005'. Online. Available at www.parlamentodegalicia.es/sites/ParlamentoGalicia/ContenidoGal/pargal_II_Xunta Electoral.aspx (accessed 15 May 2007).
Paris Match (1991) 'Sondage en Corse', 17 January 1991, pp. 12–14.
—— (1998) 'Les Corses ne veulent a aucun prix de l'independance', 26 February 1998, p. 6.
Plaid Cymru (no date) *Plaid Cymru Action Pack*, Cardiff: Plaid Cymru.
—— (1975) 'Plaid move on Brussels office', press release, 22 June 1975.
—— (1979) *Plaid Cymru Fights for Wales*, Cardiff: Plaid Cymru.
—— (1981) *Report of the Plaid Cymru Commission of Inquiry,* Cardiff: Plaid Cymru.
—— (1983) *An Independent Wales – 1983 and the Future Beyond*, Cardiff: Plaid Cymru.
—— (1984) *A Voice for Wales in Europe*, Cardiff: Plaid Cymru.
—— (1989) *Wales in Europe: A Community of Communities*, Cardiff: Plaid Cymru.
—— (1992) *Towards 2000. Plaid Cymru's Programme for Wales in Europe*, Cardiff: Plaid Cymru.
—— (1994) *Making Europe Work for Wales. Plaid Cymru European Manifesto*, Cardiff: Plaid Cymru.
—— (1995) *A Democratic Wales in a United Europe*, Cardiff: Plaid Cymru.
—— (1997) *The Best for Wales. Plaid Cymru's Programme for the New Millennium,* Cardiff: Plaid Cymru.
—— (2003) *Evidence to the Convention on the Future of Europe, March 2003*, Cardiff: Plaid Cymru.
—— (2004) *Fighting hard for Wales. A Manifesto for the European Parliament Elections 2004*, Cardiff: Plaid Cymru.
—— (2005) *We Can Build a Better Wales*, Cardiff: Plaid Cymru.
—— (2006) *Plaid. Ymlaen. Forward*, Cardiff: Plaid Cymru.
Poggioli, P. (1996) *Journal de Bord d'un Nationaliste Corse*, Saint Etienne: Editions de l'Aube.
PNC (2006) 'L'heure est à la relance du processus de paix, pas à la relance de la clandestinité', press release, 31 May 2006. Online. Available at www.unita-naziunale.org/portail/030606-PNC.htm (accessed 26 November 2006).
Simeoni, E. (1995) *Corse: La Volonte d'Etre*, Ajaccio: Albiana.
Thomas, S. (2003) 'Routemap to Independence in Europe', document presented to the Plaid Cymru National Council, November 2003.
Toro, Suso de (1991) *Camilo Nogueira e Outras Voces: Unha Memoria da Esquerda Nacionalista*, Vigo: Edicións Xerais.
Unione Naziunale (2004) *Lista d'Unione Naziunale: Un Votu per L'Unione, Un Passu pè a Nazione*, Bastia: Unione Naziunale.
U Ribombu (1979a) 'Lettre ouverte des patriotes emprisonnés', April–May 1979, p. 4.
—— (1979b) 'Non a l'Europe! Oui à la Mediterranée', July–August 1979, p. 1.
—— (1980) 'Le programme du FLNC', October–November 1980, p. 2.
—— (1982) 'Entretien avec le FLNC', April 1982, p. 5.
—— (1983) 'Le FLNC parle', February 1983, p. 4.
—— (1984) 'L'intégration européenne et atlantique', 18 May 1984, p. 3.

—— (1986) 'U discorsu internaziunale di u MCA', 22 August 1986, p. 5.
—— (1987) '1992: L'Acte unique européen aggravera la situation', 15 May 1987, p. 3.
—— (1989) 'Cunculta Naziunale – Assemblée Générale', 17 Nov 1989, p. 4.
—— (1990) 'Le projet de société du FLNC', 4 Jan 1990, p. 2.
—— (1994) 'Pour un nouveau contrat', 17 November 1994, p. 3
—— (1998) 'Presentation du nouvel executif', 9 July 1998, p. 2.
—— (2006) 'Intervention de Jean-Guy Talamoni, le 6 août 2006', No. 17, September 2006. Online. Available at www.uribombu.com/pulitica.htm (accessed 23 November 2006).
UPC (1991) *Autonomia*. Bastia: UPC.
Welsh Nation (1978) 'Your view', September 1978, p. 9.
—— (1979) 'We must have a voice', June 1979, p. 3.
—— (1980a) 'EEC? Let's get out says Phil', January 1980, p. 3.
—— (1980b) 'Scrap CAP, farmers are told', January 1980, p. 3.
—— (1982a) 'EEC has cost Wales jobs', February 1982, p. 8.
—— (1982b) 'EEC prosperity is a myth', August 1982, p. 8.
—— (1983a) 'EEC's coal policy spells death blow to South Wales', December 1983, p. 4.
—— (1983b) 'Wales and the EEC', March 1983, p. 4.
—— (1983c) 'Europe – New deal sought for Wales', September 1983, p. 1.
Western Mail (2001) 'IQ test', 21 September 2001, p. 4.
Wigley, D. (1972) 'Rethink on Europe', *Welsh Nation*, 22 September 1972, p. 1.
—— (1992) *O Ddifri*, Caernarfon: Gwasg Gwynedd.
—— (2001) *Y Maen i'r Wal*, Caernarfon: Gwasg Gwynedd.
Williams, D. (1979) 'Draft European Manifesto', presented to the Bureau of Unrepresented Nations in Paris, 27 January 1979.
Williams, E.W. (1986) 'Gwrthgyferbyniadau gwleidyddiaeth Brydeinig a strategaeth Plaid Cymru', report discussed at the Plaid Cymru Executive Committee, no specific date.
Williams, P, (1975) 'Defence policy and the EEC', in Plaid Cymru Research Group, *Wales and the Common Market*, Cardiff: Plaid Cymru.

Secondary sources

Aylott, N. (2002) 'Let's discuss this later. Party responses to Euro-division in Scandinavia', *Party Politics*, 8(4): 441–61.
Bache, I. (1998) 'The extended gatekeeper: central government and the implementation of EC regional policy in the UK', *Journal of European Public Policy*, 6(1): 28–45.
Bache, I. and Jones, R. (2000) 'Has EU regional policy empowered the regions? A study of Spain and the United Kingdom', *Regional and Federal Studies*, 10(3): 1–20.
Barberà, O. and Barrio, A. (2006) 'Convergència i Unió: from stability to decline?', in L. De Winter, M. Gómez-Reino and P. Lynch (eds) *Autonomist Parties in Europe – Volume I*, Barcelona: ICPS, 101–42.
Bardi, L. (2002) 'Parties and party systems in the European Union', in K.R. Luther and F. Müller-Rommel (eds) *Political Parties in the New Europe. Political and Analytical Challenges*, Oxford: Oxford Univesity Press, 93 – 322.
Barreiro Rivas, X.L. (2003) 'Da UPG ao BNG: O proceso organizativo do nacionalismo galego', in X.M. Rivera Otero (ed.) *Os Partidos Políticos en Galicia,* Vigo: Edicións Xerais de Galicia, 99–261.
Bartolini, S. (2000) 'National cleavage structures and the integration issue dimension', paper presented at the Colloque CEVIPOF-CERI: L'intégration Européenne entre Emergence Institutionnelle et Recomposition de l'État, Sciences Po, Paris, 26–27 May 2000.

Bibliography   183

—— (2005) *Restructuring Europe*, Oxford: Oxford University Press.
Bartolini, S. and Mair, P. (1990) *Identity, Competition and Electoral Availability*, Cambridge: Cambridge University Press.
Batory, A. and Sitter, N. (2004) 'Cleavages, competition and coalition-building: Agrarian parties and the European question in western and east central Europe', *European Journal of Political Research*, 43: 523–46.
Beramendi, J.G. (1997) *El Nacionalismo Gallego*, Madrid: Arco Libros.
Beramendi, J.G. and Núñez Seixas, X.M. (1996) *O Nacionalismo Galego*, Santiago de Compostela: A Nosa Terra.
Beulens, J. and Van Dyck, R. (1998) 'Regionalist parties in French-speaking Belgium. The Rassemblement Wallon and the Front Démocratique des Francophones', in L. De Winter and H. Türsan (eds) *Regionalist Parties in Western Europe*, London: Routledge, 51–69.
Billig, M. (1995) *Banal Nationalism*, London: Sage.
Bogdanor, V. (1999) *Devolution in the United Kingdom*, Oxford: Oxford University Press.
Bomberg, E. (2002) 'The Europeanisation of green parties: Exploring the EU's impact', *West European Politics*, 25(3): 29–50.
Börzel, T. (2002) 'Pace-setting, foot-dragging and fence-sitting: Member state responses to Europeanization', *Journal of Common Market Studies*, 40(2): 193–214.
Börzel, T. and Risse, T. (2000) 'When Europe hits home: Europeanization and domestic change', *European Integration online Papers*, 4(15). Online. Available at http://eiop.or.at/eiop/texte/2000-2015a.htm (accessed 3 February 2003).
Briquet, J.-L. (1997) *La Tradition en Mouvement. Clientélisme et Politique en Corse*, Paris: Berlin.
—— (1998) 'Le problème corse', *Regards sur l'Actualité*, 240: 25–37.
Bulmer, S., Burch, M., Carter, C., Hogwood, P. and Scott, A. (2002) *British Devolution and European Policy-Making: Transforming Britain into Multi-level Governance*, Basingstoke: Palgrave.
Butt Philip, A. (1975) *The Welsh Question: Nationalism in Welsh Politics 1945–1970*, Cardiff: University of Wales Press.
Calvet Crespo, J. (2003) 'Gobiernos minoritarios, pactos parlamentarios y producción legislativa en España', *Política y Sociedad*, 40(2): 89–103.
Capoccia, G. (2002) 'Anti-system parties: a conceptual reassessment', *Journal of Theoretical Politics*, 14(1): 9–35.
Caratini, R. (2003) *La Corse. Un Peuple, Une Histoire*, Paris: L'Archipel.
Carter, E., Luther, K.R. and Poguntke, T. (2007) 'European integration and internal party dynamics', in T. Poguntke, N. Aylott, E. Carter, R. Ladrech and K.R. Luther (eds) *The Europeanization of National Political Parties. Power and Organizational Adaptation*, London: Routledge, 1–27.
Chari, R.S., Iltanen, S. and Kritzinger, S. (2004) 'Examining and explaining the Northern League's 'U-Turn' from Europe', *Government and Opposition*, 39(3): 423–50.
Christiansen, T. (1996) 'Second thoughts on Europe's third level: The European Union's Committee of the Regions', *Publius: The Journal of Federalism*, 26(2): 93–116.
—— (1998) 'Plaid Cymru: dilemmas and ambiguities of Welsh regional nationalism', in L. De Winter and H. Türsan (eds) *Regionalist Parties in Western Europe*, London: Routledge, 125–42.
Conti, N. (2003) 'Party attitudes to European integration: A longitudinal analysis of the Italian case', *Sussex European Institute Working Paper*, No. 70. Online. Available at www.sussex.ac.uk/sei/documents/wp56.pdf (accessed 12 June 2004).

Crettiez, X. (1998) 'Lire la violence politique en Corse', *Cahiers de la Sécurité Intérieure*, 33: 195–214.
—— (1999) *La Question Corse*, Paris: Complexe.
Crettiez, X. and Sommier, I. (2002) *La France Rebelle*, Paris: Éditions Michalon.
Crewe, I. and Denver, D. (eds) (1985) *Electoral Change in Western Democracies: Patterns and Sources of Electoral Volatility,* London: Croom Helm.
Daniels, P. (1998) 'From hostility to constructive engagement: the Europeanisation of the Labour Party', *West European Politics*, 21(1): 72–96.
Davies, D.H. (1983) *The Welsh Nationalist Party 1925–1045: A Call to Nationhood*, Cardiff: University of Wales Press.
Davies, J. (1996) *Plaid Cymru since the 1960s,* The Welsh Political Archive Lecture, 1996, Aberystwyth: National Library of Wales.
Deschouwer, K. (ed.) (2008) *New Parties in Government*, London: Routledge.
De Winter, L. (1998) 'Conclusion: a comparative analysis of the electoral, office and policy success of ethnoregionalist parties', in L. De Winter and H. Türsan (eds) *Regionalist Parties in Western Europe*, London: Routledge, 190–235.
—— (2006) 'In memoriam of the Volksunie 1954–2001: death by overdose of success', in L. De Winter, M. Gómez-Reino Cachafeiro and P. Lynch (eds) *Autonomist Parties in Europe – Volume II*, Barcelona: ICPS, 11–45.
De Winter, L. and Gómez-Reino, M. (2002) 'European integration and ethnoregionalist parties', *Party Politics*, 8(4): 483–503.
De Winter, L., Gómez-Reino Cachafeiro, M. and Buelens, J. (2006) 'The Vlaams Blok: the heritage of extreme-right Flemish nationalism', in L. De Winter, M. Gómez-Reino Cachafeiro and P. Lynch (eds) *Autonomist Parties in Europe – Volume II,* Barcelona: ICPS, 47–78.
De Winter, L., Gómez-Reino Cachafeiro, M. and Lynch, P. (eds) (2006a) *Autonomist Parties in Europe – Volumes I and II*, Barcelona: ICPS.
—— (2006b) 'Introduction: autonomist parites in European politics', in L. De Winter, M. Gómez-Reino Cachafeiro and P. Lynch (eds) *Autonomist Parties in Europe – Volume I*, Barcelona: ICPS, 1–23.
Deschouwer, K. (2003) 'Political parties in multi-layered systems', *European Urban and Regional Studies*, 10(2): 213–26.
Diamanti, I. (1993) *La Lega: Geografia, Storia e Sociologia di un Nuovo Soggetto Politico*, Rome: Donzelli.
Díez Medrano, J. (2003) *Framing Europe: Attitudes to European Integration in Germany, Spain and the United Kingdom*, Princeton: Princeton University Press.
Dominici, T. (2002) 'L'Après-assasinat du Préfet Erignac. Les retombées sur le système nationaliste corse', *Les Cahiers de la Sécurité Intérieure,* 47(1): 133–63.
—— (2004) 'Le nationalisme dans la Corse contemporaine', *Pôle Sud,* 20: 97–112.
Downs, A. (1957) *An Economic Theory of Democracy,* New York: Harper Collins.
Easton, D. (1965) *A Framework for Political Analysis,* Englewood Cliffs, NJ: Prentice-Hall.
Elias, A. (2005) 'Multi-level Governance meets Arend Lijphart: the institutional adaptation of regions to European integration', paper presented at the ECPR Joint Sessions of Workshops, Granada, Spain, 14–18 April 2005.
—— (2006) 'From 'full national status' to 'independence' in Europe: the case of Plaid Cymru – The Party of Wales', in J. McGarry and M. Keating (eds) *European Integration and the Nationalities Question*, London: Routledge, 193–215.
Elias, A. and Tronconi, F. (2006) 'Minority nationalist parties and the challenges of political representation: a framework of analysis', paper presented at the conference From

Protest to Power: Minority Nationalist Parties and the Challenges of Representation, University of Aberystwyth, 28–29 October 2006.
Evans, A. (2002) 'Regionalism in the EU: Legal organisation of a challenging social phenomenon', *Journal of European Integration*, 24(3): 219–43.
Evans, E.J. (2004) *Thatcher and Thatcherism*, London: Routledge.
Evans, R. (2005) *Rhag Pob Brad*, Talybont: Y Lolfa.
Featherstone, K. (1988) *Socialist Parties and European Integration. A Comparative History*, Manchester: Manchester University Press.
—— (2003) 'In the name of "Europe"', in K. Featherstone and C. Radaelli (eds) *The Politics of Europeanization*, Oxford: Oxford University Press, 3–26.
Fernández Baz, M.A. (2003) *A Formación do Nacionalismo Galego Contemporáneo (1963–1984)*, Santiago de Compostela: Laiovento.
Flood, C. (2002) 'Euroscepticism: A problematic concept', paper presented at the UACES 32nd Annual Conference and 7th Research Conference, Queen's University, Belfast, 2–4 September 2002.
Follorou, J. and Nouzille, V. (2004) *Les Parrains Corses*, Paris: Fayard.
Franco Grande, X.L. (1985) *Os Anos Oscuros. A Resistencia Cultural da Xeración da Noite (1964–1960)*, Vigo: Edicións Xerais.
Franklin, M., Mackie, T. and Valen, H. (1992) *Electoral Change: Responses to Evolving Social Attitudinal Structures in Western Countries*, Cambridge: Cambridge University Press.
Freeden, M. (1998) 'Is nationalism a distinct ideology?', *Political Studies*, 46(4): 748–65.
Gabel, M. and Hix, S. (2002) 'Defining EU political space: An empirical study of the European elections manifestoes 1979–99', *Comparative Political Studies*, 35(8): 934–64.
Gaffney, J. (1996) *Political Parties and the European Union*, London: Routledge.
García Soto, L.M. (2000) 'Galicia, España y Europa según Castelao', *Agora: Papeles de Filosofía*, 19(2): 153–60.
George, S. and Haythorne, D. (1996) 'The British Labour Party', in J. Gaffney (ed.) *Political Parties and the European Union*, London: Routledge, 110–21.
Giordano, B. (2004) 'The politics of the Northern League and Italy's changing attitude toward Europe', *Perspectives on European Politics and Society*, 5(1): 61–79.
Giordano, B. and Roller, E. (2002) 'Catalonia and the 'idea of Europe': Competing strategies and discourses within Catalan party politics', *European Urban and Regional Studies*, 9(2): 99–113.
Giudici, N. (1997) *Le Crépuscule des Corses: Clientélisme, Identité et Vendetta*, Paris: Grasset.
Goetz, K.H. (2000) 'European integration and national executives: a case in search of an effect', *West European Politics*, 23(4): 211–31.
Goetz, K.H. and Hix, S. (eds) (2001) *Europeanised Politics? European Integration and National Political Systems,* London: Frank Cass.
Gómez-Reino, M. (2003) 'El BNG y la estrategia frentista: anatomía de los sub-partidos', paper presented at the VI Congreso de la Asociación Española de Ciencia Política, Barcelona, 18–20 September 2003.
—— (2006) 'The Bloque Nacionalista Galego: from political outcast to success', in L. De Winter, M. Gómez-Reino and P. Lynch (eds) *Autonomist Parties in Europe – Volume I*, Barcelona: ICPS, 167–96.
Gómez-Reino, M., Llamazares I. and Ramiro, L. (2008) 'Euroscpeticism and political parties in Spain', in P. Taggart and A. Szczerbiak (eds) *Opposing Europe? The Comparative Party Politics of Euroscepticism. Volume 1: Case Studies and Country Surveys.* Oxford: Oxford University Press.

Gren, J. (1999) *The New Regionalism in the EU: The Lessons to be Drawn from Catalonia, Rhone-Alps and West Sweden,* Gothenberg: SIR.
Guerrero Salom, E. (2003) 'Apoyo(s) parlamentario(s) antes que gobierno(s) de coalición. El caso espanol: 1993–96 y 1996–2000', *Política y Sociedad*, 40(2): 77–88.
Gwilym, N. (2000) 'Lleoli cenedlaetholdeb Cymreig', unpublished PhD thesis, University of Aberystwyth.
Hainsworth, P. (1983) 'Corscia: The regional assembly election of 1982', *West European Politics*, 6(2): 165–67.
Harmel, R. (1985) 'On the study of new parties', *International Political Science Review*, 6(4): 403–18.
Harmel, R., Heo, U., Tan, A. and Janda, K. (1995) 'Performance, leadership, factions and party change: an empirical analysis', *West European Politics*, 18(1): 1–33.
Harmsen, R. and Spiering, M. (2004) Euroscepticism: Party Politics, National Identity and European Integration. Special Edition of *European Studies: A Journal of European Culture, History and Politics*. 20.
Heinisch, R. (2003) 'Success in opposition – failure in government: explaining the performance of right-wing populist parties in public office", *West European Politics*, 26(3): 91–130.
Hepburn, E. (2006) 'Scottish autonomy and European integration: the response of Scotland's political parties', in J. McGarry and M. Keating (eds) *European Integration and the Nationalities Question*, London: Routledge, pp. 225–38.
—— (2007) *The New Politics of Autonomy. Territorial Strategies and the Uses of European Integration by Political Parties in Scotland, Bavaria and Sardinia 1979–2005*, Florence: Cadmus Online Publications.
Hermant, D. (1992) 'Nationalismes et construction européenne', *Cultures et Conflits*, 7: 1–7. Online. Available at http://conflits.revues.org/article.php3?id_article=473 (accessed 18 March 2003).
Hine, D. (1982) 'Factionalism in West European parties: a framework for analysis', *West European Politics*, 5(1): 36–53.
Hix, S. (1999) 'Dimensions and alignments in European Union politics: cognitive constraints and partisan responses', *European Journal of Political Research*, 35(2): 69–125.
—— (2002) 'Parties at the European level', in P. Webb, D. Farrell and Holliday, I. (eds) *Political Parties in Advanced Industrial Democracies*, Oxford: Oxford University Press, 280–309.
Hix, S. and Lord, C. (1997) *Political Parties in the European Union*, London: Macmillan.
Hix, S., Raunio, T., and Scully, R. (2003) 'Fifty years on: Research on the European Parliament', *Journal of Common Market Studies*, 41(2): 191–202.
Hooghe, L. (1995) 'Sub-national mobilisation in the European Union', *West European Politics*, 18(3): 175–98.
—— (1996) *Cohesion Policy and European Integration: Building Multi-level Governance,* Oxford: Clarendon Press.
Hooghe, L. and Marks, G. (1996) '"Europe with the Regions": channels of representation in the EU', *Publius: The Journal of Federalism*, 26(1): 73–91.
—— (2001) *Multi-level Governance and European Integration,* Maryland, USA & Oxford: Rowman & Littlefield Publishers.
Hooghe, L., Marks, G. and Wilson, C. (2002) 'Does left/right structure party positions on European integration?', *Comparative Political Studies*, 35(8): 965–89.
Ignazi, P. (2005) 'Legitimation and evolution on the Italian right-wing: sociological and ideological repositioning of Alleanza Nazionale and the Lega Nord', *South European Politics and Sociery,* 10(2): 333–49.

Inglehart, R. (1977) *The Silent Revolution: Changing Values and Political Styles Among Western Publics*, Princeton: Princeton University Press.
Janda, K. (1980) *Political Parties: A Cross-National Survey*, New York: Free Press.
Jeffery, C. (2000) 'Sub-national mobilisation and European integration', *Journal of Common Market Studies*, 38(1): 1–24.
Jiménez Sánchez, F. (2003) 'O PSdeG-PSOE (1973–2001): un caso de débil institucionalización', in X.M. Rivera Otero (ed.) *Os Partidos Políticos en Galicia*, Vigo: Edicións Xerais de Galicia, 263–344.
Johansson, K.M. and Raunio, T. (2001) 'Partisan responses to Europe: comparing Finnish and Swedish political parties', *European Journal of Political Research*, 39(2): 225–49.
Jones, J.B. (1985) 'Wales in the European Community', in M. Keating and J.B. Jones (eds) *Regions in the European Community*, Oxford: Clarendon Press, 89–108.
Kassim, H. (2000) 'Conclusion: The national co-ordination of EU policy: confronting the challenge', in H. Kassim, B.G. Peters and V. Wright (eds) *The National Co-ordination of EU Policy: The European Level*, Oxford: Oxford University Press, 235–64.
Keating, M. (1998) *The New Regionalism in Western Europe*, Cheltenham: Edward Elgar.
—— (2000) 'The minority nations of Spain and European integration: a new framework for autonomy?' *Journal of Spanish Cultural Studies*, 1(1): 29–42.
—— (2001a) *Nations Against the State, The New Politics of Nationalism in Quebec, Catalonia and Scotland*, Basingstoke: Palgrave.
—— (2001b) 'Sovereignty and plurinational democracy. Problems in political science', paper presented at the Conference on Sovereignty in Transition, European University Institute, 21–22 September 2001.
—— (2001c) *Plurinational Democracy. Stateless Nations in a Post-Sovereignty Era*, Oxford: Oxford University Press.
—— (2001d) 'So many nations, so few states: territory and nationalism in the global era', in A-G Gagnon and J. Tully (eds) *Multinational Democracies*, Cambridge: Cambridge University Press, 39–64.
—— (2001e) 'Nations without states: the accommodation of nationalism in the new state order', in M. Keating and J. McGarry (eds) *Minority Nationalism in the Changing International Order*, Oxford: Oxford University Press, 19–43.
—— (2004) 'European Integration and the Nationalities Question', *Politics and Society*, 32(3): 367–88.
Keating, M. and Bray, Z. (2006) 'Renegotiating sovereignty: Basque nationalism and the rise and fall of the Ibarretxe Plan', *Ethnopolitics*, 5(4): 347–64.
Keating, M. and Hooghe, L. (2001) 'By-passing the nation state? Regions and the EU policy process', in J. Richardson (ed) *European Union: Power and Policy Making* (Second Edition), London: Routledge, 239–55.
Keating, M. and Jones, B. (1991) 'Scotland and Wales: peripheral assertion and European integration', *Parliamentary Affairs*, 43(3): 311–24.
Keating, M. and McGarry, J. (2001) 'Introduction', in: M. Keating and J. McGarry (eds) *Minority Nationalism in the Changing International Order*, Oxford: Oxford University Press, 1–17.
Klingemann, H., Hofferbert, R.I. and Budge, I. (1994) *Parties, Policies and Democracy*, Boulder, Colorado: Westview Press.
Kopecký, P. and Mudde, C. (2002) 'The two sides of Euroscepticism. Party positions on European integration in East Central Europe', *European Union Politics*, 3(3): 297–326.
Krasner, S. (1999) *Sovereignty: Organized Hypocrisy*, Princeton: Princeton University Press.

Krasner, S. (2001) 'Rethinking the sovereign state model', *Review of International Studies*, 27: 721–46.
Ladrech, R. (2000) *Social Democracy and the Challenge of European Union*, Boulder, Colorado: Lynne Rienner.
—— (2002) 'Europeanization and political parties: towards a framework for analysis', *Party Politics*, 8(4): 389–403.
Laffan, B. (1996) 'The politics of identity and political order in Europe', *Journal of Common Market Studies*, 34(1): 81–102.
Lagares Díez, N. (2003) 'O partido Popular de Galicia', in X.M. Rivera Otero (ed.) *Os Partidos Políticos en Galicia*, Vigo: Edicións Xerais, 19–98.
Lago, I. (2004) 'La coordinación electoral del nacionalismo gallego', *Revista Internacional de Sociología*, Sept-Dec 2004, 39: 35–61.
Lago, I. and Máiz, R. (2004) 'Le nationalisme galicien: opportunités, mobilisation politique et coordination électorale', *Pôle Sud*, May 2004, 20: 25–46.
Lefébvre, C. (1992) 'Nationalismes corses et perspectives européennes', *Cultures et Conflits*, 7: 1–7. Online. Available at http://conflits.revues.org/article.php3?id_article=472 (accessed 18 March 2003).
Lefevre, M. (2000) *Géopolitique de la Corse. Le Modèle Républicain en Question,* Paris: L'Harmattan.
Leydier, G. (1994) 'Les années Thatcher en Ecosse: l'Union remise en question', *Revue Française de Sciences Politique*, 44(6): 1034–53.
Lipset, S.M. and Rokkan, S. (1967) *Party Systems and Voter Alignments: Cross-national Perspectives*, New York: Free Press.
Loughlin, J. (1985) 'The elections to the Corsican Regional Assembly, August 1984', *Government and Opposition*, 20(2): 240–50.
—— (1989) 'Regional and ethnic nationalism in France: a case study of Corsica', unpublished PhD thesis, European University Institute, Florence.
Loughlin, J. and Seiler, D-L. (2001) 'France: between centralisation and fragmentation', in J. Loughlin (ed.) *Sub-national Democracy in the European Union*, Oxford: Oxford University Press, 185–210.
Lynch, P. (1995) 'From red to green: the political strategy of Plaid Cymru in the 1980s and 1990s', Journal of Federal and Regional Studies, 5(2): 197–210.
—— (1996) *Minority Nations and European Integration,* Cardiff: University of Wales Press.
—— (1998) 'Co-operation between regionalist parties at the level of the European Union: the European Free Alliance', in L. De Winter and H. Türsan (eds) *Regionalist Parties in Western Europe,* London: Routledge, 190–203.
—— (2002) *SNP: The History of the Scottish National Party*, Cardiff: Welsh Academic Press.
McAllister, L. (2001) *Plaid Cymru: The Emergence of a Political Party*, Bridgend: Poetry Wales Press.
MacCormick, N. (1999) *Questioning Sovereignty: Law, State and Nation in the European Commonwealth,* Oxford: Oxford University Press.
—— (2004) 'The European constitutional convention and the stateless nations', *International Relations*, 18(3): 331–44.
McElroy, G. and Benoit, K. (2007) 'Party groups and policy positions in the European Parliament', *Party Politics*, 13(1): 5–28.
Macneill, S., Jeffery, C. and Gibney, J. (2007) 'Changing dynamics of regional representation in Brussels: a case study of Birmingham and the West Midlands, 1984–2004', *Regional Studies*, 42(3): 403–14.

Mair, P. (2000) 'The limited impact of Europe on national party systems', *West European Politics*, 23(4): 27–51.

—— (2006) 'Political parties and party systems', in P. Graziano and M.P. Vink (eds) *Europeanization: New Research Agendas*, Basingstoke: Palgrave Macmillan, 154–66.

Máiz, R. (1984) 'La construcción teórica de Galicia como nación en el pensamiento de Manuel Murguía', *Estudios de Historia Social*, 28/29: 133–47.

—— (1996) 'Nación de Breogán: oportunidades políticas y estrategias enmarcadoras en el movimiento nacionalista gallego (1886–1996), *Revista de Estudios Políticos*, 92: 33–75.

—— (2003) 'Making opportunities: contemporary evolution of Galician nationalism in Spain (1982–2001), *Studies in Ethnicity and Nationalism*, 3(2): 20–34.

Máiz, R., Beramendi, P. and Grau, M. (2002) 'La federalización del Estado de las Autonomías: Evolución y Déficit Institucionales', in J. Subirats and R. Gallego (eds) *Veinte Años de Autonomías en España*, Madrid: CIS, 379–424.

Marks, G. (1993) 'Structural policy and multi-level governance', in A. Cafruny and G. Rosenthal (eds) *The State of the European Community, Vol. 2: The Maastricht Debates and Beyond*, Harlow: Longman, 391–410.

Marks, G. and Hooghe, L. (2000) 'Optimality and authority: a critique of neoclassical theory' *Journal of Common Market Studies*, 38(5): 795–816.

G. Marks and M.R. Steenbergen (eds) (2004) *European Integration and Political Conflict*, Cambridge: Cambridge University Press

Marks, G. and Wilson, C. (2000) '"The past in the present": a cleavage theory of party response to European integration', *British Journal of Political Studies*, 30(3): 433–59.

Marks, G., Wilson, C. and Ray, L. (2002) 'National political parties and European integration', *American Journal of Political Science*, 46(3): 585–94.

Mitchell, J. (1998) 'The evolution of devolution: Labour's home rule strategy in opposition', *Government and Opposition*, 33(4): 479–96.

Molas, I. (2000) 'Partis nationalistes, autonomie et clans en Corse', Institut de Ciències Polítiques i Socials Working Paper, No. 181.

Moore, C. (2007) 'A Europe of the Regions vs. the Regions in Europe: Reflections on Regional Engagement in Brussels', paper presented at the EUSA Biannual Conference, Montreal, 17–19 May 2007.

Morgan, K. (1998) *Rebirth of a Nation: Wales 1880–1980*, Oxford: Clarendon Press.

Moxon-Browne, E. (1999) 'The Europeanisation of Political Parties: The Case of the Irish Labour Party', paper presented at the Sixth International Conference of the European Community Studies Association, Pittsburgh, 2–5 June 1999.

Müller-Rommel, F. (2002) 'The lifespan and the political performance of Green Parties in western Europe', *Environmental Politics*, 11(1): 1–16.

Müller-Rommel, F. and Pridham, G. (1991) *Small Parties in Western Europe*, London: Sage.

Nairn, T. (1977) *The Break-up of Britain: Crisis and Neo-nationalism*, London: NLB.

Nagel, K.-J. (2004) 'Transcending the national/asserting the national: how stateless nations like Scotland, Wales and Catalonia react to European integration', *Australian Journal of Politics and History*, 50(1): 57–74.

Neumayer, L. (2008) 'Euroscepticism as a political label: the use of European Union issues in political competition in the new member states', *European Journal of Political Research*, 47(2): 135–60.

Newman, S. (1994) 'Ethnoregional parties: a comparative perspective', *Regional Politics and Policy*, 4: 28–66.

190 Bibliography

—— (1996) *Ethnoregional Conflict in Democracies: Mostly Ballots, Rarely Bullets,* Westport, CT: Greenwood Press.
O'Reilly, C. (2001) 'Introduction: minority languages, ethnicity and the state in the European Union', in C. O'Reilly (ed.) *Language, Ethnicity and the State, Volume One: Minority Languages in the European Union,* Basingstoke: Palgrave, 20–39.
Ó Riagáin, D. (2001) 'Many tongues but one voice: personal overview of the role of the European Bureau for Lesser Used Languages in promoting Europe's regional and minority languages', in C. O'Reilly (ed.), *Language, Ethnicity and the State, Volume One: Minority Languages in the European Union,* Basingstoke: Palgrave, 20–39.
Observatório Político Autonómico (2005) *Sondeo de Opinion del Observatório Político Autonómico: Part II – Evolución 2001–2005.* Online. Available at www.opa151.com (accessed 26 June 2007).
Olivesi, C. (1998) 'The failure of regionalist party formation in Corsica', in L. De Winter and H. Türsan (eds) *Regionalist Parties in Western Europe,* London: Routledge, 174–89.
Olsen, J. (2002) 'The many faces of Europeanisation', *Journal of Common Market Studies,* 40(5): 921–52.
Osmond, J. (1998) *National Assembly Agenda,* Cardiff: Institute of Welsh Affairs.
—— (2000) 'Devolution relaunched', *Monitoring the National Assembly,* December 1999 to March 2000. Cardiff: Institute of Welsh Affairs.
—— (2003) *Birth of a Welsh Democracy,* Cardiff: Institute of Welsh Affairs.
Panebianco, A. (1988) *Political Parties: Organization and Power,* Cambridge: Cambridge University Press.
Pedersen, M. (1982) 'Towards a new typology of party life-spans and minor parties', *Scandinavian Political Studies,* 5(1): 1–16.
Pérez-Nievas, S. (2006) 'The Partido Nacionalista Vasco: redefining political goals at the turn of the century', in L. De Winter, M. Gómez-Reino Cachafeiro, and P. Lynch (eds) *Autonomist Parties in Europe – Volume I,* Barcelona: ICPS, 31–64.
Peterson, J. (1994) 'Subsidiarity: a definition to suit any vision?', *Parliamentary Affairs,* 47(1): 116–32.
Poguntke, T. (2001) 'From nuclear building site to cabinet: the career of the German Green Party', KEPRU Working Paper, No. 6, University of Keele.
Poguntke, T. (2002) 'Green parties in national governments: from protest to acquiescence?', *Environmental Politics,* 11(1): 133–45.
Poguntke, T., Ladrech, R., Aylott, N. and Luther, K.R. (2003) 'The Europeanization of national political parties: a framework for analysis', paper presented at the 2nd General Conference of the ECPR, University of Marburg, 18–21 September 2003.
Poguntke, T., Aylott, N., Carter, E., Ladrech, R. and Luther, K.R. (2008) (eds) *The Europeanization of National Political Parties. Power and Organizational Adaptation,* London: Routledge.
Pomponi, F. (1977) 'Le régionalisme en Corse dans l'entre deux-guerres, 1919–39', in C. Gras and G. Livet (eds) *Régions et Régionalisme en France du Xviiieme Siècle à Nos Jours,* Paris: Presses Universitaires de France.
Prezeworski, A. and Teune, H. (1970) *The Logic of Comparative Social Inquiry,* New York/Chichester: Wiley Interscience.
Radaelli, C. (2000) 'Whither Europeanization? Concept stretching and substantive change', *European Integration online Papers,* 4(8). Online. Available at http://eiop.or.at/eiop/texte/2000-2008.htm (accessed 3 February 2003).
Radaelli, C. and Pasquier, R. (2006) 'Concpetual issues', in P. Graziano and M.P. Vink (eds) *Europeanization: New Research Agendas,* Basingstoke: Palgrave Macmillan, 35–45.

Raunio, T. (2003) 'Relationships between MEPs and domestic parties: a comparative analysis of regionalist parties', paper presented at the ECPR Joint Sessions of Workshops, Edinburgh, 28 March–2 April 2003.
Ray, L. (1999) 'Measuring party positions on European integration: results from an expert survey', *European Journal of Political Research*, 36: 283–306.
Reif, K. And Schmitt, H. (1980) 'Nine second-order elections: a conceptual framework for the analysis of European election results', *European Journal of Political Research*, 8(1): 3–45.
Rich, P. (1996) 'Visionary ideals of European unity after World War I', in P. Murray and P. Rich (eds) *Visions of European Unity*, Boulder, Colorado: Westview Press, 21–38.
Rihoux, B. and Rüdig, W. (2006) 'Analyzing Greens in power: setting the agenda', *European Journal of Political Research*, 45(1): 1–33.
Riker, W. (1993) *Agenda Formation*, Ann Arbor: University of Michigan.
Risse, T., Cowles, M.G. and Caporaso, J. (2001) 'Europeanization and domestic change: introduction', in M.G. Cowles, J. Caporaso and T. Risse (eds) *Transforming Europe: Europeanization and Domestic Change*, Ithaca: Cornell University Press, 1–20.
Rivera Otero, X.M. (ed.) (2003) *Os Partidos Políticos en Galicia*, Vigo: Edicións Xerais.
Rokkan, S. and Urwin, D. (1983) *Economy, Territory, Identity. Politics of West European Peripheries*, London: Sage.
Roux, C. (2005a) 'Les "îles sœurs". Une sociologie historique comparée de la contestation nationalitaire en Corse et en Sardaigne', unpublished PhD thesis, University of Lille.
Roux, C. (2005b) 'Corse: vote à gauche, île de droite', in B. Dolez, A. Laurent and C. Patriat (eds), *Le Vote Rebelle. Les Élections Régionales De Mars 2004*, Dijon: Editions Universitaires de Dijon, 169–77.
Rüdig, W. (1996) 'Green parties and the European Union', in J. Gaffney (ed.) *Political Parties and the European Union*, London: Routledge, 254–72.
Ruzza, C. (2006) 'The Lega Nord: towards electoral stability and modest success', in L. De Winter, M. Gómez-Reino Cachafeiro and P. Lynch (eds) *Autonomist Parties in Europe – Volume II*, Barcelona: ICPS, 219–46.
Sartori, G. (1976/2005) *Parties and Party Systems: A Framework for Analysis*, Cambridge: Cambridge University Press/Essex: ECPR Press.
Sasse, G. (2005) 'EU Conditionality and Minority Rights: Translating the Copenhagen Criterion into Policy', EUI RSCAS Working Paper, 2005/16. Online. Available at www.iue.it/rscas/wp-texts/05_16.pdf (accessed 12 June 2005).
Scully, R. (2005) *Becoming Europeans?* Oxford: Oxford University Press.
Scully, R. and Elias, A. (2008) 'The 2007 Welsh Assembly Election', *Regional and Federal Studies*, 18(1): 103–9.
Seiler, D-L. (1982) *Les Partis Autonomistes*, Paris: PUE.
—— (1995) 'A historical overview on non-state wide parties in Western Europe', in L. De Winter (ed.) *Non-State Wide Parties in Europe*, Barcelona: Institut de Ciències Polítiques i Sociales, 15–22.
Sherrington, P. (2006) 'Confronting Europe: UK political parties and the EU 2000–2005', *British Journal of Politics and International Relations*, 8(1): 69–78.
Sitter, N. (2002) 'Opposing Europe: Euro-scepticism, opposition and party competition', Sussex European Institute Working Paper, No. 56.
Spiering, M. (2004) 'British Euroscepticism', *European Studies*, 20: 127–49.
Strøm, K. and Müller, W. (1999) 'Political Parties and Hard Choices', in K. Strøm and W. Müller (eds) *How Political Parties in Western Europe Make Hard Decisions*, Cambridge: Cambridge University Press, 1–35.

Szczerbiak, A. and Taggart, P. (2003) 'Theorising party-based Euro-scepticism: problems of definition, measurement and causality', Sussex European Institute Working Paper, No. 69.

Taggart, P. (1998) 'A touchstone of dissent: Euroscepticism in contemporary west European party systems', *European Journal of Political Research*, 33: 363–88.

Taggart, P. and Szczerbiak, A. (2008) *Opposing Europe. Volume 1: Case Studies and Country Surveys,* Oxford: Oxford University Press.

Thorlakson, L. (2006) 'Party systmes in multi-level contexts', in D. Hough and C. Jeffery (eds) *Devolution and Electoral Politics*, Manchester: Manchester University Press, 37–52.

Thrasher, M. and Rallings, C. (2007) *British Electoral Facts 1832–2006,* Aldershot: Ashgate.

Turner, C. (1998) 'Plaid Cymru and European integration. An empirical study of multi-level governance', unpublished PhD thesis, University of Wales Aberystwyth.

Türsan, H. (1998) 'Introduction. Ethnoregionalist parties as ethnic entrepreneurs', in L. De Winter and H. Türsan (eds) *Regionalist Parties in Western Europe,* London: Routledge, 1–16.

Ugarte, B.A. and Gómez-Reino, M. (2003) 'Towards an understanding of the ideology of nationalist parties: Dimensions and comparative framework', paper presented at the ECPR Joint Sessions of Workshops, Edinburgh, 28 March–2 April 2003.

Van Atta, S. (2003) 'Regional nationalist party activism and the new politics of Europe: the Bloque Nacionalista Galego and Plaid Cymru', *Regional and Federal Studies*, 13(2): 30–56.

Van der Eijk, C. and Franklin, M.N. (2004) 'Potential for contestation on European matters at national elections in Europe', in G. Marks and M.R. Steenbergen (eds) *European Integration and Political Conflict*, Cambridge: Cambridge University Press, 32–50.

Van Hecke, S. (2003) 'The principle of subsidiarity: ten years of application in the EU', *Regional and Federal Studies*, 13(1): 55–80.

Vilas Nogueira, X., Maíz, R., Dominguez Suárez, F.C. and Rivera Otero, X.M. (1994) *O Sistema Político Galego*, Vigo: Edicións Xerais.

Vilas Nogueira, X. and Fernández Baz, M.A. (2004) 'El BNG: definición y evolución de su estructura organizativa', *Revista de Estudios Políticos*, January-March 2004, no. 123: 201–22.

Volkens, A. and Klingemann, H. (2002) 'Parties, ideologies and issues: stability and change in 15 European party systems 1945–98', in K.R. Luther and F. Müller-Rommel (eds), *Political Parties in the New Europe: Political and Analytical Challenges*, Oxford: Oxford University Press, 143–67.

Walker, N. (2001) 'Late sovereignty in the European Union', paper presented at the European Forum, European University Institute, Florence, 15 February 2001.

Wyn Jones, R. (1996) 'O 'sosialaeth gymunedol' i quango Wales: ymdaith ddeallusol hynod Dafydd Elis Thomas', *Tu Chwith*, Haf 1996: 46–58.

—— (1999) 'Saunders Lewis a'r blaid genedlaethol', *Cof Cenedl*, XIV: 163–92.

—— (2007) *Rhoi Cymru'n Gyntaf: Syniadaeth Plaid Cymru,* Cardiff: University of Wales Press.

Wyn Jones, R. and Scully, R. (2004a) 'Minor tremor but several casualties: the 2003 Welsh election', *British Elections and Parties Review*, 14: 191–207.

Wyn Jones, R. and Scully, R. (2004b) 'Must Plaid lose?', *Agenda*, Haf 2006: 60–62.

Wyn Jones, R. and Scully, R. (2006) 'Devolution and electoral politics in Wales', *Publius: The Journal of Federalism*, 36(1): 115–34.

Wyn Jones, R. and Trystan, D. (2000) 'A "quiet earthquake": the first national elections to the National Assembly for Wales', CREST Working Paper, no. 85, September 2000. Minority nationalist parties and European integration.

Index

A Cuncolta Naziunalista (aCN) 112, 175n5
Accolta Naziunale Corsa (ANC) 112, 127, 176n7, 176n10, 177n21
Action Régionaliste Corse (ARC) 111, 112, 113, 115
Alianza Popular (AP) 82, 174n17
Alsace 65, 122, 176n
Asamblea Nacional-Popular Galega (AN-PG) 173n4
Associu di u Patriotti Corsi (APC) 112, 113
Aylott, N. 33

Baggioni, Jean 135
Basque Country 5, 8, 13, 133, 174n19
Beiras, Xosé Manuel 82, 84, 85, 92, 95, 99, 106
Belgium 1, 10, 31
Bloque Nacional-Popular Galego (BN-PG) 79, 80
Bloque Nacionalista Galego (BNG): constitutional policy 79, 88–9, 97, 100, 107–8; history 77–8; in coalition government 107–8, 154–5; internal party organisation 93–4, 106
Bomberg, E. 39
Briquet, J.L. 177n23
Brittany 50, 122, 170n8, 176n18
Bureau of Unrepresented Nations 64
bypassing the state 37, 38, 101, 110

Capoccia, G. 172n10
Castelao, Daniel 79
Catalonia 13, 108, 174n19 *see also* Convergència i Unió
Chari, R.S.: *et al.* 170n4
Charter on European or Minority Languages 11, 128, 170n6
clientelism 110, 117, 131, 135, 139

Coalición Galega (CG) 174n7
Collectivité Territoriale de la Corse see Corsican Assembly
Committee of the Regions 5–6, 10; party evaluations of 59, 68, 86, 147, 160
Common Agricultural Policy (CAP) 54, 129
Conference of Nations without a State in Western Europe (CONSEO) 99, 124
Congress of Deputies: elections to 81, 87, 96
Convergència Democràtica de Catalunya (CDC) 41
Conservative Party: British 33, 52, 56, 61, 63, 154, 156; Welsh 70
Conti, P. 27, 171n8
Convention on the Future of Europe 69
Convergència i Unió (CiU) 1, 8, 30, 41, 103, 174n19; constitutional goals 3, 7, 97; *see also* Galeusca
Corsica Nazione: constitutional goals 128–9, 136, 146; ideology 131–2
Corsica Viva 113, 176n7, 176n8
Corsican Assembly 118–9, 130, 132, 137; elections to the 113, 119, 120, 130, 133
Corsican nationalist movement: composition of 13, 111–13, 126, 127–8, 133, 137
Council of Ministers 6, 10, 18, 162
Crettiez, X. 124, 131, 176n20; and Sommier, I. 113
Cuncolta di i Cumitati Naziunalisti (CCN) 112, 175n5

Dafis, C. 59
Daniels, P. 172n2
De Winter, L.: and Gómez-Reino 41, 171n6; *et al.* 170n2, 170n7

Declaration of Barcelona 96 *see also* Galeusca
de-ideologicalisation 131, 150
Deschouwer, K. 36
developments in European integration 2, 4–6, 8–11; BNG response to 80, 83–6, 88–9, 101, 104–5; Corsican nationalist responses to 123–5, 127, 129–30, 131–2, 133–4, 147; impact on party attitudes 39–40, 146–7, 160–2; Plaid Cymru response to 63–4, 68–9
Diamanti, I. 8
Downs, A. 29

Easton, D. 171n8
Economic and Monetary Union (EMU) 68, 88
Elis Thomas, Dafydd 44, 45, 57, 172n6; political ideas 51; strategy 61, 62
enlargement 10, 68, 88, 133
Erignac, Claude 113, 128
Esquerda Galega (EG) 173n3, 173n4, 174n6
Esquerda Nacionalista (EN) 78, 174n9
Esquerra Republicana de Catalunya (ERC) 8, 99
Europa sí pero non así 86, 89
Europe of Markets 121
Europe of Nations 50
Europe of Nations without States: *see* Corsica Nazione, constitutional policy; *see* FLNC, constitutional policy
Europe of the Peoples: *see* BNG, constitutional policy; *see* UPC, constitutional policy
Europe of the Regions 2, 4, 9, 20, 24, 36, 143–4
Europe of States 50, 68, 69, 121
Europe Yes, EEC No 49, 50
European Bureau for Lesser Used Languages 6
European Commission 62, 132
European Constitution 8; referendum in France 18, 133–4, 151, 171n3; referendum in Netherlands 18, 171n3; referendum in Spain 8, 89, 101, 105, 151
European Free Alliance (EFA) 41, 162–3; BNG in 99–100, 144, 162–3; Corsican nationalism in 115, 122–3, 162–3, 176n16; Plaid Cymru in 56–7, 61, 64–5, 69, 144, 162–3

European integration, dimensions of 23–7, 42
Europeanisation: 'bottom-up' 20–1, 22; of political parties 12, 18–22, 171; 'top-down' 19–20
European Parliament 6, 18; minority nationalist parties in 10, 158–9, 37; party groups in 17, 19, 40–1 172n11; socialisation 40, 162–3
European Parliament elections 5, 10, 18, 37; role of 38–9,152, 159–60; European elections in Corsica 122, 123, 124, 176n17; European elections in Galicia 85, 87–8, 92, 98–9, 103, 175n21; European elections in Wales 50, 54–5, 56–7, 62–3, 65, 69
European regional policies 5, 64, 85, 147, 160; Cohesion Fund 86; Structural Funds 64, 135, 147, 177n25
Euro-scepticism, causes of 34–36, 153
Euskadi 'Ta Askatasuna (ETA) 175n, 177n22
Eusko Alkartasuna (EA) 8, 175n
Evans, Gwynfor 44, 48, 49–50, 51, 54
Evans, R. 54

factionalism: in the BNG 93–4, 103–5, 106–8, 109; in the Corsican nationalist movement 126–7, 127–8, 133–4, 137; impact on party attitudes 32–4, 150–2; in Plaid Cymru 52, 55
Featherstone, K. 28, 32, 152, 171n5
first-past-the-post 62, 63, 173n11
Flanders 13, 170n8
Flood, C. 27
Fraga Iribarne, Manuel 90, 174n17
France 10, 11, 111, 113, 135; French Presidency 132, 137; Jacobin tradition 110, 117, 128
Franco, General Francisco 77, 79, 80, 84
French Parliament: elections to 117, 176n12
French Basque Country 176n
Front de Libération Nationale de la Corse (FLNC): 'canal habituel' 112, 127, 176n7; 'canal historique' 112, 113, 127, 128; constitutional policy 116, 125, 146; ideology 116–17, 118, 125–6; 'Union des combatants' 113, 137, 176
Fronte Régionaliste Corse (FRC) 111

galeguismo 77, 79, 173n1
Galeusca 96–7, 103–4, 174n18

Index   195

Galician Parliament 89–90, 158; elections to 82, 90, 91
George, S.: and Haythorne, D. 172n2
Giudici, N. 131
Gómez-Reino, M. see De Winter, L.
Government of Wales Act 1998 66
Green Party: British 61; and the EFA 41, 162, 170n, 172n11; French 122, 123, 124; see also new politics

Harmel, R.: et al. 32
Haythorne, D. see George, S.
Herri Batasuna (HB) 99, 175n22
Hix, S.: and Lord, C. 3; et al. 171n1
House of Commons 50, 62, 158, 172n3; elections to 46, 53, 55, 62, 72, 73

ideology: impact on European attitudes 28, 29–31, 149–50; see also Bloque Nacionalista Galego, ideology; see also Corsica Nazione, ideology; see also FLNC ideology; see also Plaid Cymru, ideology; see also UPC, ideology
Iles de la Méditerranée Occidentale (IMEDOC) 135
Intergroup of Nations without States 100
internal enlargement 66, 173n13

Janda, K. 32
Johanssen, K.M.: and Raunio, T. 28, 33
Jones, T. 172n4

Keating, M. 7, 9
Kinnock, Neil 62
Kopecký, P.: and Mudde, C. 24, 171n8

La Chjama 133, 175n6, 176n10
Labour Party: British 2, 51, 56, 62, 156, 172n3; Welsh 45, 70, 73, 74
Ladrech, R. 18–9, 40, 171n4
Lago, I.: and Maíz, R. 97
Lefébvre, C. 138
Lefevre, M. 128, 131
Lega Nord 2, 8, 31, 41, 170n4
Lewis, Saunders 44, 48–9, 50, 52, 58, 59–60
Lipset, S.M. 29
Lord, C. see Hix, S.
Lynch, P. 170n8

Maastricht Treaty see Treaty on European Union (TEU)
MacCormick, Neil 69

Mair, P. 171n2
Maíz, R. 80, 106, 173n2, 174n12; see also Lago, I.
Mella, Carlos 98
Molas, I. 131
Morgan, K. 53
Mouvement des Radicaux de Gauche (MRG) 177n23
Movement du 29 Novembre 111
Movimentu pà l'Autodeterminazione (MPA) 112, 127, 176n7
Mudde, C. see Kopecký, P.
multi-level governance 9
Murgía, Manuel 79
Muvimentu Corsu per l'Autodeterminazione (MCA) 175n5

Natali, Paul 135
National Assembly for Wales (NAW) 2, 62, 66, 70, 74; elections to 45, 47, 66, 70, 73
new politics 31, 95, 102, 148
new regionalism 58, 102
Nogueira, Camilo 93, 99–100, 103, 106, 173n3, 175n25
Northern Ireland 52, 177
Nós-Unidade Popular (Nós-UP) 105, 174n10

Occitanie 122
Olsen, J. 28, 171n5
Opik, Lembit 70
opportunity structure: in Corsica 118; European 5, 20, 23, 75, 147; in Galicia 80, 106; regional 157; in Wales 66
Osmond, J. 173n10, 173n14

Panebianco, A. 32
Parti National de la Corse (PNC): constitutional policy 133, 136
Partido Comunista de España (PCE) 83
Partido Galegista (PG) 79, 77, 78, 173n, 174n7; see also PNG-PG
Partido Galego do Proletariado (PGP) 173n3
Partido Nacionalista Vasco (PNV) 1, 4, 8, 22, 41, 65; constitutional goals 5, 97; see also Galeusca
Partido Nacionalista Galego-Partido Galeguista (PNG-PG) 78, 174n7
Partido Obrero Galego (POG) 173n3
Partido Popular (PP) 174n17
Partido Popular de Galicia (PPdeG) 90, 106, 174n17

Partido Socialista de Galicia (PSdeG-PSOE) 90, 106, 107
Partido Socialista Galego (PSG) 77, 78, 79, 80
Partido Socialista Galego- Esquerda Galega (PSG-EG) 92, 93, 174n6, 174n8, 175n21
Partido Socialista Obrero Español (PSOE) 83, 96
Partitu di a Chjama 134
Partitu Sucialistu Per l'Indipendenza (PSI) 134, 176n10
party attitudes, categorisation of 23–7, 42, 141–8
party competition 19, 165–6, 171n2; and the BNG 90, 96, 98, 105, 106; and Corsican nationalism 117–8, 131–2, 135, 136–7, 153; impact on party attitudes 34–6, 152–5; and Plaid Cymru 51, 61–3, 70–1
Party of European Socialists (PES) 40, 172n11
Pasquier, R. *see* Radaelli, C.
Piñeiro, Ramón 77, 79
Plaid Cymru: 'full national status' 7, 45, 48–9, 57–8, 59–60, 65; history 44–5; in coalition government 73–4, 154–5; ideology 44, 54, 55–6, 58–9; 'independence in Europe' 66–8, 70; referendum on devolution 1979 52–3; referendum on UK membership of EEC 50–2
Poggioli, Pierre 112, 176n15, 177n21
Poguntke, T.: *et al.* 19
political space: in Corsica 134–5; in Galicia 90, 105–6, 107; impact on party attitudes 36, 155–7; in Wales 51, 61–2, 70–1
political violence 118, 119, 126, 133, 137, 176–7n20
post-sovereignty/post-sovereigntist 5, 7; Plaid Cymru and 43, 67, 72, 75, 146, 149
process Matignon 132
proportional representation 63, 66, 98, 118, 173n11
public opinion: in Corsica 134; in Galicia 105–6; impact on party attitudes 37–8, 159; in Wales 71–2

Quintana, Anxo 106

Radaelli, C.: and Pasquier, R. 171n5
Rainbow Group 122, 170n5; *see also* Green Party, and the EFA
Rassemblement pour la République (RPR) 135, 177n23
Raunio, T. 38 *see also* Johansson, K.M.
Ray, L. 3
regionalisation 1–2; in France 118, 119, 132, 134, 176n14; in Spain *see* state of autonomies; in the UK 65–6
Régions et Peuples Solidaires 123
Reif, K. 38
Rinnovu Naziunale (RN) 176n7
Rodriguez, Francisco 87
Rokkan, S. *see* Lipset, S.M.
Rossi, Jose 135

Scelta Nova 112
Schmitt, H. *see* Reif, K.
Scotland 13, 50, 52, 61, 170n8, 172n3
Scottish National Party (SNP) 2, 4, 7, 61, 69, 172n3
Scottish Parliament 2, 66
Scully, R. 40 *see also* Wyn Jones, R.
second-order elections 38, 159
Simeoni, Edmond 111, 112, 118
Simeoni, Max 112, 122–3
Single European Act (SEA) 56, 85, 125
Sinn Fein (SF) 99
Sitter, N. 32, 35
Sommier, I. *see* Crettiez, X.
sovereignty, changing nature of 3, 4–5
state of autonomies 1, 80, 106
Statut Joxe 118, 176n14
Statut Particulier 118, 119
statute of autonomy: Catalan 108; Corsican 114; Galician 107–8, 174n13
subsidiarity, principle of 6, 10, 59, 68, 122, 160, 173n13

Taggart, P. 32, 34
Talamoni, Jean-Guy 130, 132
Thatcher, Margaret 53, 55–6, 61, 62, 63
transition to democracy 76, 77, 79, 80, 152, 157, 174n17
transnational co-operation 19; impact on party attitudes 28, 40–1, 162–3; *see also* European Free Alliance
Treaty of Amsterdam 68
Treaty of Nice 68
Treaty of Rome 14, 51, 166
Treaty on European Union (TEU) 5–6; BNG responses to 89, 90, 93; Corsican responses to 122, 127, 134, 177; French referendum on 122, 127, 134; Plaid

Cymru responses to 59, 64
Turner, C. 54

Unidade Galega (UG) 78, 92–3, 99, 102, 174n8
Unió Democràtica de Catalunya (UDC) 41
Unión de Centro Democrático (UCD) 82, 174n7
Union pour un Mouvement Populaire (UMP) 177n23
Unione di u Populu Corsu (UPC): constitutional policy 114–15, 121, 128; ideology 115–16; internationalisation strategy 114
Unión do Povo Galego (UPG) 77, 79–80, 82, 87, 173n3

Unione Naziunale 113, 133–4, 137, 176
Unione pour la Démocratie Française (UDF) 135
Unità 113
Unita Naziunale 119
U Rinnovu 134

Vandemeulebroucke, Jaak 65
Vlaams Blok/Vlaams Belang 31
Voce Popular 134
Volksunie 4, 65

Wigley, Dafydd 45, 51, 52, 55, 67, 172n7
Wyn Jones, R. 53, 60, 172n1; and Scully, R. 70

eBooks – at www.eBookstore.tandf.co.uk

A library at your fingertips!

eBooks are electronic versions of printed books. You can store them on your PC/laptop or browse them online.

They have advantages for anyone needing rapid access to a wide variety of published, copyright information.

eBooks can help your research by enabling you to bookmark chapters, annotate text and use instant searches to find specific words or phrases. Several eBook files would fit on even a small laptop or PDA.

NEW: Save money by eSubscribing: cheap, online access to any eBook for as long as you need it.

Annual subscription packages

We now offer special low-cost bulk subscriptions to packages of eBooks in certain subject areas. These are available to libraries or to individuals.

For more information please contact webmaster.ebooks@tandf.co.uk

We're continually developing the eBook concept, so keep up to date by visiting the website.

www.eBookstore.tandf.co.uk